D0853879

Philosophy and
Personal Relations

Much of the preparatory work for these studies was carried out within the framework of GRIPH, Groupe de Recherche Interculturelle et Philosophique, of Montreal.

A grant from UNESCO to help in meeting the costs of the work involved is gratefully acknowledged.

CE

Philosophy and Personal Relations

An Anglo-French Study

Edited by
Alan Montefiore

Routledge & Kegan Paul   London

Universitas
BIBLIOTHECA
Ottaviensis

312464

First published in 1973
by Routledge & Kegan Paul Ltd
Broadway House, 68–74 Carter Lane,
London EC4V 5EL
Printed in Great Britain by
Clarke, Doble & Brendon Ltd
Plymouth
© Routledge & Kegan Paul 1973
No part of this book may be reproduced in
any form without permission from the
publisher, except for the quotation of brief
passages in criticism

ISBN 0 7100 7661 4

BJ
1012
.M625
1973b

Contents of this volume

Contents of the French volume

Philosophie et rapports inter-personnels

Notes on authors of this volume

Jean Austin Read Classical Mods and Greats at Somerville College, Oxford (1937–41). Married and started a family as undergraduate and spent the following twenty years looking after a husband and four children. Started to teach philosophy in 1960; Fellow of St Hilda's College since 1964. No very specialized philosophical interests, but has always found the traditional problems and their constant recurrence in modified forms intriguing. Still feels something of an amateur among professionals.

Larry Blum Born in 1943. B.A. Princeton University, 1964. At present working on a Ph.D. at Harvard on 'Individualism in the moral and social theories of Kant and Mill'. Main interests include Merleau-Ponty, the later Wittgenstein, moral, social and political philosophy.

J. A. Brook Born in Edmonton, Canada in 1943 of working-class parents. From 1961 to 1966 studied as undergraduate and subsequently graduate at the University of Alberta; from 1966 to 1967 as a graduate at the University of Oxford. At present Assistant Professor of Philosophy at Carleton University, Ottawa. Topic of doctrinal thesis – 'Self-consciousness and reference to self'.

M. W. Hughes Born in 1944. Educated at Birkenhead School, in the north of England, and Balliol College, Oxford. After spending some time as Lecturer in Philosophy at the University College of North Wales, Bangor, completed a B.Phil. at Oxford in 1971. Is now a member of the Department of Philosophy at the University of Newcastle-on-Tyne.

Alan Montefiore   Read P.P.E. – Politics, Philosophy and Economics – at Balliol College, Oxford from 1948 to 1950. From 1951 to 1961 taught philosophy, a lot of it moral and political philosophy, at the then new University College of North Staffordshire, now the University of Keele. In 1961 returned to Balliol as Fellow. Is interested in what he would rather reluctantly call the nature of evaluation.

W. Newton-Smith   Studied mathematics and philosophy at Queen's University, Kingston, Canada. Subsequently took an M.A. in philosophy at Cornell University and then came as a graduate student to Balliol College, Oxford, where he is now a Fellow. Is working on a doctrinal thesis on 'The nature of time'.

Derek Parfit   Born in 1942. Read Modern History at Balliol College, Oxford, and then went to America for two years, where he changed his subject to philosophy. Is now a Fellow of All Souls College, Oxford, and is working on a doctoral thesis on Personal Identity.

Michael Schleifer   Was born in Montreal in 1943 and obtained a B.A. at McGill University in 1964. Then went to Oxford and obtained the B.Phil. in 1966. Returned to McGill to teach philosophy and to do research in psychology. Has recently completed his doctorate at McGill in the area of moral development in children. Is married, with three children.

David Wood   First studied philosophy at Manchester University, where he was introduced to phenomenology. As a graduate student went to New College, Oxford, where he became interested in the relation of sociology and philosophy; is writing a thesis on 'The conceptual relationship between beliefs and social contexts'. Recently appointed to the staff of the Department of Philosophy at the University of Warwick. Plans a book on Suicide as a concrete attempt to reconcile philosophical and sociological perspectives on a concrete issue.

Notes on authors of the French volume

Françoise Armengaud   Born in Paris in 1942. Has studied at the Sorbonne and at Sèvres. 'Professeur agrégé' in philosophy, 1965. Is working on a thesis on G. E. Moore.

Vincent Descombes   Born in Paris in 1943. Studied both sociology and philosophy at the Sorbonne. 'Professeur agrégé', 1967, Ph.D. 1970. Has already published *Le platonicisme* (Presses Universitaires de France) and intends to publish *L'Origine de la Sociologie* before long.

Jocelyne Gérard   Born in the province of Quebec in 1949. 'Maîtrise' in philosophy, 1970. At present teaching in the C.E.G.E.P. of Vieux-Montréal.

Francis Jacques   Born in Strasbourg in 1934. 'Agrégé' in philosophy after having studied at the Sorbonne. Has published articles in *Recherches et Débats* (Fayard) and in the *Revue de Métaphysique et de Morale* (A. Colin). Is interested in the origins of English and American analytic philosophy. At present working on a study of the history of the Theory of Descriptions and on a French translation of *Über Annahmen* by Meinong.

Claude Panaccio   Born in Montreal in 1946. Studied at the University of Montreal. M.A. in philosophy (memoir on Merleau-Ponty) and in medieval studies (memoir on 'La Situation du Langage dans la *Summa Logicae* de Guillaume d'Occam'. Is working on a doctorate on the treatment of language in Occamist logic. Has a special interest in the philosophy of language.

Jacques Poulain   Born in France in 1942. Studied philosophy at the Institut Catholique de Paris and at the Sorbonne (1961–8). 'Agrégé' in philosophy, 1968, Ph.D. (Paris) 1969. At present 'professeur adjoint' in the Department of Philosophy at the University of Montreal. Teaches philosophy of logic and of language. Has published an article, written in 1967 and published in 1970, on 'Le Mysticisme du Tractatus Logico-Philosophicus et la Situation Paradoxale des Propositions religieuses' in *La Recherche en Philosophie et en Théologie* (Editions du Cerf, Paris).

1 Introduction

Alan Montefiore

This volume of essays contains half of the first fruits of a study, whose originating points and further horizons I must try in this introduction to explain. The other half is contained in a companion volume, written by French-speaking philosophers and published in French by Les Presses Universitaires de Montréal. Each volume contains details of the contents of the other (see pp. vi–x) as well as a closely parallel version of the same introduction.

There are several distinct themes of interest to be found in or, hopefully, beyond these present studies; but the two principal ones are that which appears in the title of these two volumes, and that more general interest which may be found in any attempt by philosophers of the 'analytic' and 'continental' traditions to explore the possibilities of working towards each other through the discussion of a specific topic in some sense common to them both. It cannot be pretended, however, that the whole project, as it now stands, actually derives from one masterly unifying conception already present at its birth and guiding its development throughout. It has, in fact, behaved in a far less well-ordered way; indeed, the two main themes were not even linked at the outset. Not only did the study start as something small and relatively straightforward before beginning to grow; it did not even start all in one piece. So although I must apologize for the semi-narrative style of much of what follows, to explain the background to how the papers actually came to be written does seem the clearest and most honest way of introducing these two collections.

There is one other point of preliminary explanation or warning that should be made right away. The need to understand and to bridge the notorious gap between analytic and continental ways of doing philosophy has been felt for a long time. This idea for a philosophical study of personal relations had to start off with, however, no consciously international dimension; it was in fact conceived in the purely internal context of analytic philosophy conducted, as it most typically is, in English. This meant that when, subsequently, French-speaking philosophers were invited to participate in an expanded version of the original venture, they were being asked to work on a theme which had already been chosen without reference to whatever their interests might be and which, furthermore, had been articulated in terms of analytic presuppositions about the nature of philosophical enquiry. This explicitly analytic presentation of the theme in turn meant not only that there were bound to be differences between the ways in which it is for the most part treated in the French and the English volumes – which was not only to be expected, but positively to be looked for; but also that the French philosophers may run a greater risk of finding the intended point of their contributions misconstrued than do the English philosophers. To this must be added the risk that this introduction by someone who learnt his philosophy at Oxford may, with the best will in the world, itself involve some degree of distortion of the nature of the non-analytic contribution. In particular, while I am well placed to tell the story of how and why certain analytic philosophers came to invite some of their French colleagues to join with them in writing on the theme of personal relations, I am evidently in no position to explain just what this invitation looked like and why they decided to accept it from the French point of view. If, then, one is to have any hope of avoiding it, one must explicitly recognize the risk that this inevitably analytically orientated introduction may somehow obscure the *joint* nature and balance of the final enterprise – a risk that may be increased by the fact that to explain its first 'analytic' origins in proper narrative order means devoting much of the first part of the introduction to essentially analytic concerns. It remains to be seen, indeed, whether there can even in theory be a standpoint from which to explain the origin and growth of such an enterprise, from which all distortion of this kind or another may be finally eliminable. Be this as it may, the point should be emphasized as strongly as possible that whatever interest either of these volumes may have on their own, they should each of them take on substantially greater interest in the light of the other. Indeed, they can take on their full sense in relation to the project as a whole *only* when so considered.

Where, then, can this project be said to have begun? In practical terms its immediate starting point lay in a smallish graduate seminar held in Oxford during the spring term of 1969, under the title of 'Philosophy and Personal Relations'. But of course there was, even then, already a certain background to this choice of subject.

The general background was something like this: most analytic philosophers are more or less familiar with the complaint, coming sometimes from their students, often from members of the cultural public to which analytic philosophy 'belongs', that in their hands philosophy has lost all contact, has indeed given up any claim to such contact, with the 'real problems of life'. There is, to be sure, a great deal of disagreement, uncertainty and confusion as to the nature and direction of the 'real', over whether it is to be found in the ordinary and everyday, in the religious or the metaphysical, or in radical politics or in-depth psychology. No matter, moreover, that the accusation of indifference and irrelevance to 'real' life has been cast from one direction or another against philosophers and philosophy of all types and ages. Analytic philosophers have seemed to many contemporaries to be quite peculiarly out of touch, with their apparently obstinate insistence on limiting themselves to the study of how people do or might speak, without any direct concern for the issues which they actually want to speak about. The comparisons that may be drawn, either implicitly or explicitly, are varied, sometimes mutually overlapping, sometimes mutually incompatible; with classical metaphysics, with openly normative moral or political philosophy, with Marxism, with Freudianism (which may be thought of as a family of generalized derivatives of psychoanalysis, but which are perhaps already contained in ambiguous seed within classical psychoanalytic theory itself), with structuralism, with existentialism, even with that highly academic (and on the continent now beginning to be a little old-fashioned) backbone of much so-called existentialist writing, phenomenology. Philosophers of all these persuasions, it seems to have appeared to many exasperated members of the English-speaking cultural public, at least try to talk about something; analytic philosophers are peculiar in that they only try to talk about talking. And insult is added to injury when they react to this complaint by proposing to discuss the word 'real'.

Now, one may have a number of reservations about taking analytic philosophy, or indeed any other kind of philosophy, so seriously as to allow it to dominate every aspect of one's life (if, indeed, one is in any way entitled to demand of philosophy this sort of relevance); but, whatever other justifying grounds it may have, this particular complaint would seem to be peculiarly mistaken, if 'reality' is conceived as having somehow to do with the problems of non-philosophic life.

If the complaint is mistaken, it has to be admitted, however, that it has received considerable support from the tacit practice, and sometimes the explicit assertion, of many of the most influential practitioners of analytic philosophy up to the present day. Indeed, with certain outstanding exceptions, most of them *have* been largely absorbed in problems, the solutions to which they conceived of as having no bearing at all on issues of 'real' non-philosophical life – the life to which Hume returned each time that he came out of his study. Perhaps this may be because the more general and fundamental the theoretical issues, then (whatever the idiom in which they may be identified and explored) the remoter must be their relevance to the particular problems of particular individuals in the particularities of their own lives. It may also be traced to a certain professional reluctance to give the appearance of any allegedly professional involvement in non-theoretical affairs; and this in turn may be traced partly to a certain professional understanding (or misunderstanding) of the relations between theory and practice and partly, perhaps, to the influence of certain forms of educational institutions. But whatever the reasons may be for the most frequent choices of topics or for the ways in which most analytic philosophers may have understood what they have been doing up to now, there seems to be nothing in the *method* of analytic philosophy as such to justify the view that this kind of philosophy is in principle peculiarly incapable of having anything to do with 'real' life.

In fact this point is already being made in one way or another by an increasing number of philosophers trained in general analytic methods and outlook, who are nevertheless coming to be sceptical of their predecessors' views of their subject as a strictly 'academic' discipline. Many of their arguments amount to the simple point that to talk about the way in which to talk about X is, willy nilly and even if indirectly, itself to talk about X. This is true and, even if a trifle obvious on second reflection, still worth remembering and elaborating. On the other hand, it is also true that to talk about X is not itself and need not further involve actually doing (or feeling) anything about X; indeed for many values of X it may be very unclear what further behavioural difference *could* be seen as implied in believing one set of things about it rather than another. There are, of course, certain theories of belief in the light of which this would seem to need qualifying. All the same, it is at least very unobvious what differences one should look for in the behaviour of even the most consistent of men who were divided on such questions as those concerning the eliminability of particular terms, the possibility of actually proving that the world did not begin only five minutes ago, or that of translating all statements referring to one's experience of the material objects of the world into other (sets of) statements referring to nothing but what some philosophers have called 'sense data' – all topics which have provoked a great deal of analytic writing. And even at a more finely controversial level it is still far from evident that anyone struggling to think his way through his own life must, in so doing, grapple with such theoretical problems as those of whether one is entitled to speak of knowledge of one's own pains, of the pros and cons of treating the proposition that P is necessary as itself a necessary proposition, or of the precise logical status of causal explanation.

All in all, the temptation to conclude that analytic philosophy must for all practical purposes leave the non-philosophic world precisely as it finds it, is no more foolish than it is strong. Nevertheless, it seems to be mistaken.

To argue the case for regarding it as a mistake, however, clearly calls for a great deal of detailed support and exemplification. In some ways the most likely areas in which to seek this may seem to be those of moral and political philosophy, for both of them have again become the active concern of analytically trained philosophers (and maybe one should add the philosophy of religion to the list). Here, surely, one could hope to show how positions taken up with respect to even the most apparently abstract issues in philosophical logic might determine those that one should or could take up in moral, political and social philosophy (and philosophy of religion). One would further need to show, of course, that it might, *in so far as one was consistent*, actually make some difference to one's practical moral or political stance that one should hold one view in moral or political philosophy rather than another; but this too, it may be thought, should not be too difficult to do, given that the once largely taken for granted autonomy of value judgments from statements of fact and the propositions of conceptual analysis has once again become a matter for wide and academically respectable controversy.

In fact I do myself believe that some version of this line of argument can be successfully pursued in the end; but also that it may turn out to be more difficult, and perhaps less easily convincing, than one might first suppose. My main reasons for caution are concerned with certain reservations in regard to the precise applicability of the restrictive condition 'in so far as one was consistent'; as well as with a range of problems concerning the interpretation of the concepts of 'the moral' and 'the political'. There is, for example, one fairly common level of understanding at which people are inclined to say that politics is simply a device for the institutionalized avoidance of truly human, living concerns, and that 'morality', if it does not refer simply to the prejudices and conventions of a blinded, self-blinded, partially dehumanized society, is a word to which they can no longer easily attach any meaning. I should not myself go along more than a very limited distance with either branch of such an argument. But that is not at all to say that it is always unimportant or merely silly. Nor that any serious attempt to uncover its incoherences or its limitations could be carried through without coming at some point to grips with problems of personal or interpersonal relations.

Personal relations: one's relations with oneself and, paradigmatically perhaps, one's relations with other individuals; the dimensions of experience that many distant and some not so distant critics (and, if it comes to that, defenders) of analytic philosophy feel to be left out of account by its methods and objectives, but which, so they seem to think, have been the more or less direct concern of at any rate a great deal of recent 'continental' philosophy. Nietzsche, Kierkegaard, Mounier, Sartre, Camus, Simone de Beauvoir, Marcel, Buber, Heidegger and Jaspers are among the most frequently cited names. Above all, perhaps, the kinds of relations and experience that to many contemporaries, forsaken by religion and increasingly sceptical of politics, constitute what, if anything at all, is 'real' about so-called 'real life'. If anything is worth thinking about this is; if philosophers *qua* philosophers cannot think about it, then so much the worse for philosophers *qua* philosophers; if it cannot be thought about at all without its distorting transformation into an object of manipulation, then so much the worse for thinking.

Here, then, was one powerful reason for wanting to work on the subject of personal relations : to examine at what might seem to be the point of sharpest contrast the widely held view that there were radical discontinuities between philosophical (at any rate analytic philosophical) and non-philosophical ways of thought and practice. Another, it goes without saying, was the interest of the subject in its own right; was there a proper or even necessary use for general philosophical considerations in certain situations of purely personal problem or discussion? There was, however, virtually no tradition of analytic philosophical discussion of personal relations as such to give any specific theoretical background or context to further study of the topic. In this sense my approach to it was characteristically *non*-continental. Here was a problem, together with the further problems of whether the first could be seen as a problem in philosophy; if so, how; if not, why not? But it was a problem without any obvious immediate history in the philosophical tradition within which I hoped to examine it.

This last assertion stands, no doubt, in need of certain qualification. Some analytical philosophers *have* after all written, and written interestingly, on certain aspects of personal relations. Here I am thinking not so much of G. E. Moore, who declared personal relations to be among the objects of the highest intrinsic value, but who hardly treated them as objects for sustained philosophical analysis, as of philosophers such as Peter Strawson on the difference between objective and personal-reactive attitudes; Herbert Fingarette and Patrick Gardiner (among others) on sincerity and self-deception; R. S. Downie and Elizabeth Telfer on respect for persons; Thomas Nagel on sex; and so on. . . . There are examples to be found all right. But we may acknowledge their existence and still be uncertain as to how exactly they count. Perhaps they provide no more than descriptive analyses of a region of thought and experience in which all that happens

B

or exists does so in logical independence of all such analyses; perhaps they offer ways of classifying and talking about phenomena that cannot in themselves be affected by the ways in which one may choose to classify or talk about them? If so, anyone actually involved in personal relations would be temporarily stepping out of his involvement for whatever time he devoted to the philosophical discussion of how best to understand his involvements; and philosophy would still not have any very close or genuine interaction with the 'real', for all that it might in some way 'be about it'.

I do not myself think that this *is* necessarily or always the situation; and indeed it may never be so entirely. (Here, of course, the analytic philosopher *can* situate himself within a recognizable tradition of debate as to how to understand the relationship between a given area of philosophical discourse and the actual subject-matter of that discourse itself.) But if we are to examine the matter more precisely, it seems necessary to pin down somewhat more closely exactly what we may be trying to talk about in speaking of personal relations. At any rate, the working hypothesis from which I started was roughly as follows: (*a*) that we may take it as a necessary defining condition of personal relations that the beings between whom they do or could hold should be capable in principle of forming for themselves some conception of the existence and nature of whatever relationship is in question; and (*b*) that if not all, then in certain cases at least the actual nature of the relationship would be a partial function of the conceptions or misconceptions (or failure to form any conceptions) that one or more of those involved had or might have of it. From this it would seem to follow that in so far as philosophical considerations might be brought to bear to sustain or to modify the understanding that anyone had of the key concepts that might enter into his understanding of such relationships, such considerations must have a direct potential bearing on the nature of the relationships themselves. (If the nature of the relationship between us is in part at least a function of the way in which I view it, then arguments which might oblige me to change my view, could *ipso facto* lead to the bringing about of a change in the nature of the relationship itself.) Finally, I should want to argue that there are in fact cases in which philosophical considerations may be seen to have this peculiar relevance and force –

cases in which a philosopher may in effect relevantly say to himself or to another, 'Look, you really have, in all lucid consistency, to look at, and hence to live it, in this way rather than in that.'

This, of course, is only the rough outline of a thesis and no attempt will be made here to work it up into even a first version of a fully articulated whole. But there are certain remarks which it may already be useful to record :

(1) I am uncertain still as to how my opening partial definition should be construed to stand with respect to such apparently marginal cases as relationships with oneself and with babies, idiots and even animals. On the face of it, it would seem preferable for them to be in one way or another bringable into the purview. The 'proper' meaning (or meanings) of self-respect, and its loss, can hardly be argued out without any reference to what it might be to have respect for others; and vice versa. The same is true for self-deception. One way of stretching this first formulation to enable it to cover these cases might be to allow a man to regard himself as more than one being for the sake of this form of analysis. It is clear that there exists some considerable conceptual (not to speak of psychological) impetus in this direction, for example in some of the ways in which such concepts as self-respect and self-deception are built up. As against that, it would seem unwise to risk begging in advance any expressible questions relating to the unity and identity of the self, especially as this may be one of the very cases in which philosophical considerations may impinge on ways in which people may actually view and so, in the relevant sense, experience themselves and others. So perhaps it will turn out to be better to build some extra clause into this condition to allow one to talk of 'personal relations with oneself' without thereby committing oneself to claiming or admitting any sort of double existence.

(2) As for animals, babies and the more or less like, there would seem, *prima facie*, to be at least two possible directions in which to move. One might insist on the disputed uncertainty of interpretation (and perhaps even ineliminable residual opacity) of the expression 'capable in principle of forming for themselves some conception'. What is it exactly 'to form for oneself a conception'? What is the principle of 'capable in principle'? Would it, for example, let in babies on the grounds that, given normal development, they will one day be able to exercise full human capacities,

while excluding animals on the ground (if finally established) that they belong to species incapable of developing language? What, then, about low-grade human monsters? And so on. . . . In one way, I should take it to be a positive advantage of any definition that it should allow of, even perhaps encourage, disputable cases at the margins. For of course there will be more or less cases of personal relations, relations which approximate to the fully personal in some respects while falling far short in others. And of course there will be deeply felt disagreements arising out of and feeding back into different ways of ordering the relevant concepts, as to whether certain relationships, such as those of some people with some animals, are to be classified as genuinely personal or not. And if so, moreover, why? Some people, for instance, might concede to the dog-lover not so much a personal relationship *with* his dog as, maybe, a special kind of personal relationship with himself mediated back *via* his dog. Surely, any preliminary formulation at least should leave such issues open for further exploration.

The other possible direction of movement might, however, be simpler: namely, to relax the formulation of the first partial defining condition so as to read not that it is a necessary condition of relationships being personal that 'the beings between whom they do (or could) hold should be capable in principle etc . . .', but that 'at least one of the beings between whom they do (or could) hold should be capable in principle etc. . . .'. On balance, however, my initial inclination would be not to avoid the complexities, but on the contrary to seek to bring them out; and so to move in the first direction.

(3) There is also a problem about the proper status to be accorded to the consideration that 'in certain cases at least, the actual nature of the relationship in question would be a partial function of the conceptions or misconceptions that one or more of those involved in the relationship had or might have of it'. (One should remember in passing that criteria of what might be counted, and by whom, as misconceptions of a relationship may vary fairly widely.) Is it, that is to say, a hypothesis to be further refined and tested or, on the contrary, another element of partial definition? And if it is partly definitory, definitory of what exactly? Of a sub-class of personal relations? Or might it turn out conveniently to contribute to the definition of personal rela-

tionships in general? In which case might it be already somehow implied by my first partially defining formula – or rather by what might be the most suitable interpretation and/or possible extension of it? These are questions to which I have as yet no comprehensive answers. For the moment it would seem to be enough that there should exist at least certain important cases in which this consideration would clearly apply. For instance : if A and B are both adults and in a relationship in which, *inter alia*, A believes himself to be responsible for B, then the nature of this relationship must be changed by any line of thought that leads A to revise his conception of responsibility in such a way that, for further example, he no longer thinks it possible for any adult being to be responsible for any other.

(4) One should emphasize as strongly as possible the distinction between the purely causal influence that the consideration of any line of argument might have on anyone and what may be called its rational impact. In causal practice, of course, a man's consideration of any given line of argument may have all sorts of more or less weird effects upon him, depending on the circumstances in which he may consider the argument, who puts it to him and so on; counter-suggestion is among the least uncommon of such effects. No one can say *a priori* what strange effects the subjection to philosophical types of argument may have on a man. But these are not the issues of immediate concern. *They* may be brought into focus by thinking of them in the context of a man facing (or somehow refusing to face) problems of his own personal relationships. 'I have always thought of myself as in some way responsible for you (or him or her), but now I have doubts about the very concept of responsibility. . . .' Notoriously, a man cannot normally seek *merely* to influence himself in causally manipulative ways by his own reflective reasoning. No doubt that he may in fact do this, and no doubt too that this may be among his aims. (He may, for example, seek to calm himself by forcing himself to reflect.) But in as much as his thinking is subject to rational criteria, this cannot be all. The immediate issues, then, are those that may confront a man in the course of his own rational thought and may lead him, in so far as he can see and accept the implications of his own line of argument, to think differently about himself and his relationships from the ways in which he thought before; and so, if my hypothesis

is correct, contribute either to modifying or to consolidating the nature of the relationships themselves.

It was this thesis, rough and uncertain as it was, that I tried to present to the 1969 Oxford Graduate Seminar; uncertain at any rate in its details, though at some rather high level of generality the only really remarkable seeming thing about it was that anyone should consider it remarkable. What was clearly needed, however, both in order to provide material for the further study necessary to refine the rough patches and in order to exhibit the exact relevance of the general thesis to particular cases, was some extended work on a number of detailed examples. Clearly, too, it would be a much better test of its viability if other people, whose sole commitment to the thesis was that it was worth further testing examination, would undertake the study of their own chosen examples in their own chosen way.

It was in this context, then, that some of the participants in this seminar agreed to work systematically, each on their own chosen themes, themes which (*a*) they could envisage as relating to problems arising within a context of 'real' personal relations; and which (*b*) raised issues which were of interest to them as philosophers. In this way they hoped to show *either* how the consideration of the 'real' problem led on into areas of thought which it would be unnatural not to regard as philosophical, and how in turn the systematic thinking through of the philosophical issues might lead back to a modification of the terms of the original problems; *or* that the whole hypothesis was ill formulated or mistaken and that coming to philosophical conclusions on their chosen topic need have no bearing on how anyone actually saw or lived their lives.

It was – I am now rather ashamed to say – only after we had got going in this way that the idea occurred of seeking to expand the scope of the investigation in what could turn out to be a most rewarding way. As I have explained, one of its starting points had lain in the feeling that there was among the English-speaking 'cultural public' a widespread misapprehension as to the different implications of the methods of 'analytic' and 'continental' philosophy. But to try to dispel this misapprehension by an investigation conducted in analytic terms alone was, when one came to think of it, an absurdly one-sided way of going about the matter. If the different patterns of philosophic thought really did connect with problems of personal relations, and if there really were substantial, and not merely stylistic, differences between 'analytic' and 'continental' philosophy, then if continental philosophers were to work on the same general theme, one should expect to find substantial differences probably in their choice of particular topics, surely in the manner of their treatment. The very nature of these differences (or, improbably, the lack of them) should be deeply instructive. None of this would, of course, be at all *easy* to interpret. There would already be difficulties, indeed, in the way of settling on criteria for determining whether and when two philosophers, operating in different styles and on the basis of different presuppositions, might in fact be deemed to be dealing with the 'same problem' or the 'same theme'. But the thing was worth trying, if one could. Might it not be possible to find people interested in working on similar themes in Paris and, maybe in a bilingual and bi- or tri-cultural group, in Montreal?

Of course, these ideas did not spring simply out of some sudden, wild interest in pursuing the theme of the Oxford seminar in as many different places as possible at once; it was rather a matter of running together two already existing interests. As noted at the beginning, there has long seemed to be something of an intellectual and cultural scandal in the apparent inability of 'analytic' and 'continental' philosophers even to recognize each other as having intelligible and challenging things to say or as taking part in genuine intellectual controversy or debate. More specifically, it has seemed to be a weakness in these respective groups of philosophers that they should have proved in general equally incapable of giving any convincing account of the sense of what was going on in the other. No doubt, there have been quite a number of attempts to bring the two sides somehow together. Most of them, however, have remained at a rather high level of generality at which each side has talked about its own interests and methods without ever coming actually to grips with those of the other. There have been, so to speak, exchanges of view at a distance, but very few exchanges of closely reasoned discussion. But the problem – the philosophic problem – of re-establishing communication between such different descendants of what was once a common tradition will surely never be solved merely by talking about it; one needs, rather, to jump into an actual effort of communication in the hope of learning more about its difficulties and possibilities by looking back at oneself from time to time as one struggles along. For these purposes the choice of a particular theme for discussion is far less important than the decision to pick a particular theme. Inevitably there will be difficulties in defining a theme in terms that both sides can confidently regard as common; and no doubt many of these difficulties will only emerge to disconcert one as one goes along. But then they *will* only emerge if one is prepared to take the theoretical gamble of starting out as *if* one had determined a common area of debate.

Here then were two largely independent reasons why the analytic philosophers already concerned should turn to seek French co-operation. First, in order to see what could be learnt about the relations between philosophy and personal relations from joining in discussion with philosophers coming at the matter from an apparently very different angle. Second, in order to learn more about the theoretical bases of communication and its possible breakdown between philosophers of such different traditions from an attempt to discuss with them the particular theme which was offered – from this point of view quite arbitrarily – by the topic of personal relations.

But why, one may ask, both Paris and Montreal? The detailed background to this side of the story is largely a matter of personal accident. It so happened that I was myself already involved with various French- and English-speaking colleagues in commitments to try to develop some sort of cross-fertilizing contacts in regular exchanges between Oxford and Paris, and also to create some persisting centre for such studies in Montreal under the joint auspices of the English language and philosophically 'analytic' University of McGill and the French language and philosophically 'continental' Université de Montréal. It seemed natural enough in these circumstances to think of these places when seeking people interested to see what might come out of an attempt to work on the same general lines as we were already following at Oxford, by writing on such topics of their choice as might come under the general rubric of 'Philosophy and Personal Relations'.

'It seemed natural enough . . .' but, in spite of what I have just said about the necessity of 'jumping in' to a discussion, it was (and is) deceptively easy for an analytically trained philosopher to underestimate the complexity of what we were suggesting to our French-speaking colleagues. (I certainly started out by underestimating this complexity myself.) An analytic philosopher may perhaps appreciate something of the awkwardness of their situation when faced with such a request, if he imagines himself having to respond to an invitation to contribute to an international study of, say, the relationship between philosophy and the understanding of Being. It is not so much that he would have nothing to say on the subject – indeed, he may in a sense feel that he had a great deal that he would like to say – as that he would have somehow to reinterpret it before being able to treat it as a philosophical subject at all, with the consequent risk of being after all interpreted as if he had nothing to say on the theme actually proposed.

The theme of personal relations is in fact one which French philosophers will naturally associate with certain movements in French philosophy which are now as far from the focus of explicit attention as only movements of the recent past can be – personalism and a certain kind of existentialism. (English critics are wholly wrong if they imagine that philosophers such as Sartre or Marcel remain at the centre of burning contemporary debate.) In any case, as one of them put it to me, even an analysis of the concepts actually employed by people in working out their personal relations seems at first sight condemned to bog down in what many contemporary French philosophers would regard as the out-worn confusions of phenomenological and existential analysis and such of its fictions as those of 'real life', 'immediate experience' or 'concrete existence'. Moreover, to quote another comment, 'The immense influence of psychoanalysis upon philosophy has meant that the link between my relations with others and what I might *say* about them has become for us extremely enigmatic.' This means that the French philosopher can hardly see himself as simply extending in more systematic form the same basic lines of reflection that any individual might pursue in the expectation that the insights of philosophy might in turn result in some transformation of that experience. He starts rather from the presupposition that ' "the reality" of the relations to be studied is not to be found simply within the conscious awareness which those concerned have of them', and that his task is rather to describe or to reconstruct the 'organizing principles' that *underlie* these relations. [One might compare the way in which Chomsky conceives his task of elucidating the rules of deep grammar, which the ordinary man knows full well how to follow, but which he is quite incapable of calling to explicit consciousness.]

> In consequence the standard by which philosophical enquiry has to be assessed, is neither the proper understanding of the concepts that may be employed in the ordinary experience of personal relations nor that of the reality of the transformations which such relationships may undergo in the light of such an understanding. The author's basic commitment is to be found rather not so much in his choice of the particular sorts of personal relations to be analysed as in the ways in which he orders both the philosophical problems which he sees as arising out of them and the replies which he may give to these problems.

In other words, the French philosopher invited to take part in a project presented in terms such as I have outlined, may risk (*a*) finding his contribution interpreted as providing proof that he has neither feet anywhere near the solid ground of everyday reality which the English philosopher claims to walk with such purposeful tread; and (*b*) being unable straightforwardly to object that he is as close to that ground as anybody, since it is in his view no more than a confused and unwarranted assumption that any such unproblematically solid ground exists.

There were, of course, other and more immediately practical reasons why one could not hope simply to duplicate in Paris or in Montreal the working conditions which we had enjoyed in Oxford. Oxford is a small place in which people can meet easily and often; this is not true of Montreal and even less of Paris. At Oxford not only was it a straightforward matter of working on an analytically formulated theme with philosophers taking the presuppositions of analytic philosophy for granted, but it was at the same time possible to do this in large part within the framework of the normal university programme of graduate seminars. In Paris and in Montreal, on the other hand, it was a matter of asking people to go out of their normal way to join in an enterprise which would impose on them wholly additional burdens. All of which meant that while the whole general point of the invitation was to take part in a *common* enterprise, the terms on which those who accepted could do so were bound both in principle and in practice to be different in Montreal and Paris from what they had been in Oxford.

Against this background we were very fortunate to find so many 'continentally trained' philosophers actually interested in taking part in the project, in order to see what might be learnt from an effort to work alongside analytic philosophers, if not yet on a common problem, at any rate on some *prima facie* common general theme. In both Montreal and Paris, as of course in Oxford, not all of those who showed such an interest, nor even all those who took leading parts in discussions, found themselves able actually to contribute papers. The total published contribution from philosophers working in these two places is nevertheless substantial. This means that the 'English' volume contains as well as seven papers written from Oxford, so to speak, one that was written from Montreal (though, as will be apparent from the biographical notes, by no means all the Oxford contributors are in fact Englishmen). The 'French' volume contains four papers written from Montreal and two from Paris; or, to split it another way, four by authors of French origin and two by French-Canadians. It is also worth noting that, with very slight exception, almost all the contributors to both volumes belong to the new generation of philosophers in their respective countries.

If, as I have tried to explain, it was built into the very conditions under which this study came to be conceived that the French and English participants could neither in principle nor in practice enter into it on the same terms as each other, it is equally true that it was impossible – again in principle as well as in practice – for them to pursue their work under exactly the same conditions. In particular it seems that when all due allowance has been made for the misleadingness of over-rapid generalizations, philosophical discussion has come to have a somewhat different sense and to play a somewhat different role within the two traditions. Within the analytic or critical tradition, discussion tends to mean detailed argument over the precise meaning, logical implications and methods of confirmation or disconfirmation of what is explicit or at least evident not only in the thesis as a whole, but also in each of the separate affirmations contained within it. Moreover, such arguments typically take place around efforts to deal with some problem in which those concerned are primarily engaged; it may, of course, be relevant to refer to the writings of past philosophers, but the problem, if it is not simply one of exegesis, exists, so to speak, in its own right as a focus for debate between those among whom the discussion takes place. Continental philosophers, on the other hand, are in general at once much more distrustful of what can be seen as explicit in a text, much less inclined to concentrate on the meaning or validity of separate affirmations and much more conscious of working within a developing history. To make the point by way of what is, I hope, a justifiable exaggeration, there are for them no philosophical problems outside the history of philosophy, through which every philosopher has to re-make his way to pick up the threads of its problems at the stage at which his predecessors have left them. This, as one of the Montreal contributors pointed out, makes it easy to understand why much of the discussion there tended to turn on the meaning and relevance of a proposed contribution *taken as a whole*. While an analytic philosopher tends to structure his work in terms of trying to adjust to and to ward off objections at every point of detail along his path, and while discussion is therefore often most relevant to him as he tries to tighten up the nuts and bolts of his argument, a continental philosopher is relatively much more concerned with the total sense of his position. Much of the discussion, therefore, tends to take place at a level of setting one overall view or interpretation against another rather than at one of testing for the truth or validity of particular arguments or assertions that may occur within them. There is also a very real sense in which many continental philosophers find it at least as significant to take part in debate with the leading figures of their own history as with their colleagues in the next room; or rather, debates with their next door colleagues tend to be at the same time three-cornered debates with their colleagues of the past. All this goes some way to explaining why, glancing only occasionally at each other across the unfamiliar distances of the Channel, analytic philosophers have tended to regard much continental philosophy as somewhat lacking in rigour and why continental philosophers have tended to regard much analytic philosophy as somewhat superficial and parochial; while often neither side is able to appreciate even the intended point of the criticisms of the other.

I am uneasily aware that I may in this last paragraph have provided a far better example than I should have wished of the impossibility of limiting this introduction to the presentation against their originating background of these first studies without slipping into questions of potentially controversial or one-sided interpretation. As far as possible, however, it seems better to keep such questions for what is envisaged as the next stage, which will be for all those concerned to assess their reactions towards the papers that have been written out of the other tradition and the nature of the whole enterprise. Meanwhile, whatever the shortcomings of this present account, I hope to have given some idea of how these two volumes came into being and of what, in some very general sense, they are about. I hope, on the other hand, that I may not have exaggerated their differences. After all, some of the 'English' contributions are much less explicitly directed to the problems suggested by my particular presentation of the theme than are others; the 'French' contributions are not all equally 'non-analytic' in their approach. Nevertheless, the differences exist and present indeed one of the most interesting themes for further comparison and study.

For the moment, however, it seems best to leave the papers to speak for themselves. The particular themes of each one of them may be indicated fairly enough by the lists of their titles. For myself, I should like to end at this present stage by adding just three somewhat disparate reflections :

(1) We have seen why it would be only too naturally easy for an analytic philosopher to derive and to pass on the impression that he was after all in much closer contact with 'real' problems than his continental opposite number; while from the opposite standpoint it might be equally natural to suppose that the analytic philosopher's so-called closer contacts were simply the confusions of 'ordinary' concepts, from which he had not yet even seen the need to escape. It remains, nevertheless, the case that, contrary to what many English critics would apparently have expected, it is on the whole in the French papers that the distance between problems concerning the interpretative study of personal relations and problems that may demand to be dealt with in the actual course of the relations themselves *seems* greatest and most resistant to any but the indirectest of crossings. It may be, however, that this too is an illusion; or, to put it another way, that the

extent of the distance may be no measure of the depth of the influence. Can it really be true that one may acquire a new conscious perspective on the context of one's 'personal' problems and yet leave one's experience of them totally unchanged? At any rate this – though I speak here only and no doubt controversially for myself – is one of the questions that I hope it may be possible to pursue in what is to follow.

(2) The papers that are actually contained in these two volumes I leave, as I said, to speak for themselves. What does seem worthy of immediate mention, however, is the way in which two themes, which at early stages took a major share of the attention on the one hand of the Oxford group and on the other of the French-Canadian members of the Montreal group, ended up by receiving little explicit treatment in the papers that have emerged for publication. The first meetings of the Oxford seminar, and the early drafts of papers on which its discussions were based, were extensively preoccupied with the problems that might be thought to arise in different contexts of personal relationships from a serious personal commitment to one form or another of utilitarianism. This preoccupation with utilitarianism seemed to have no counterpart among the preoccupations of the 'continentally' trained philosophers. Conversely, the French-Canadian preoccupation with the implications of a rejection of any standards of 'absolute' or 'objectively' given morality for very often the same type of personal relationships that appeared to the Oxford philosophers to be callable into question by utilitarianism, seemed to be peculiar to them. This concern does indeed remain central to Claude Panaccio's paper – though one could not deduce, from finding it treated in this one paper alone, the extent to which it dominated the earlier discussions among the French-Canadian participants. There are, no doubt, not very mysterious explanations to be given for the converse existence and virtual non-existence of these concerns among the respective groups. What is perhaps more interesting to speculate on is whether there is any general explanation to be given for their subsequent recession in the course and perhaps in the partial light of discussion. This once more is a topic that may be worth taking up again. For the moment I do no more than record the phenomenon.

(3) I return finally to the question of discussion. If it is true that it tends to take one form among members of the one tradi-

tion and a somewhat different form among members of the other, then one may suppose that discussion across the traditions must be, to say the least, much more difficult, with the purposes much more likely to become crossed, than discussion *within* one tradition or the other. And this is, of course, in fact the case. To me at least it now seems quite clear, however, that it would be completely mistaken to suppose that such discussion is actually impossible or that it may not in the end be among the most rewarding. My own experience in trying to write this introduction may, I hope, provide some testimony to this possibility; for that it is not considerably more inadequate than it is, is due to the very tough, detailed and constructive criticisms that I received from my friends among the French as well as among the English contributors to whom I showed earlier versions. I cannot suppose that any of them will be entirely satisfied with the result as it now stands; but that it is not much worse is entirely due to the lessons that they were able to teach me, the 'continental' philosophers in particular driving their lessons home with as much patient, detailed reference to the text as the minutest of philosophers could demand. It has been the chastening experience of finding myself convinced by my French friends of the need for extensive rewriting that has, as much as anything, convinced me at the same time of the real possibility of worth-while exchange in continuing vigorous discussion. In registering my very grateful thanks, therefore, to all those who have worked so hard on their contributions to both volumes, I should record my especial gratitude to those who have saved me from at least the worst of the one-sided effects of writing, without proper awareness that I was doing so, simply as an analytic philosopher for others of the same enclosed family.

It may be appropriate to conclude this introduction with a quotation from a philosopher who came from the continent to make his home in England. In his preface to the English edition of *The Logic of Scientific Discovery*, written in 1958, Karl Popper wrote of the different 'methods' of rational discussion, singling out one method in particular as worthy of special mention.

It is a variant of the (at present unfashionable) historical method. It consists, simply, in trying to find out what other people have thought and said about the problem in hand :

why they had to face it : how they formulated it : how
they tried to solve it. This seems to me important because it
is part of the general method of rational discussion. If
we ignore what other people are thinking, or have thought
in the past, then rational discussion must come to an end,
though each of us may go on happily talking to himself. Some
philosophers have made a virtue of talking to themselves;
perhaps because they thought that there was nobody else
worth talking to. I fear that the practice of philosophising on
this somewhat exalted plane may be a symptom of the
decline of rational discussion. No doubt God talks mainly to
Himself because He has no one worth talking to. But
philosophers should know that they are no more godlike
than other men.

None of the contributors to these volumes risks confusing himself with God.

2 Teaching moral philosophy

Jean Austin

When this paper was suggested to me, the subject seemed an interesting one, and one in which I was myself particularly interested: a subject with which I was genuinely concerned. It was not until I had made futile attempts at some outline of my thoughts on the matter that I realized that the actual writing is bound to be a reflection, perhaps an example, of the sort of muddle of which I am complaining in myself. The epithet that most naturally attaches to it in my mind, and of which my mind cannot rid itself, is 'disreputable'. Muddled thinking is reprehensible, one is ashamed of it and tries to avoid it, but at least something is gained by a genuine attempt and perhaps failure at clarification; one is not, then, dwelling on, or exploiting, in what is felt to be a non-philosophical manner, the sort of mess that one feels that a training in philosophy is supposed to enable one to avoid: *that* is disreputable. That is one thing; another is that when it comes down to it, there is actually very little to say apart from rather banal generalities or embarrassing but not very interesting personal revelations. That too is disreputable. If it was a question of analysing in terms of causal explanation, or perhaps better, whatever exactly is meant by it, conceptual connection, the difficulty and frustration one feels in attempting to teach moral philosophy, someone, no doubt, could do that very well. But phoneyness is not a qualification for that enterprise and it is phoneyness in my case that has to be faced. 'Phoneyness' is a fairly general term of disparagement – and in many contexts not very serious disparagement: but it can be perhaps the most damning of any condemnation. It might be regarded as the contrary of the philosophically rather unfashionable 'integrity'. There may have been attempts at an explicit analysis of integrity, but I am not familiar with any, nor, obviously, can one be attempted

c 23

here. Very grossly one might say that it was associated with the preservation of personal values – most relevantly the preservation of values both in a moral context and in an intellectual context. A failure of artistic integrity would be all-disastrous to an artist, and one of political integrity to an administrator. Philosophy, whether it is regarded as primarily metaphysical, speculative or analytic, has traditionally always made the highest demands on the intellect: the loss of intellectual integrity, unclear again though it may be what precisely is entailed by this concept, is equally disastrous to the would-be philosopher. On the other hand, moral philosophy has always had rather a special position. 'Systems' have not always prevailed, but when they have, it has tended to have pride of place in them. Even where metaphysics or epistemology have in fact occupied most of the scene, their place has been seen as leading to, explaining or supporting the relevant moral system. Whether 'reason' played or did not play the dominant part within morality, this itself lay with 'reason' and depended upon the nature of 'reason' to determine. Intellectual integrity is therefore of paramount importance here, too; but given that moral philosophy is overtly concerned not only with man but man as an inevitably egocentric individual faced with the problem of somehow getting along with at least some number of other such individuals, it is perhaps at the same time ancillary to moral integrity whatever that may be. I have perhaps already made too many vague and general statements, but it seems to me that the most general background with its most general obscurities does have some relevance to the particular problem that faces one today and perhaps special relevance to the personal problem of which I complain: a feeling of lack of integrity of any kind in attempting to teach the subject.

To sell out further on intellectual integrity, a few more generalities first. This difficulty does not apply, of course, simply to moral philosophy (nor really for that matter *simply* to philosophy at all). An attempt at clarity, argument and precision, or if not clarity, argument and precision, then a self-conscious obscurity which presupposes these in order to deny them, has always been characteristic at least of Western philosophy, though the favoured methods of achieving these have varied and sometimes seemed to be subordinated to its other characteristic – imaginative and systematized speculation. But to the extent that intellectual acceptance is required, argument must be a necessary vehicle, and objective precise argument has often in itself been a favoured ideal. This is an ideal most nearly realized in mathematics and its allied discipline of formal logic. The essentially artificial languages within which these operate make it possible to satisfy the demand for validity that any argument must raise, and it is a tempting model. But anyone trying to teach elementary logic to undergraduates beginning a philosophy course knows to his cost how remote such a model appears to them, and such skills as they may acquire are normally treated as quite detached from any common 'critical' approach. The apparatus makes the understanding of quasi-technical terms easier, and awareness of such things as the analogies and differences between formal and natural logical constants are useful by-products; they may help with the attempt to impart that skill, the passing on of which may be felt to be the greatest professional obligation – the manipulation of analytic techniques. Such techniques do represent, quite properly, for the ordinary undergraduate, a far more obvious attempt at relevant clarification of thought. To grasp that problems about the relationship between mind and body can at one level be solved or dissolved by examining the presuppositions involved in the use of the terms, can give satisfaction to the pupil who has never previously considered giving any thought to such traditional philosophical problems. Most undergraduates will not have indulged in epistemological speculation until they are forced to treat this branch of philosophy in a formal critical manner, and that usually means treating it as the subject-matter for being drilled in analytic techniques. A few, of course, do have some spontaneous interest, and a few more may find interest awakened; for all these the sorts of problem facing anyone trying to teach them may approach, though I do not think it reaches, the sort of problem I am complaining of being very frequent in teaching moral philosophy. To limit oneself for the moment to moderately competent ('Second Class') pupils – for the majority of these the very absence of engagement or position-prise makes it easier for them, if they profit at all, to acquire the relevant skills in this area. But if, and one counts oneself fortunate if it happens, they do so acquire them, such skills tend to be seen at best as healthy exercise having its own place – probably beneficial in the long run, but without other or immediate relevance to anything else. And perhaps this is as it should be; perhaps if this is achieved, what one is being paid to do has been achieved. But I am not at all clear even about this. Without some interest in the subject matter, drilling itself is far more difficult and, even if it can be done, more barren. A few, the best no doubt, of those pupils who have a natural speculative interest, will find a satisfaction in the tidying up operation that one may be able to offer them; but the less good, and those in whom one can perhaps spark off some temporary interest, are likely to feel at least as much frustration as satisfaction : to work within the limits of articulacy, and of the acceptance of those limits, when dealing with problems which have often beset them in one form or another ever since they became self-conscious and articulate beings, may not seem a pointful exercise. And the normal undergraduate is both impatient and ambitious. So, even at this stage there are likely to be two groups of undergraduates who, while being in a sense successful, may cause one to worry : those who flounder in philosophical bogs without adequate means of extricating themselves, and those, the smaller group, who have mastered the techniques but remain unaware of any bogs too deep for this means of escape.

In teaching elementary epistemology, at least within the present system and with the final examination test in mind, one knows to some extent what one ought to be doing, even if one is not very successful at doing it. At least there is not the same consciousness of a split that seems to show itself in the attempt to teach moral philosophy. Here I find myself not knowing at all what it is I am supposed to be doing. As I implied earlier, part of the trouble, I think, is inherent in the nature of the subject. Intellectual argument must be primarily directed towards intellectual acceptance. Perhaps the most efficient tools of intellectual argument are objectivity and precision, and though analytic techniques can be, and are, useful in moral theory, moral terms notoriously lack to some extent both objectivity and precision. Again, what one requires of moral theory may be intellectual acceptance, but how far moral theory or moral concepts are subject to analysis in isolation, as detached from substantive content, is itself a question moral philosophers have legitimately raised, with no unanimity of answer. There seems to be, even at the conceptual level, confusion as to both methodology and content; and about this I hope to say a little more later. It seems clear that there is a conceptual element in the situation of which I complain, but to what extent this can be distinguished from the more obviously causal elements is far less clear and it is perhaps this that is itself so uncomfortable. What, from the teacher's point of view, most patently marks moral philosophy off from other branches of the subject is, of course, the fact that unlike epistemology or logic, its 'subject-matter', however this is interpreted, is expected to be familiar. This fact in itself produces immediately a further split for, being familiar, the question arises almost inevitably of the place within the discipline that should be given to any first order thinking : and this is where the split in my own approach shows itself. That is what I am inclined to say, though even that may be too objective, for of course it may again be the way in which one sees the situation that determines what is.

However this may be, it seems to me that most undergraduates, with even a minimal training in analytic techniques, are usually prepared – sometimes to the point of prejudice – to find it abstract, second-order and dry; that is to say that on the whole they are prepared to jettison as irrelevant any previous concern they may have had with the 'subject-matter'. But adolescents and young adults are inevitably very much preoccupied with problems related to their own personalities, and though there are those, largely the group I identified earlier as finding their chief satisfaction in the expertise of analytic techniques as such, who remain content to reproduce and criticize traditional and contemporary moral theory in a more or less orthodox way, the majority do find themselves faced with the sometimes frustrating attempt to relate their problems to second-order theorizing and analysis. They find this : but of course it is really I who find them finding it, and again the split is apparent. And this is so without any deliberate attempt or indeed the least intention on my part to approach the subject or the teaching of it in a personal way, in the sense in which one would aim at probing into the personalities of one's pupils or trying at all to indoctrinate them or, from my point of view, 'worse', guide their private lives. There are few things I should be more reluctant to do. For one thing I am not at all clear what my 'views' are; for another, and perhaps more importantly, as teaching an academic discipline, my obligation would seem to be rather to insist on rigour, and in this case, intellectual rigour in the form in which I suppose I have been trained to recognize it. And this is where what I have called 'intellectual integrity' comes in, for whatever exactly is meant by this rather pompous term, it seems to have something to do with one's own standards of performance, such standards as are inculcated, presumably, by one's own training, and to offend against them can produce a sense of betrayal of oneself. If one were an ideal, or even a very good, teacher, one might be able to combine the two stresses, and stress of *some* sort there does seem to be, of academic rigour with attention to questions of substantive moral thinking : but here again only, it seems to me, if his first order moral views were clearly defined and their presuppositions were for him not questionable. Some starting points in any branch of philosophy have to be assumed, but it is a truism that those in moral philosophy lack the objectivity of those in other areas. Mere coherence will not do – arguments directed to a 'language of morals' themselves entail the holding of certain moral views. And so a further split is generated by doubt as to how much weight should be given to substantive moral questions, and if one admits this, uncertainty and lack of clarity of what, in the moral dimension, one is up to.

This paper does not so much describe as exemplify these splits in approach, for whatever the truth may be, I see this difficulty arising from a causal personal factor. If one has spent a large part of one's life primarily concerned with bringing up one's children, and this is well known to one's pupils, one's role as teacher must be to some extent affected – perhaps in two main respects. In bringing up children, one of the questions that faces one, and may do so explicitly, is of course the question of what sort of people, given their inheritance, one would like them to be. There may in fact be – almost certainly is – very little or nothing that one can actually do about it, but one fusses on nevertheless. A fairly basic point is that in so far as one's values are values, one must want one's children to share them; what one believes to be most important is what one would like them to believe to be most important. But against this, one also wants them to be fully adult and to see themselves as being so. An adult's values must be seen as his own in order to be his own; values seen as merely inherited are scarcely fully adult values. Though, as I have said, some pupils – 'competent' ones – are content to remain detached in their approach to moral philosophy, many respond by an explicit or implicit, official or unofficial, introduction of their own first order personal 'moral' problems – and whether I approve or not, I find myself encouraging this. All this must be particularly true at the present moment, when practically every undergraduate is self-consciously aware of his need for establishing and determining at some level or other his own system of values, whether or not he sees this as a 'moral' question. Moral integrity must also be a matter of the standards and values one accepts, but this is a far more complex affair, or may be a far more complex affair, than the acquiring of intellectual skill.

It is no historical accident that orthodoxy and authoritarianism are so much out of fashion. Fairly obvious explanations could be given in historical terms. What is relevant is that they are out of fashion. It does not seem to be a merely personal, but a fairly general assumption, that an adult is responsible for his own determination of these. Mere acceptance or blind obedience or conformity, though they must have a place, conspicuously within the more authoritarian religions, are not generally considered admirable, or even passable. Values seem in need of personal justification : but in what does such a justification consist ? And again there is a split, for merely to raise the question of justification is to deny at any level at which this happens, the possibility of presupposition. Intellectual acceptance demands coherence and a rationale – this has most often been the legitimate object of moral philosophers; human, personal problems are traditionally more intransigent and, even if complete intellectualization at this level were possible, it could not be sufficient. Split after split is again generated as one sees that this very process of intellectualization and clarification, though it may for oneself appear to have some ultimate value, may not, in some perhaps dubious sense of the word, be 'right' even for undergraduates reading philosophy, let alone for everyone. Pupils who have been brought up as members of authoritarian churches can suffer very really by being encouraged to probe their premises, and though such suffering can be regarded as either healthy or trivial, it all, without exaggerating one's own importance in these things, produces a frustrating sense of lack of clarity. One has a feeling of both moral and intellectual integrity being undermined.

Of course, this is all very subjective : and it is a subjective point of view that this is necessarily so – that the moral philosophy (and perhaps its teaching) necessarily reveals the nature of the man. Less controversially, there seems no doubt that those who hold or adopt moral systems that seem to themselves clear and consistent are not likely to be beset in their teaching by the kind of strain to which I confess. This was confirmed by a seminar in which papers were read on the teaching of moral philosophy. Viewpoints probably appeared more extreme than they actually were, but it was noticeable that at one extreme, moral argument on more or less utilitarian lines, together with an analysis of the relevant concepts, seemed an entirely satisfactory method of procedure; at the other extreme, with which I should certainly not wish to identify myself, self-conscious inarticulacy and incoherence was offered as the only honest position. To some, the strain – and split – seemed, even given the common ground of working in terms of human wants and needs, to come at the point where it was seen that though many of these could perhaps be supplied, and should be so supplied, by some sort of universalized principle or set of principles of behaviour, the most deeply felt human wants and needs could be satisfied only by some sort of spontaneity of feeling – producing a contradiction and essential lack of coherence. To others, rather differently, given that substantive moral values could not be entirely intellectualized, the strain and split arose at the point at which the question of respect for the values of others came up and the degree to which one's own could or should be imposed or those of others influenced. Incoherence would again seem to arise from an insistence that each must choose, in a quasi-Sartrian way, for himself, this insistence being itself an ultimate but personal value.

Such questions as these can be seen, and have been seen, themselves to be within the legitimate province of moral philosophy. To see them in this light however is, in my own case, to react instinctively to a need for intellectual clarification. 'Intellectual integrity' is at stake again. But to make efforts to right this is scarcely relevant to the situation of teaching beginners' moral philosophy. It is not the abstruse intellectual aspect that is distressing here – though it may be indirectly relevant; it is rather the fact that it is only too easy to allow oneself to neglect almost completely what one regards as philosophy at the cost of giving one's attention to the first order moral or personal worries that tend to be triggered off in the tutorial setting. The role of 'listener' is not an uncongenial one, and the, I think, increasing seriousness with which undergraduates in the present climate of opinion tend to take their moral and political problems might well justify time spent in this way: but though one may neglect philosophy almost completely, it is hard to do so quite completely. Clarity is an intellectual virtue which, however elusive it may be, is hard to dismiss deliberately: indeed it may be very hard not to see it as a moral virtue in itself. Clarity in some respects must be demanded, but it is easy for oversimplification to masquerade as perhaps half-baked clarity – or again, though in some contexts it may be an end in itself, in others it scarcely should be given this honourable place. Pupils – not the best – have made use of the name of clarity to justify the increasingly legalistic system they wish to see adopted in college and university administration. They may well be right in this, but in this particular argument the name may blind them to the fact that the more precise the machinery, the greater the risk of failure of human trust and, given a failure of human trust, the greater the further risk of total abuse. Natural language is distorted by the strait-jacket of formal logic and human justice by an attempt at over-precise anticipation. This is a fairly superficial example of the sort of muddle, however one looks at it, that I am inclined to call half-baked; and it is perhaps not irrelevant that the pupils involved were overtly concerned with their own 'integrity'. Sadder cases are those to which I have already alluded, where a pupil's loyalty to an authoritarian religion may struggle with the attempt to see himself as a fully moral agent only if he takes responsibility for his own decisions. It would be possible, but hardly necessary, to display more phoneyness with the proliferation of examples – enough seems to have been said. That there is a genuine problem and a very interesting one can scarcely be doubted: it is an additional frustration that, no doubt for good psychological causes, even a negative exposition seems to reveal only split and block.

Any attempt to be entirely articulate seems almost inevitably self-defeating: that is a personal confession and one that is intended not only as a redundant apology for one's own fairly obvious limits, but to explain also what may more generally account for the sense of there being a problem at all. Intellectualization, articulacy and clarity should go together; and perhaps this process starts with the formulation of the question that is being raised. A question that cannot in principle at least be properly formulated is no proper question. Moral terms may lack the ἀκρίβεια of logical or epistemological terms, but that is not necessarily to say that within the relevant discourse they lack clarity : clear answers can no doubt be given where clear questions can be asked. It is no new thought that the use of such terms as 'character' for instance, though it must maintain some objectivity, is not amenable to the same standards as that of more rigid impersonal terminology. It is only this very general presupposition that gives a possible use to such terms. But this general presupposition generates or may generate the problem that in operating with such terms, in attempting to 'clarify' or sort out what I have called second order moral theory from first order moral tenets, much has to be taken for granted. And what is taken for granted has, literally, to go without saying : one may state that the answer is taken for granted, but in so stating, one is acknowledging that the question has been raised; 'taking for granted' no longer has what I should like to call its full force. At this level one may see oneself as 'knowing' one's premises – this would be comfortable. But one may 'know' that, at least in the narrower sense of the word, one is not, or may not be, fully 'rational'. One may find oneself holding moral premises that, were they ascribed to anyone else, one would be inclined to describe as dogmatic, unjustified, prejudiced – being one's own, one cannot view them in this light, or again so far as one does so view them, one cannot hold them in the way I suggest. It is a matter of the sort of person one is : one may find, trivially or not so trivially, in 'real', 'first order' life that one can be no other – and this may be not only without the support of reason or reasons, but as one sees it, counter to reason or reasons. Truth, 'getting it right', seems to be a demand both of intellectual and of moral integrity, and truth requires not merely honesty, but veracity. Honest doubt is all very well, and honest muddle has its place, even in philosophy – confusion and obscurity are another matter; they may have defenders, but I should prefer not to place myself among them. No doubt the resolution between first-order moral premises and second-order theory can be seen as a philosophically respectable intellectual problem – and this is how I should myself like to see it and feel strongly that it ought to be so seen. To be intellectually inadequate, which would be one's trouble if this were all that was the matter, is uncomfortable, but something with which one is anyhow forced to come to terms. It is more distressing to find oneself in a position in which one is both committed to setting a very high value on clarity at all levels, and aware that one is ultimately unclear without the advantage of being open-minded, at the first-order ('presupposition') level; one is not clear as to the mode in which one is operating. Even the attempt to state all this in such a paper seems to induce a kind of pretentiousness, for such statements must reflect a claim to importance, which in itself is out of place.

3   Deceiving, hurting and using

Larry Blum

Human beings mistreat each other. We have many ways of describing, explaining, and understanding this fundamental aspect of human life. We say, for example, that people use, manipulate, hurt, deceive, are unfair to, are cruel to, harm, humiliate, torture, are inconsiderate towards, are spiteful towards, are insensitive towards one another.

Some mistreating takes place in a context of personal relationships and some does not; some descriptions of types of mistreatment can apply in both contexts. For example, I can deceive a business associate in regard to a business deal in which we are both involved; I can also deceive a lover about my feelings for her. I can humiliate a friend by telling people about some conduct of his of which he is ashamed; I can also humiliate someone I hardly know, for example a prisoner or a subordinate in my place of work. The distinction between 'personal relationships' and other forms of human interaction and association is not a sharp one. Friends, lovers, many types of familial relationships will fall into the former category; salesman and customer, workers in different parts of the same factory, residents of the same neighbourhood, people riding the underground together will usually fall into the latter category. Of course, merely by the institutional structure or form of the relationship one will not know whether the persons are involved in a personal relationship or not; the point is that certain institutional forms will not count, in themselves, as personal relationships. Thus a doctor and his patient may be close friends, but their doctor–patient relationship is not itself a personal relationship.

In this paper, I will focus on one type of description of mistreatment important in the morality of personal relationships : the notion of *using people*. I will first describe several examples of what seem to be fairly standard cases in which we would say that one person is using another in the context of a personal relationship. I choose to describe several such cases rather than just one in order to give some evidence of the different kinds of things which can go on in instances of using.

Example 1 A has ambitions to rise above his present social status. To help him realize these ambitions, he forms an attachment with a girl who likes him very much and through whom he is likely to meet and become acquainted with a group of (what he considers) socially superior people. Despite this ignoble motive for promoting this relationship A is not cruel or unkind to the girl, but on the contrary is kind and considerate towards her. Nevertheless, when A eventually comes to feel that he is accepted on his own by the group of the girl's friends he slowly and as painlessly as possible allows the relationship with the girl to end.

Example 2 A is introduced to B whom he discovers to be fond of children, though having none of his own, and to have a house on Cape Cod where he regularly goes for the summer. With the thought in mind that if he becomes friendly with B, B is likely eventually to invite A's children to his house for the summer, and that the children would be happier spending part of their summer at such a house than they would with the facilities available to A, A attempts to become friendly with B, although, in the absence of B's having the house, he would not make this attempt for he is not so genuinely fond of B. Eventually A and B become (what B regards as) fairly close friends, close enough for B to invite A's children to his home during several summers.

Example 3 Joe is a man who feels that he needs to have women around him. At present he is going through a difficult period in his academic work, as he must turn in his dissertation in six weeks. He meets Gwendolyn who seems to fancy him, but with whom under ordinary circumstances he would not want to have a sustained relationship. Nevertheless she offers him the prospect of some emotional security and stability, as well as a good deal of affectionate care, during the next six weeks. And so he decides to, and does, maintain a romantic involvement with her until his thesis is in.

Example 4   Marlene is writing her Ph.D. dissertation about which she has great anxiety. She meets Ed and feels as if she likes him, but because she is preoccupied with her work, she does not give much directed thought to Ed or to how she feels about him. Ed does know that he likes Marlene and they begin going out and soon begin living together. From nearly the beginning of their romantic involvement Marlene finds her anxiety about her work decreasing and she is much better able to write her thesis. That Ed's presence has a greatly beneficial effect on her and on her ability to work is regarded by Ed and Marlene as a normal and natural effect (or aspect) of their having a good relationship, that is, a relationship which has a genuine basis in mutual caring and feeling, independent of the security and lessened anxiety which Marlene received as a result of it. For example, it is taken for granted, without being given much thought, that the relationship will continue without any substantial change in feeling after Marlene finishes her thesis. (And it would be in general unnatural if they *did* give this much thought.)

Despite this, however, in actuality Ed and Marlene's relationship would *not* continue on this plane in the absence of her working on her dissertation. For Marlene does not really like and care for Ed as much as she and he think she does. We can imagine that after the thesis is turned in the relationship begins to deteriorate and eventually Marlene terminates it. It would be true to express Marlene and Ed's situation by saying that for Marlene the attachment to Ed, and thus her part in the relationship, is based primarily on the security, lessened anxiety, etc., which she receives as a result of it.

I am portraying this as a case of deception and self-deception. And something must be said about how Marlene and Ed could have remained ignorant of the true nature of Marlene's feelings for Ed. It is not, I think, hard to imagine. No doubt there was evidence of lack of real feeling on Marlene's part – incidents in which Marlene was unresponsive or imperceptive about Ed's needs and feelings and moods; times in which she was mean and insensitive, perhaps occasional quarrels. But such indications can always be misread; they are seldom conclusive evidence of a real lack of feeling. In any case people just *are* often imperceptive about such evidence of others', and of their own feelings, especially when circumstances would make it unpleasant and difficult to acknowledge the evidence objectively. In this example, we can imagine that Ed is disposed to be indulgent with Marlene because of the dissertation and thus tends to attribute her unresponsiveness, etc., to her general anxious situation, or to a bad mood.

These considerations apply both to Ed and to Marlene, but in her case the lack of recognition of the true situation (i.e. her self-deception) requires accounting for more than in Ed's case, since she is the person whose feelings are in question.[1] We could perhaps imagine that she is a bit self-centred in general and this trait in the context of her preoccupation with her thesis could account for her not attending to the kinds of things which might lead her to realize how she feels about Ed.

I will leave these four examples of one person using another as they are described. Yet it is obvious that they are not described fully or convincingly or plausibly enough. The descriptions do not present us, I feel, with situations which we recognize as ones which seem sufficiently real that we know what to say about them from a human or moral point of view. A typical example of the inadequacy of description is this: I have tried to describe example 4 so that it differed from the previous three in the important respect that the person who was using the other was aware of doing so in the first three examples but not in the fourth – it is this which occasions the much lengthier description in example 4. But it is evident that on this dimension the first three are oversimplified. In example 1, for example, I say, 'To help him realize his ambitions A forms an attachment with a girl. . . .' One might get the impression, though it is not explicitly stated, that A says something like this to himself, 'Since I want to make it socially and since Jean is a classy girl with classy friends, if I can just make it with her, I'll be able to meet them and get in with them, and then I'll drop Jean, since I don't really care much for her anyway.' This form of callousness is perhaps not so common. Generally, a person is not so conscious of his motivation if he is using another person in this sort of way. More typically, the case would be something like this: A would notice and be drawn to the girl because she seemed to him a 'classy' girl, *one* of the things involved in this being that she had socially superior friends. He would not think to himself that he was interested *only* in her 'classiness' and not in *her*; he would not really make this distinction, and he would not distinguish sharply and consistently his interest in her friends from his interest in her. Nevertheless, his real and *relatively* conscious interest in the girl is in her friends. In the case thus more fully described the description given in example 1 is still applicable. We just *can* say 'A has ambitions to rise above his present social status. To help him realize these ambitions, he forms an attachment with a girl etc.', even though A does not have a totally explicit awareness of his motives. One could further describe these cases so as to justify saying that the person doing the using was *partly aware* of doing so, or that he was *more* or *less* aware (than in another case). Thus it is perhaps more useful to regard all the examples as lying on a dimension of more or less consciousness of using, with the first example near one end and the fourth near the other.[2]

I want now to focus on an important aspect of using, as exemplified in these examples, and that is that a person who is being used by another person is not necessarily being hurt or made unhappy in being used. The person who is doing the using (whom we will henceforth refer to as 'A' in the absence of a specific name given) is not necessarily mean, nasty, or cruel to the person being used (whom I will refer to as 'B'). Thus in example 3, one can imagine Joe being reasonably attentive to G's wishes, considerate of her feelings, and not selfish in his interactions with her; in such a case we can imagine Gwendolyn being quite happy in their relationship. The same could be said of the man and woman in example 1. Nevertheless in both cases one person is using the other.

One may still feel uneasy about this and want to say something like 'It isn't *real* considerateness (kindness, niceness) that Joe is showing here. Certainly one is not being *really* considerate (kind, nice) to someone if one is using him.' There is some point to this response and I am not certain that I can say flatly that it is false; but it does express some confusion. The valid point in the response is this: the kindness and considerateness cannot, as it were, go very *deep*. The user cannot, in being kind and considerate, be giving too much of himself to the other person or it will no longer make sense to say that he is using him. A 'deeper' kindness would involve a level or degree or form of caring and giving which would be incompatible with using someone. One might say, then, that there is a *limit* to the depth of kindness and considerateness which is compatible with using someone. But the presence of such a deeper kindness and considerateness is not necessary to saying that one person is 'kind' or 'considerate' to another. One can be kind or considerate to someone (in some types of situations) while nevertheless lacking those kinds of feelings for that other person which also naturally express themselves in kindness and which may seem sometimes to be the really important part of kindness. So being kind and considerate to someone is certainly compatible with using him, and being used is compatible with not being hurt and with being happy or satisfied in a relationship.

In spite of a response which would want to deny these facts, the facts can, on the other hand, seem so obvious as to be of negligible interest. Of course Gwendolyn is not hurt, since she does not *realize* she is being used; if she did realize it she would be hurt. This *is* obvious, but not uninteresting. For it brings out that using as a type of moral misconduct is a very different kind of thing from being cruel, being inconsiderate, being nasty, being not nice, being insensitive. It is characteristic of the latter group that the person who is the object of this type of misconduct is hurt, offended, made unhappy, etc., by it; whereas it seems not characteristic of being used (within a personal relationship) that some type of (what we might call) a 'negative psychological reaction' is produced in the person being used.[3] This is of course connected with the fact that a person being used (within a personal relationship) characteristically does *not* know that he is being used, whereas a person who is the object of someone's being cruel, mean, inconsiderate, etc., does characteristically know it and it is part of what it is to know it that characteristically a 'negative psychological state' is produced in him.

But why are the differences between using and hurting interesting? Here I must backtrack for a moment. 'Using someone' has been taken to be something which it is (*ceteris paribus*) wrong or bad to do.[4] In examining the notion of 'using people' we will want to know *why* it is wrong or bad to use people, *what* is wrong with using people, what is *morally objectionable* about using people. These are things which we can, it seems, fail to know, while yet knowing *that* it is morally objectionable to use people (knowing *that* it is wrong to use people etc.).

D

But how does one *show* the moral objectionability of some morally objectionable type of conduct? One way, it seems, is to show that the type of conduct involves *hurting someone*. If we are concerned with some type of behaviour which seems to be morally objectionable and we are wondering what makes it morally objectionable, to see that it involves someone's being hurt is to know what makes the behaviour morally objectionable; or so it would seem. Thus when we see, as we did above, that using people, though morally objectionable, nevertheless does *not* characteristically involve hurting people, we might find this strange. It might seem, in fact, that unless the user hurts the person being used there is nothing morally objectionable about using him. Alternatively one can feel certain that using *is* genuinely morally objectionable in itself and conclude that the person being used *must* be being hurt in *some* way, even though perhaps not in the obvious way involved in being the object of cruelty or meanness or unkindness. Both of these reactions involve the common assumption that (at least in a context of personal relations) there *must* be some connection between what is morally objectionable and what hurts people.

I want to examine the issue of the actual role hurting plays in understanding what it is to use people and in understanding what is morally objectionable in using people. Does hurting explain (what is wrong with) using people as it may seem to? In discussing this, I will have to deal with the general question, 'What role does hurting play in explaining or understanding morally objectionable behaviour?'

The first thing to note is that 'hurting' does not itself need explaining in the way that using does. We do not wonder why it is wrong to hurt. We do not look for an account of what it is to hurt someone in the way we look for an account of what it is to use someone. We do not find ourselves confused about what it is to hurt someone in the way we do about what it is to use someone. We are more likely to run across people who seem genuinely not to see that there is anything wrong with using someone unless it involves hurting him than people who genuinely do not see what is wrong with hurting people.

These observations are perhaps somewhat oversimplified. Sometimes we do *not* wonder what is wrong with using people any more than we wonder what is wrong with hurting people.

In some cases if I can show that in A's conduct toward B, A is using B, then one can feel that I have said all that needs to be said about the moral objectionability of A's conduct. Kant some-times seems to say that the idea of treating people as means rather than ends (a notion closely related to that of using people) is the fundamental type of moral objectionability in terms of which the others are to be explained and understood. Nevertheless, it does seem generally right to say that the question 'What is morally objectionable about using people?' needs the kind of answer which the question 'What is morally objectionable about hurting people?' does not.

Thus hurting does not need explaining in the way that using does. This fact is one of the conditions which enables hurting to be the kind of concept which is *capable* of explaining the moral objectionability of using.

Though we now understand better what it means for a concept like 'hurting' to explain[5] the moral objectionability of using, we have previously seen that it cannot actually explain using, for hurting people is not involved in all (morally objectionable) in-stances of using. Nevertheless, in understanding the relations be-tween using and hurting the following fact is surely important: if someone discovers he is being used, he is likely to, he charac-teristically will, feel hurt. If this is important, then the fact that the person being used does not know he is being used, i.e. the fact that he is being *deceived*, must also be an important con-sideration in understanding the moral objectionability of using people. I will thus consider the role of deception along with hurting in understanding using people; and I will try to discover this role by showing ways in which neither of these types of morally objectionable conduct can be seen as providing an *ex-planation* of using.

If one is confused as to the moral objectionability of some purported misconduct, to recognize that it involves deceiving the person can appear to clear up this confusion and explain what is wrong with the type of behaviour in question. In this way *deception* has the same status as *hurting* with regard to their capability of explaining using. But in another respect they are different; for, unlike hurting, deception can itself seem to need explanation as to *its* moral objectionability. We can wonder 'What is wrong with deceiving people (if they are not hurt)?' Despite this disparallel with hurting it still remains true that deception is more obviously morally objectionable than using, and hence is, like hurting, a candidate for explaining the moral objectionability of using.

There are two types of case to be considered in regard to the truth that someone who is being used but is not aware of it *would* characteristically be hurt if he *were* aware of it.

(1) In some cases the person being used is likely to find out that he is being used or was being used (in a relationship already terminated). For example, in example 2 when A's children are older and no longer enjoy spending summers at the Cape, then A, as we have portrayed him, will no longer have any reason to keep up his acquaintance with B and will perhaps make no attempts to see B and will not respond to B's natural attempts to continue their friendship. Perhaps B will soon come to understand A's motivation in pursuing and maintaining their friendship previously and he would certainly be hurt by this realization. Similarly in example 3 Gwendolyn might well come to realize (after she and Joe have stopped seeing each other) the nature of Joe's feelings and intentions towards her and she would certainly be hurt by this realization. In this type of case what could explain what is wrong with using the person is that the person is likely to be hurt as a result of the expected outcome of the relationship. Though this is different from the person's actually being hurt in being used, nevertheless the role of hurting in explaining what is wrong with using is essentially the same in both cases, i.e. using is wrong because it involves or is likely to involve someone's being hurt.

(2) In many other instances of people being used, although the conditional statement remains true, nevertheless the person being used never does realize that he is being or has been used (and *a fortiori* is never hurt as a result of being used). For example, in example 3 one can easily imagine the romance breaking up without Gwendolyn ever realizing Joe's lack of feeling for her and his intentions in regard to her. One can imagine Joe telling her that he has simply stopped caring for her, he does not know why; such things do happen, so one can imagine Gwendolyn accepting this explanation. She would perhaps be confused and hurt and sad that the relationship was over, but she would not be hurt as a result of being used but only as a result of the relationship no

longer existing. In cases of this type it is not necessary to envisage that the person being used has *false* beliefs about why the relationship terminated. In example 3 Gwendolyn might just resign herself to being *confused* about why she and Joe broke up: 'I don't know what happened exactly; after Joe got his thesis in, things just didn't seem to work out right', she might say to herself. This is hardly uncommon. One can easily imagine a similar outcome in the first and fourth examples.

In these cases (type 2) the conditional statement that if the person being used realized it, he would be hurt, remains true; but the role which the hurt plays in understanding the moral objectionability of using is different than in the type 1 case, since no *actual* hurt is ever involved. These cases, unlike type 1, remain problematic from the point of view of understanding the connection between using and hurting.

Clearly deception plays a significant role in these cases; it is the deception which prevents the person from being hurt. If in considering such cases one were to try to construct an explanation of the moral objectionability of using in terms of hurting and deception, one might do it in these terms: deception involved in maintaining a situation in which one person would be hurt, if he were aware of the true nature of that situation, is what explains what is wrong with using someone (in cases in which no hurt is involved). But this cannot be right; for keeping someone from being hurt is the kind of thing which *justifies* or at least *mitigates* deception, rather than contributing to the moral objectionability of the behaviour. For example, suppose I am aware that A is using B and I do not tell B because I believe that he would be hurt. Clearly *my* behaviour is less condemnable than A's (deception in) using B; but the above explanation in terms of deception and potential hurt, does not make any moral distinction between my position and A's in this situation, since we are both deceiving B in a situation in which B would be hurt if he realized the true situation. Hence the proffered account fails to explain (the moral force of) the using involved in cases of type 2.

Let us now focus on the concept of deception directly. Consider the following case: Jim meets Paul and in a vague attempt to impress him tells him that as a child he spent a year in a school in Switzerland, which is not the case. Throughout their acquaintance Jim, out of embarrassment, fails to correct this misimpression; but in fact very little of Paul's opinion of Jim is connected in any way with his belief that Jim spent a year in a school in Switzerland, and Jim realizes this.

In this example Jim is deceiving Paul. But we would not be likely to view this as a serious moral failure on Jim's part (some might even find the term 'moral failure' too strong). And we would certainly not regard it as serious a moral failure as the conduct of the people doing the using in the various examples we have considered. But common to those examples and the one just considered is that morally objectionable behaviour in the form of deception is involved.

Thus, when deception is involved in a context of one person using another, it seems to be a more serious moral fault than in at least some other cases in which using is not involved. One thing which follows from this is that the mere fact that deception is involved in an instance of using cannot fully account for, fully explain, the moral objectionability of using someone. There must be some morally relevant difference other than the deception itself which accounts for the difference in moral weight or force of the deception as it is involved in cases such as that of the sociologist as compared to the deception involved in cases of using.

The idea that deception cannot *by itself* explain using is hardly surprising once we can grasp the idea of deception-by-itself at all. But it is this notion (deception-by-itself) and its relation to the idea that deception is evaluated differently in different circumstances which requires some comment. The idea that deception might be evaluated differently in different circumstances might come to no more than this: that in situations in which deception is involved the behaviour of the person doing the deceiving will be evaluated taking into account not only his deception, but also other morally relevant considerations (e.g. that he is hurting someone) and that the final evaluation will depend on the weighing of the evaluations of all the morally relevant considerations. An obvious example could be of someone's lying to save an innocent friend from harm. Here the deception, one might say, is bad *in itself*, but saving an innocent friend is so good (in itself) that it far outweighs the deception, and thus the conduct *as a whole* is good. It may be, this view would grant, linguistically permissible to say

'Lying is good in some cases, but bad in others', but this will mean no more than that when a given morally relevant consideration is present in a situation, other morally relevant considerations may also be present which will affect the overall evaluation of the behaviour in that situation. This would not contradict the idea that deception in itself has a particular moral weight or force which does not vary in different situations; one could still maintain that in cases of using people there are other morally relevant considerations besides the deception which, along with the deception, fully account for the moral objectionability of using someone; and it would still be our task to identify these other morally relevant considerations.

What might these other morally relevant considerations be in the case of using? Clearly using itself cannot be a candidate, the most obvious reason being that one would have then abandoned the attempt to *explain* using, in so far as deception was supposed to be a part of that explanation. A more fruitful approach would be to say that in cases of using, the deception involved is of a type involving the feelings and attitudes of one person for the other in a context of a kind of relationship in which those feelings and attitudes are an essential part; whereas in the school in the Switzerland case (see pp. 43–4) the deception involved concerns something less significant, that is, where a person went to school when he was young. This is surely an important element in understanding the different situations from a moral point of view. However, as it is stated, this consideration is not of the form of *another* morally relevant consideration or feature *alongside* or together with the deception. Rather it is more like this: one might classify deception into different *types*, depending on what the deception is *about*, e.g. one's past, one's feelings, one's work (and also depending on the kind of setting or situation or context of those feelings, e.g. a personal relationship).

Utilizing the idea of 'types of deception', then, one might say that there is one type of deception, i.e. deception about one's feelings toward another person in a close relationship, which can explain the moral objectionability of using. That is, that it is because using involved deceiving another person about one's feelings and attitudes toward him that using is morally objectionable (at least in cases in which hurt is not involved).

But this view is also wrong. Consider the following case:

Example 5   Patsy and Eric have been going together. Eric cares for Patsy very much, but the feeling is not reciprocated by Patsy, though it used to be. The waning of her former feelings for Eric is something Patsy has only recently become conscious of. But she does not tell Eric this, primarily because she cannot yet bring herself to do something which she knows will cause Eric great pain. (This is not to say that it is the *unpleasantness to her* of having to face Eric's reaction to her confessing her lack of feeling which motivates her. Such a case would be more a matter of selfishness and less one of the genuine concern for Eric which I am attributing to Patsy.) Patsy maintains, for the present, a semblance of fully participating in the relationship. Since this state of affairs has had only a temporary existence, we can imagine that Eric has not yet realized (or has done so only in a confused and inexplicit way) that Patsy has lost her strong feelings of attachment to and affection for him.

In this example Patsy is deceiving Eric about her true feelings for him, just as Joe is deceiving Gwendolyn in example 3 – in both cases one person represents himself as caring for the other in a way in which he, in fact, does not care for the other. And so there is, in the language we are now using, the same 'type' of deception going on in both cases. But do we regard the conduct as a whole of Patsy as equally morally objectionable as that of Joe? I think not. Patsy's conduct seems clearly less objectionable than Joe's (if it is objectionable at all).[6] Hence this one type of deception cannot account for the moral objectionability of using someone.[7]

Throughout the discussion so far the notion of *explaining* or *accounting for* the moral objectionability of some type of conduct has been left vague (see note 5). Its primary content so far has been the idea that some concepts denoting morally objectionable types of behaviour, such as 'hurting' and 'deceiving', do not appear to require explanation as to their moral objectionability in the way that the concept 'using' does. And that if it could be shown that deception and hurt are involved in all cases of using which are morally objectionable, then one would have succeeded in providing an explanation of using. Thus the general model for such an explanation would seem to be that the moral objectionability of a concept X, which denotes a morally objectionable type of conduct, is explained or accounted for by showing that in every instance of it other concepts Y, Z . . . which connote moral objectionability and which do *not* stand in need of such explanations, also apply. But my subsequent discussion has not always operated with this model. For in every case of using so far presented, deception has been involved; nevertheless I have argued that deception cannot explain the moral objectionability of using. Thus I have brought in other elements beyond that model of explanation which must be included in anything which is to count as an explanation of using. I now want to make these elements explicit.

Even if a concept Y meets the given requirements (to be an explanation) for a given concept X it may still be the case that X carries a *stronger moral force or weight* than Y. This is what has been shown in the case of deception and using. If one attempts to consider deception *by itself* (within the context of personal relations), it does not carry nearly the moral force of the concept of using and hence cannot account for its moral objectionability; and when it is seen that the moral force of the concept of deception itself varies in different circumstances, so that we can speak of different types of deception, nevertheless there do not seem to be any immediately plausible ways of picking out a particular type of deception which will account for the full moral force of using someone (within a context of personal relations).

Thus, to supplement the original model of explanation we have to add the condition that the concept which is doing the explaining must carry the *same moral force* as the one which is being explained, that is, they must both involve the same 'degree' of moral objectionability. It is this more adequate model in terms of which hurt and deception have been shown *not* to explain using. I now want to give some kind of positive account of the kind of moral force the concepts of 'hurt' and 'deception' have and what role they play in the understanding of using people within the context of personal relationships. I begin with deception.

It is an obvious fact about deceiving people that it is characteristically done with some purpose. In some cases that purpose can be characterized (roughly) as, bringing about some state of affairs for which the following two conditions hold : (1) in order to bring about this state of affairs the deceiver needs the noninterference, co-operation, or participation of the person deceived; and (2) the person being deceived would be unlikely to co-operate, participate, or not interfere if he knew the true situation (i.e. the intentions of the deceiver). Thus I might lie to a guard at the Pentagon and tell him that I am going to visit my cousin who works there, although I am really looking the place over as part of a plan to blow it up.

Of this class of cases of deception there is a large class in which the reason that the person being deceived would not co-operate, etc., if he knew the true situation, is that he finds the deceiver's purposes *objectionable*. The above example does not necessarily fall into this class; the guard may well not think that blowing up the Pentagon is objectionable, but might nevertheless not refrain from interfering with my plan (if he knew of it) because of fear of being found out. Typically, however, he would find my plan objectionable. Of the above sub-class of cases a large sub-class would be cases in which the person being deceived would find the deceiver's purposes morally (as opposed, e.g. to aesthetically) objectionable. The guard at the Pentagon would be likely to meet this description.

In this latter group of cases, in which deception which is morally objectionable is going on, the *context* of that deception involves moral objectionability in another way also: the moral objectionability, to the person being deceived, of the purposes of the deceiver. This second aspect of the moral objectionability is, of course, not generally reducible to, or identical with, the moral objectionability of the deception itself.

It is evident that using is such a type of case. It is because being used is something objectionable to the person who is being used that the deception is required. That the user acknowledges this objectionability is shown in his recognition of the necessity of that deception. Obviously he does not (generally) go through an explicit process of reasoning, that in order to be able to treat X in the way he wishes, he must deceive him; for this fact is so obvious that the deception is, as it were, already contained in the decision toward the person in a way which constitutes using him.[8]

How does the user know that being used is (characteristically) objectionable to the person being used? Obviously this is not merely an empirical matter; the user does not, and does not need to, look for *evidence* that the person would object to being used.

Rather, involved in understanding that it is *using* which one is doing to another person *is* understanding that one is doing something (characteristically, *ceteris paribus*) objectionable to that person.[9]

These considerations make clear that some understanding of the moral objectionability of using is involved in understanding the role of deception in the context of using, and hence that deception can never *explain*, or account for, using. In the discussion so far I have considered only cases of using which also involve deception. An accurate picture of the role of deception in using requires recognition that it is not necessary to using that the person used be deceived. Consider the following example:

Example 6 Ann and Bill are going together. Ann cares very much for Bill, but the feeling is not reciprocated. Bill is no longer very sensitive or considerate towards Ann. He is too often unwilling to interest himself in her concerns, to respond to her moods, and to take her feelings and wishes into account in the regulation of his life. He is often indifferent to her presence. On the other hand he finds her more intellectually congenial and stimulating than most people he knows and he also still finds her sexually attractive. In honest moments he admits to himself, and occasionally to Ann, that for him the sex and the intellectual stimulation are his only reasons for maintaining his part in the relationship and that the deeper feelings of concern and affection for her, which once were so intimately bound up with their intellectual and sexual relationship, are no longer really present. Though Bill does acknowledge this situation in honest moments, the recognition of his lack of caring for Ann is seldom so explicitly present in his mind. The satisfactions to him of their intellectual and sexual interactions (though so importantly different and less fully satisfying than they were before, when they were bound up with his and Ann's mutual affection and caring), allow Bill not to be constantly aware of the deep inadequacy of his part in their relationship.

Ann is willing to tolerate this state of affairs because she really does care for Bill. Like him she regards as honest moments those in which he articulates his lack of feeling for her and his motivation in maintaining the relationship; but like him, it is very seldom that she thinks so explicitly about the state of their relationship. She can find in her day-to-day interaction with Bill ways of responding to him and of viewing their situation which allow her *not* to be explicitly aware of his feelings and attitudes towards her. Further, although she has no reason to believe that Bill's feelings will change, she nevertheless continues to hope – as persons in her situation might naturally do – that he may come to reciprocate her feelings for him. And so she has chosen to continue in this relationship at least for the present – though she tells herself that she may want to break it off sometime in the future when the situation becomes too much for her to take, when she comes to feel that it is perhaps just too degrading. Sometimes she wishes that she had the strength to break it off now, but this sentiment is not a dominant one.

In this example Bill is using Ann. This is so because, although he did not *enter into* the relationship with a view only to what benefits, comforts, and pleasures he would derive from Ann's sexual and intellectual companionship, at this point these are essentially his sole reasons for wanting to maintain the relationship. Formerly his motives included a genuine caring for Ann, which is no longer present. As in example 4 we can say that for Bill the relationship is based primarily on the intellectual and sexual companionship which he receives as a result of it, and it is therefore a case of using. Involved in Bill's using Ann is also that he is not trying to extricate himself from the relationship nor is he trying to make it easier for Ann to extricate herself. (His trying to extricate himself, or at least making it easier for Ann to extricate herself, would still be compatible with Bill's deriving benefits and pleasures from the relationship, as he is now doing, but would not be compatible with these benefits and pleasures *accounting for* why he still maintains the relationship, and hence such cases would not be instances of Bill's using Ann.)

Although Bill is using Ann he is not deceiving her. She is aware of the nature of Bill's feelings for and intentions toward her and, despite this, she has chosen not to break off the relationship. In this case, as in the others, being used is objectionable to the person being used; this was the central aspect of using which helped us to understand the role of deception. But using does not, as the example shows, *require* deception. What it does require is that the fact that the person being used does not discontinue the relationship requires some explanation. The most characteristic explanation involves deception, so that the person does not realize that he is being used. But there are also cases in which the objectionability is in some way overcome (rather than masked). One example of this would be a case in which the person being used would suffer more if he did not go along with the using than he would if he did. An instance of this would be physical coercion, e.g. rape at knife-point. Example 6 exhibits a more common type of case of using without deception in which coercion is not involved.[10]

To summarize the main points of my discussion of deception and using: deception is more obviously morally objectionable than using, but deception is not always involved in using people (cf. example 6) and for this reason could not explain using. However, a more fundamental reason why deception cannot explain using is that the moral objectionability of using is presupposed in understanding the role which deception plays in using people. That using people must be acknowledged to be objectionable on its own is seen also in cases in which deception is not involved.

I will now consider *hurting* and its role as a concept connoting moral objectionability, especially in contexts of using. We have seen that there are cases of using people in which the person being used is not hurt nor is likely to be hurt in the future. Hence hurting cannot explain using. Nevertheless it is still natural to presume that in instances of one person using another in which the person used *is* eventually hurt as a result of being used, what explains what is wrong with the using is that the person is hurt. Although this position does not fit very well with a recognition that it is objectionable to use someone even if one does not hurt him, nevertheless it is a very natural position to take and it is necessary to confront it head on in order to see that hurting can *never explain* what is wrong with using people in *any* situation.

If hurting is to explain using (in cases in which both are present), then it is not sufficient that some degree of hurt be involved in a given instance of using. For as in the case of deception, the moral force of the fact of hurt must be the same as the moral force of the using, if hurt is to explain using. Thus if A mistreats B in a certain way and B is slightly hurt by this, then, according to the position that the hurt explains the moral objectionability of the conduct, the moral objectionability of A's conduct is correspondingly slight. But if the same (slight) degree of hurt is caused B by A's using B, and if one thinks that the moral objectionability of A's conduct[11] is greater than in the previous case, then the hurt will not be (fully) accounting for or explaining (the moral objectionability of) the using. Thus, to consider hurt as explaining using, the position must be that the moral force of using is a reflection of the degree that the person who is used is hurt. According to this position different instances and types of conduct will produce different amounts of hurt, and in evaluating any given conduct from the point of view of moral objectionability one need look only at the amount of hurt produced.[12] In this sense the *context* in which the hurt is produced is irrelevant from a moral perspective, for one need not look at it in order to determine the moral objectionability of the conduct. One need determine only the hurt, and this will tell us all we need to know of the moral objectionability of the conduct.

I now want to argue against this view. In order for the degree that someone is hurt by the behaviour of a person R in a situation S to be the sole criterion (determinant) of the degree of moral objectionability of the behaviour of R, the degree of hurt must be (theoretically) *determinable independently* of the behaviour or the situation; for if we could not determine the degree of hurt independently of any characterization (from a moral point of view) of the situation and of the behaviour which produced the hurt, then we could not, of course, use the degree of hurt to measure the moral objectionability of the behaviour. It is plausible to think that the degree of hurt *is* so determinable (theoretically); for we can just *ask* a person how hurt he is and he can say that he was mildly hurt by Z, deeply hurt by W, more hurt by X than Y, etc. This might not be a foolproof method for learning how hurt someone is, since the person may lie to us. Nevertheless even in that case *he* will know how hurt he is, even though he will not tell us honestly. So the hurt will still be *determinable independently* of the behaviour which caused it, even if we cannot *in fact* determine it. And this is all that is being claimed in the position being considered.

But this view of how one determines how hurt someone is, is incorrect. A person's verbal report (plus evidence of his honesty in reporting) are not the only criteria for determining whether and how hurt someone is. Consider the following example: suppose, in example 3, that soon after Joe and Gwendolyn stop seeing each other Gwendolyn discovers through friends that Joe never cared for her very much and was only using her for some kind of emotional stability until his thesis was in. (We have assumed that she had been unaware of this throughout the relationship.) Suppose that her response to this knowledge, after it has had some time to sink in, is to claim that she does not feel hurt by this, though she is angry and resentful towards Joe for having treated her in this way. Suppose also that she seems genuinely to believe that this is the way she feels and gives no indication of consciously keeping her true feelings from us.

How would one be likely to regard Gwendolyn's denials that she feels hurt at having been used? From the view of hurting which I am considering, it would not even *make sense* to wonder whether Gwendolyn was really hurt, once we were convinced that she was not consciously deceiving us about her feelings. But obviously the natural response to this situation is precisely to wonder if she is not deceiving *herself* about how she has been affected by this realization of having been used.

In fact it would be natural to think that she probably is very hurt, but that she does not want to acknowledge such painful feelings, and so she represses them. Part of the reason for not acknowledging such feelings is just that they *are* so painful, and part of it may also be that she is ashamed for having allowed herself to be deceived and used by Joe.

Whether we are actually correct in thinking this about Gwendolyn (and the example has not been described sufficiently to determine whether this is so), is less important here than the fact that it is a coherent possibility; for it is this latter fact which shows that we acknowledge that being hurt is something one can be unaware of, and hence that in determining whether and how hurt one is, we cannot go solely on the basis of how hurt he thinks or feels that he is.

To say that one can say that someone is hurt even though he denies it, is not to say that the criteria for saying this of him, in contradiction to what he says, will justify us in making that judgment *no matter what* he says. On the contrary the person himself will be able to, and sometimes will, regard the presence of these other criteria as reason for *him* to think that he is more hurt than he realizes or feels. And the criteria in question will not carry the same force, if we feel that the person himself is aware of their presence and yet still denies that he is hurt.

In order to dispose fully of the idea that the existence and degree of hurt are (theoretically) determinable independently of the context of the hurt, we must discuss the role of the behaviour of the person in question subsequent to the events which led to his being hurt. For it might be thought that if we make a judgment contrary to the person's own avowals of how hurt he is, we must be doing this on the basis of his *behaviour*. For instance, in the case we are considering we can imagine that Gwendolyn often becomes very upset when Joe's name is mentioned in her presence, that she gets angry at people who say nice things about Joe, that she spends much time being depressed and unable to do her work, or makes forced and occasionally semi-hysterical attempts to form new relationships. Such behaviour would typically be taken as evidence that Gwendolyn has been more hurt by the realization that Joe was using her than she realized.

In this case Gwendolyn's subsequent behaviour *is* a criterion of hurt which is independent of and sometimes capable of overriding what she says. But the question is What does this fact show? Let us compare to this case one in which someone has *not* gone through an experience like the one Gwendolyn has had with Joe, but in which she nevertheless manifests behaviour similar to Gwendolyn's. In such a case would we take this sort of behaviour as a criterion of the person's being hurt? In fact it is far from clear what such a case is like. For example, in what relation to the woman is the person analogous to Joe whom the woman is manifesting such agitation about, being upset by references to, etc.? From the description given, her behaviour could well be a manifestation of her wishing to repress the memory of her having mistreated this person (rather than her *having been* used or otherwise mistreated). Her inability to work, her depression and forced attempts to establish relationships could signify any number of things, given that we know nothing else about the situation; they could mean nothing, as it were, beyond that she cannot work now, that she is depressed and finds it difficult to establish relationships (though she wants to). Or, the depression could come from the inability to work, or vice versa, or the three aspects could well not be so intimately related in the way they are likely to be in Gwendolyn's case.

The point of all this is that what *makes* Gwendolyn's behaviour a criterion or indication of her being hurt is the *context* of this behaviour, i.e. that she has recently been mistreated in an intimate and important relationship. Whereas, without any such context having been indicated, such behaviour is not obviously a criterion of anything.[13]

So it is our understanding that a relationship can appropriately be described as 'using' which allows us to take certain kinds of behaviour as indications or criteria of someone's being hurt.

Thus, applying the concept 'hurt' in a context of using *presupposes* an acknowledgment of the moral force of the concept of using. Thus it cannot be the moral force of the concept of hurt which *explains* the moral force of the concept of using. In some cases, at least, we cannot determine how we are going to evaluate some type or instance of behaviour by way of determining the degree of hurt caused by this behaviour; for what we will count as the 'degree of hurt' is not determinable independently of some understanding of the morality of the (type of) behaviour which caused it. In arguing for these propositions I am not, of course, arguing that what we will call 'the degree of hurt' of someone in a particular situation will be *fully* determined by our judgment of the moral status of the conduct which produced the hurt. The important complexity of the concept of '(degree of) hurt' for our enquiry is that its application is governed *partially* by the conduct which produced the hurt and *partially* by what the person says about how hurt he is or feels (and also partially by his behaviour). It is because it is not governed solely by the latter criteria that it cannot always be used to *determine* our judgment on the moral status of some (type of) behaviour which caused the hurt. But it is because it is not governed solely by the former criteria that it is capable of carrying *some* moral weight independently of the conduct which produced the hurt. Thus different people may be more and less hurt by the same conduct, and this difference may justify some difference in our evaluation of the conduct which produced the hurt in the different cases.[14]

To recapitulate my argument about *hurting* and *using*: hurting cannot explain (the moral objectionability of) using, because in order to do so it would have to be the case that the degree to which a person is hurt in being used is determinable in every instance, independently of knowing the behaviour which pro-

E

duced the hurt; but this is not the case. What is the case is that in recognizing some behaviour as an instance of using, one has already acknowledged the moral objectionability (*ceteris paribus*) of that behaviour, and this to some extent controls our judgments about the hurt caused to the person being used.

I began by talking about using people and it is still my primary purpose to get at this notion; but I have spent most of this article on the ideas of hurt and deception. Why have I felt this to be necessary? The reason is that both in moral philosophy and in practical life there is a strong tendency, a temptation, not to be able to see past the notions of 'hurt' and 'deception' (and ones like them, such as pain and pleasure in the first case and lying and truth-telling in the second) in understanding morality within the sphere of personal relations. So often it seems as if these two notions are the only two aspects of morality which one can really maintain a grip on. Everything else – such as 'using', 'exploiting', 'treating people as objects', 'degrading people' – can seem insubstantial, ephemeral, over-subtle, metaphysical. 'It's all right to do such-and-such, as long as you don't hurt anyone (. . . as long as you don't deceive anyone etc.')': this is a typical sentiment, heard often in contexts of moral choice. It is expressed in moral philosophy, in utilitarian theories of morality (in which deception too falls on the insubstantial side) : what really counts is people's happiness, pleasure, avoidance of pain or hurt – the rest is metaphysics, blind authority, etc. The fact is that utilitarian sentiments and doctrines often arose historically to combat false moral principles which derived from outworn religious, metaphysical, or political doctrines and which were unconnected with any human good. And in our own lives we still get entangled in principles which appear to us compelling, but which in particular instances have no genuine application and serve only to confuse the issues. Morality and human life being what they are, it is difficult to see how this type of confusion could ever completely cease to arise. In these situations the sentiment expressed as 'If it hurts people it's bad; if it doesn't it's all right' can be useful and liberating.

Sentiments such as these lead on to the idea that concepts like 'hurt' (and, less often, 'deception') are really the root ideas in the morality of personal relations in terms of which the others must either be explained or abandoned as obfuscating and misleading.

What I have tried to do in this paper is, firstly, to show that the notion of 'using' must be treated as having a morally pejorative force in its own right, not reducible to that of hurting and deception. The temptation to try to reduce it must be overcome. Secondly, I have tried to indicate, without really developing the point, that not only must other terms of moral objectionability (besides 'hurt' and 'deception') be granted status as root moral notions alongside deception and hurting, but that in a certain sense hurting and deception are *not* themselves fundamental, but are secondary moral notions, dependent for their full moral status on other notions, such as 'using'.

Notes

1 In saying this I mean to be making a quite ordinary remark about feelings. I do not draw support for it from, nor wish to be open to objections to, doctrines regarding 'privileged access' to one's own feelings. I do think that it is not at all obvious how one does know what feelings one has (or what it is to have a feeling), especially in contexts such as this one, but I also do not think that the discussion in recent philosophy about privacy and privileged access really touches on these problems in more than a peripheral way.

2 I raise the general issue of inadequacy of description because I think its importance has been greatly unappreciated in Anglo-American moral philosophy. By 'inadequate description' I mean that situations, persons, and actions are described in such a way that features which are necessary to our being able to treat the situation as one which we would find realistic and would know what to say about it, are absent. I cannot discuss this important and complex matter in this paper, but a few sketchy remarks are in order to indicate the perspective from which I am here working. I feel that moral philosophers have been overconfident in thinking that they know what kinds of aspects of situations are and are not relevant to the moral understanding of a situation, that they have been overconfident in their particular understanding of the concepts involved in moral description and evaluation, and moreover that this overconfidence leads them to accept, as adequately described, cases which are not adequately described. In fact, I think that much useful moral philosophy could be done just by trying to describe fully, accurately, and realistically certain typical moral situations and attempting to face the problems inherent in this task, without one's philosophical presuppositions about what counts as a morally relevant consideration and what does not. (Obviously I believe also that there are deep-rooted reasons why philosophers go astray in this area.) These large claims would of course have to be explained and justified, and I cannot do that here. Such claims are in any case more plausible

in the context of personal relations than elsewhere, where it is evident that feelings, emotions, and subtleties of behaviour play an important role, and these aspects are often not so easily described as are the morally relevant features in other types of moral situations.

3 I recognize that my use of 'characteristic' in 'X is characteristic of Y' is unclear, in that a philosopher will naturally feel that he wants to know more about the kind of connection I am asserting to exist between X and Y, e.g. whether it is analytic, necessary, empirical, etc. I cannot answer this request for clarification; but it is also not evident to me that it does clarify the kinds of issues and concepts I am working with to try and apply such categories. (I cannot justify these doubts here.) In any case I do think that the claims I am making which utilize the term 'characteristic(ally)' are true, if that term is taken in a fairly ordinary sense.

4 This innocent-sounding remark in fact requires much qualification. Outside the sphere of personal relationships we often speak of 'using people' in contexts in which it seems totally unobjectionable, e.g. I might use someone to help me jack up my car, or to work out a physics problem to which I need an answer. One might even say that A uses B whenever A hires or otherwise induces B to perform a task useful to A. And obviously within the sphere of personal relations this can also happen: I can use a friend to help me build my house. It is tempting to say that I am in this paper concerned solely with cases of using within personal relations which *are* morally objectionable and that I am not concerned with cases which are not. But this would be unfair. First, because there will be disputed cases and second, because an understanding of using should *explain* why using is objectionable in some contexts and not in others. Nevertheless I am unprepared at this point to make very helpful remarks on this. One thing I can say is that the cases I will be considering will be ones in which in some sense the fact that A is using B is a *fundamental* aspect of the relation between A and B, as it is not, for example, when I have a friend help me build my house. One more disclaimer: even in types of contexts in which the notion of using does carry a morally negative force, what that negativity comes to is very complicated and unclear. For instance, it will not be a consequence of what I am arguing that we should be so overconscious about not using other people that we avoid personal relationships at all (and hence avoid using people in that context). Nor will I be saying anything that implies that we should not be more open and giving in our personal relationships for fear of using and being used. Obviously, in instances in which using is an issue there will be other aspects of the situation which will weigh with the using and may outweigh its negativity. So sometimes it will be all right – perhaps even good –to use someone. For example, a person may need to feel needed by someone else and this consideration may be more important for him than the objectionability of being used. Nevertheless I think it is important and also not obvious that there is some morally negative

force to the concept of 'using people'; but I think it is also very far from clear what it means for this to be true. Though I do have many thoughts on this, it is a topic essentially beyond the scope of this paper.

5 Beyond the brief remarks I have made here, I do not have a clear idea what 'explaining' comes to in this sort of context. As my argument develops the concept will to some extent become clearer.

6 But example 5 could easily become like example 3 if Patsy began to maintain the deception *because* she found the status quo convenient and beneficial to her, e.g. if Eric provided her with intellectual companionship or status with her friends. In such a case she would be using Eric, though that would not have been her motive for getting involved with Eric in the first place. As the example is described, however, she is not keeping up the deception because she benefits from the situation; rather she would like to end it, but because of Eric's feelings she sees no easy or unpainful way to do so.

7 It is true, however, that within the context of a personal relationship deception about feelings seems generally a more serious matter than deception about one's past profession.

This example does not show that there is *no* characterization of different types of deception (in the sense we are using) which could account for the moral objectionability of using; but by taking a quite natural characterization of what might be such a type (i.e. deception about feelings) one sees, I think, the general implausibility of this way of trying to explain using. The example also does not prove that there are no other considerations which in the case of using weigh along with the 'type' of deception involved and which together account for the (moral objectionability of the) using, though I do think that such a position is somewhat implausible.

8 The account would have to be modified for cases of *self*-deception in using, but the basic point still holds, that in deceiving the other person (as well as oneself) one evidences a recognition of the objectionability of one's behaviour.

9 To say this is not, of course, to deny that one can describe types of cases in which someone might *not* object to being used. (Such a case is described in note 4.) As previously stated (note 4) I am far from clear as to what the force of the 'negativity' of using in the context of personal relationship is, and this unclarity is intimately involved with the unclarity about the nature of *'ceteris paribus* objectionability' of being used to the person being used. One reminder here is that I am considering only cases in which the using is a reasonably fundamental aspect of the relationship and not, for example, an isolated *act* of using.

10 Example 6 presents some important difficulties of description. How would we describe why Ann goes along with a situation in which she is being used? It is not, I think, correct to say that she feels she is deriving 'benefits' from the relationship which outweigh, as it were, the 'costs' of being used. Nor is it a matter of a rational calculation and weighing of the amount of suffering involved in the two alternatives

(continuing the relationship or breaking it off). It is correct to say that her attachment to Bill is so great that she does not leave; this is a kind of explanation of her conduct, and is a reason she might give for why she remains with Bill. But it is not a kind of reason or explanation which counts for showing that she is *rational* to continue with Bill or which shows that she has valid reasons or good reasons to continue. (Nor does it say that she is *irrational*.) The difficulties in describing this example in terms of these sorts of categories of rationality are not a consequence of having picked an unusual example, but are endemic to describing behaviour within personal relationships. (See note 2.)

11   In this paper I have in general not made use of the distinction between the badness of an action and the moral blameworthiness of someone for doing it. This is not a distinction which can always be made out clearly, especially in the area of personal relationships where concepts which refer to the 'actions' (e.g. deceiving, using) refer partly to aspects of human interaction (e.g. motives, feelings, attitudes), which in other areas of moral conduct (e.g. institutional morality) are primarily relevant *only* to the moral blameworthiness of the agent and not to the badness of the action itself. Thus the badness of a nurse not fulfilling her duties in a hospital has little to do with her feelings or attitudes. (It has to do with her duties being an integral part of an institution which serves human welfare.) But her feelings or motives are certainly relevant to her moral blameworthiness, e.g. she was upset by her husband beating her that morning and so she was lax in her duties. But the badness of using someone in a personal relationship itself involves (lack of) feelings and attitudes (e.g. not caring for someone one is using etc.). Despite all this, the distinction between badness of actions and blameworthiness of agents *can* often be made in the kinds of cases I have been discussing. I think that my arguments are merely less clear, rather than false, for not generally having been explicit about the distinction.

12   The idea of the 'degree (or amount) of hurt' can be misleading. I do not mean to imply that in every situation in which someone is hurt, the hurt can (even theoretically) be placed on a quantitative scale of hurts. The simple facts about our notion of 'hurt' which do underpin the concept of 'degree of hurt' are that we sometimes speak of people as being 'more (or less) hurt' (by some behaviour as compared to some other), as being 'very hurt' or 'slightly hurt', etc. To some extent hurt just *is* a 'comparative' notion and it is only to the extent which it actually is such a notion that the position I am considering need to claim that it is. If A causes B to be hurt and C causes D to be hurt and if B's hurt and D's hurt are not comparable, then, according to this position, one cannot say which of the two behaviours (C's or A's) was the more morally objectionable.

13   In this discussion I have not tried to use 'criterion' in a way common in discussions of Wittgenstein's use of that term, but hopefully in a way somewhat closer to ordinary usage. Nevertheless I do think that the points I am making are relevant to a discussion of 'behavioural

criteria' (in the Wittgensteinian sense) of 'psychological predicates' in Wittgenstein and to the general current discussion and debate on behaviourism.

14 A fuller discussion of the concept of *'hurt'* would, among other things, try to show the kind of picture of what it is to be hurt which is involved in the idea that one determines how bad a (type of) behaviour is by how much hurt it causes. I will make some brief remarks on this insofar as it is difficult to get fully clear on the concept of using without clearing up some fundamental problems with the concept of 'hurting'. It is necessary to see that we sometimes have *feelings* or *sensations* of hurt, but what it is to *be* hurt is not merely to have such sensations. I can be hurt, even deeply hurt, without at some particular time having any sensations or feelings of hurt. If one does view being hurt on a model of having certain feelings or sensations, then it is natural to view that which *causes* the hurt as fully separable and distinct from the hurt itself. But if one acknowledges the greater complexity to the notion of hurt, which I have tried to bring out in my argument, this picture of the separability of the cause of the hurt from the hurt itself ceases to force itself on one. To make these points out and to establish their importance would require an excursion into recent philosophy of mind, which is beyond the scope of this paper. All these issues are important for a general understanding of utilitarian views of morality and the views of the central 'psychological predicates' on which these moral views depend (i.e. pleasure, pain, happiness), 'hurt' being such a utilitarian-like concept. Though I am not primarily concerned with utilitarianism and am not very clear about how what I am arguing here bears on it in general, I want to indicate one utilitarian position regarding hurting which I am *not* arguing against. I *am* arguing that 'degree or amount of hurt' cannot be *determined independently* of the context and type of behaviour which caused that hurt (where the behaviour is described by use of concepts which have some moral force, e.g. 'using'). I am *not* arguing that the badness of some behaviour is not in some sense proportional to how much hurt it causes, so that the hurt is in some way a *measure* of the badness of the behaviour which caused it. (I do, however, believe that this view is also false.) My main task has been to show that hurting cannot *explain* using and it is not necessary to refute the latter position to show this, but only the former.

4 How to treat persons as persons

J. A. Brook

Recently, various institutions and persons have been the object of demands that they treat persons as persons, not things. The people making these demands complain that they are being used as mere objects, as cogs in a machine, as means to others' ends, that they lack real human contact, that they are isolated from other people, that their lives are increasingly mechanized, depersonalized, dehumanized, that relations among persons are impersonal and alienated. On the other hand, they demand that they be treated as human beings, as equals, as though all men were brothers. The language in which these complaints and demands are expressed is not graced by clarity. However, one thing stands out – the distinction between treating persons in ways thought to be appropriate, perhaps uniquely appropriate, to persons, and treating persons as (mere) objects, as things.

The notion of treating persons as persons, on which this paper will mainly dwell, might be thought to have mainly or even entirely a moral import, so that we could translate it, 'treating persons as they ought, morally, to be treated'. This translation is both ambiguous and not altogether correct.

It is ambiguous because it does not distinguish 'treating persons as they ought, morally, to be treated by virtue of being persons' from 'treating persons as they ought, morally, to be treated by virtue of what they have have done'. If A has killed B, we might well believe that A ought, morally, to be punished. However, few of us believe that persons, just because they are persons, ought, morally, to be punished. (Some religious doctrines do contain that belief.) When we speak of treating persons as persons, we speak of how they ought to be treated *prior* to any consideration of what treatment they *merit*, as the sort of person they are or by their actions.

That it is not altogether correct can be brought out by some comparisons. Consider, for example, a knife. Treating a knife as a knife consists of two things : using it primarily as a cutting device, and not abusing its capacity to perform this and other functions. It is, in general, a matter of respecting its potential for satisfying our fairly stable and long-term interests in such objects. Or consider treating an inanimate object, say a teddy-bear, as a person. In adults such behaviour is inappropriate because inanimate objects do not have the power to satisfy the desires and expectations contained in such behaviour. In these two examples, the notions of appropriate (and therefore inappropriate) treatment have a descriptive, as well as an evaluative (though not moral) content. So does the notion of treating a person as a person, which is why the translation above is not entirely correct.

Even the general characteristics of this descriptive content are by no means obvious. With knives, and tools generally, it consists largely of using them for the function(s) for which they were designed. With many other things (for example, teddy-bears) it is at least partly our having only those desires and expectations which the things have the power to satisfy. Neither will do as an account of what we are saying when we describe someone as treating another as a person. Persons do not have a specific function, none at least which anyone has ever succeeded in describing in a convincing manner. And many of our desires and expectations concerning other people which they quite clearly have the power to satisfy are sharply in conflict with treating them as persons. Indeed, no simple analysis of what counts as treating persons as persons is possible. In virtually every example which one can imagine, a variety of different principles is at work and no one of them by itself is sufficient to justify describing the case as treating a person as a person. Defending this claim, by describing a few of the relevant principles, is a main aim of this paper.

Some might question whether we have a concept of treating a person as a person which is even remotely precise. Given its practical importance, we should hope so. Only the paper itself, tested against our sense of what it is right to say about the concept, can answer the question. With the notion of treating persons as persons, unlike the notion of treating tools as tools, there is no easy way to drive clear wedges between elements of the descriptive content and elements of the evaluative content, and we shall try to do so only rarely.

For brevity, let us call principles which work to satisfy our demand to be treated as persons 's-personal', and those which comprise situations in which persons are being treated 'as objects' 'objective'.

Situations which are s-personal have something of importance in common with situations which are objective. Very casual encounters, for example, are neither s-personal nor objective. A condition of our intelligibly treating someone either s-personally or objectively, is that our encounter with him have a certain degree of complexity. He must matter to us in some way (perhaps only as an object of control or treatment), and we must be disposed to embark on a wide and somewhat systematic range of activities concerned with him. Duration is not essential : a sexually-charged glance (s-personal) lasts about as long as a casual wave (neither). Rather, the complexity must be sufficient to provide the material for taking up a policy regarding him.

The difference, however, between the s-personal and the objective is not simply a difference between two kinds of policy; indeed, the two need not have in common even a disposition to take up a policy. Although objective treatment seems to include at least a disposition to take up a policy, s-personal treatment clearly need not. Consider a father playing happily with his child. Here no policy, indeed no conscious goal, moral belief or purpose at all, need enter.[1] Or consider happy lovers, or close friends. Here the partners need have no policy, no thought-out plan of action, towards each other. In such circumstances, in fact, policies are widely thought to be injurious. Policies are similarly unnecessary for unpleasant s-personal treatment, such as might contain or consist of hate, anger, moral indignation, enmity, punishment or some acts of hostility, though a policy could hardly injure them. In both the pleasant and the unpleasant cases, what we do have is all the material to take up a policy; that is what objective and both sorts of s-personal treatment have in common and what distinguishes them all from very casual encounters.

An analysis of some principles of objective treatment would provide a useful contrast for the discussion of s-person-ness to come. Detachment is one such principle. (Its contrast, involvement, might be thought to be a principle of s-person-ness, but problems await such a view.) If I am detached from a person, I do not feel, and organize my ways of viewing him so as not to feel, towards him what Strawson² calls personal reactive attitudes, e.g. resentment, gratitude, hostility or affection. My interest in the person is intellectual (e.g. with researchers) or professional (e.g. with doctors). In my relationship to him, nothing which he does can affect me emotionally, not directly at least. He may cause me sadness because he disproves a theory of mine (if I am a researcher) or because he proves me inept (if I am a poor doctor). But I cannot feel sadness simply at what he does, or because of the attitudes which he adopts towards me. Detachment, with its complexity of connections with a person, could be contrasted with indifference, a total lack of interest in a person.

One principle of treating someone objectively is detachment, a kind of attitude. Another is using someone for our ends, a kind of motive. Using someone for our ends need not be selfishness, if our benefit is not an end for which he is used. For example, one might use employees to strengthen a corporation with no end in view other than strengthening the corporation. The objectivity consists in one's having ends, with respect to the employees, other than the employees' benefit. The intensity of objectivity varies inversely with the extent to which the employees' own benefit and ends are taken into account – if the account taken of the ends is not merely precautionary; if, that is, the employees' ends are taken into account just because they are the employees' ends.

Detachment and using someone for our ends are logically independent. Using someone for our ends is quite compatible with, for example, friendship, and also with most other s-personal attitudes, acts and relations with respect to that person. An obvious exception is using someone for our own ends and acting exclusively for his sake. These are incompatible, and acting for someone's sake is, as we shall discover, one aspect of treating him s-personally. Being detached from someone, on the other hand, is not compatible with friendship, and it is quite compatible with acting for his sake.

Both detachment and using someone for our ends must be distinguished from literally treating a person as a non-animate object. Using him for our ends will almost certainly be one feature of such treatment, but it will also include a total unconcern for his interests, desires, etc. (even, probably, for learning what they are), utter lack of consideration for his 'feelings', and many other things. This kind of treatment is a third principle of objectivity. It is logically independent of the other two.

All three seem to have in common three further principles, not any of them plausible principles of objectivity by themselves, but each part of what lends objectivity to the principles we have discussed : (1) any person, M, towards whom we direct exclusively objective acts, attitudes or relations could, in principle, be replaced without loss to us by another person, N, having relevantly similar characteristics; (2) how the persons, such as M, to whom we direct our attitudes, etc., see their interests seldom matters to us, or seldom acts as a determinant of our behaviour, except in so far as noticing them is relevant to furthering our ends; and (3) we are disposed (especially if our attitudes, etc., are objective according to more than one of the first three principles) to interfere, if necessary with physical force, in another's life with no more than precautionary regard for his opinions on the matter. Much, much more could be said about objectivity. However, we have said enough to provide an adequate contrast for our enquiry into s-person-ness.

Earlier we called such attitudes as hate and moral indignation, such emotions as anger and such acts as punishment and acts of enmity and hostility unpleasant s-personal. The above analysis of objectivity might lead us to ask whether they are, not s-personal, but in fact objective. Punishment is not a good example because the class in which it belongs is determined by the motives behind it. It seems right to call the rest s-personal. Contrast them with such acts as economic exploitation, mass oppression and mass extermination, all of which are paradigmatically, if dramatically, objective. Unpleasant s-personal attitudes, emotions and actions may not be what anybody wants to receive, but most people would agree that persons having such attitudes and emotions and performing such acts towards them are treating them as persons. Later, even stronger arguments will become available to support the soundness of this classification.

Philosophers analysing concepts similar to our concept of s-person-ness have, at one time or another, put certain kinds of attitudes, certain kinds of motives for action, and certain characteristics of personal relationships at the centre of their respective theories. Principles of s-person-ness can be found in each of the three. Kant,[3] who was perhaps the first philosopher to stress the moral importance of treating persons appropriately, emphasized actions and motives for actions: he distinguished treating persons as ends in themselves from treating them as means. Martin Buber[4] laid his main emphasis on certain kinds of relationships, specifically what he called I–thou relationships. More recently P. F. Strawson ('Freedom and Resentment'), in discussing a distinction similar to our distinction between s-person-ness and objectivity, has emphasized what he calls personal reactive attitudes. Beginning with Strawson's discussion, let us examine attitudes first. Our interest is, of course, in finding principles of s-person-ness, not in what philosophers have said about them.

Strawson characterizes, first, what both he and we call objective attitudes, and contrasts them with personal reactive attitudes and emotions, as follows ('Freedom and Resentment', p. 79):

> To adopt the objective attitude to another human being is to see him, perhaps, as an object of social policy, as a subject for what, in a wide range of sense, might be called treatment; as something certainly to be taken account, perhaps precautionary account, of; to be managed or handled or cured or trained. . . . The objective attitude may be emotionally toned in many ways. . . . But it cannot include the range of reactive feelings and attitudes which belong to involvement or participation with others in inter-personal human relationships; it cannot include resentment, forgiveness, gratitude, anger or the sort of love which two adults can sometimes be said to feel reciprocally, for each other.

Notice that Strawson, in his description of objective attitudes, refers implicitly to both detachment and using others for our ends, without (here or elsewhere) recognizing them as principles of the objective. Notice, too, that he contrasts the objective attitude and involvement. The latter notion might seem to be just the place to open an enquiry into s-person-ness. In fact, it is not. It is too vague a concept, no clearer, in fact, than s-person-ness itself. Considered as a principle of s-person-ness, the main feature unique to involvement is the suggestion of strong emotional attachment. We shall see later that such attachment is not an important part of what most of us mean by s-person-ness. Finally, since involvement is more than a matter of attitude and emotions, it is not even an exact contrast to detachment, or objective attitudes in general.

As examples of personal reactive attitudes and emotions Strawson mentions resentment, gratitude, forgiveness, hostility, contempt, anger and (some kinds of) love. They are distinct from, though, he tells us, analogous to, moral reactive attitudes and emotions such as moral indignation, disapprobation and approval, and self-reactive attitudes and emotions such as guilt, shame, remorse, regret, and feeling responsible, obliged and morally bound. Neither moral reactive nor self-reactive attitudes and emotions are plausible principles of s-person-ness, though in situations where *only* moral reactive or objective attitudes are appropriate, it may well be more s-personal to adopt the moral reactive ones.

Personal reactive attitudes and emotions seem to be characterized by the fact that in having them, we become open to injury or benefit, not just from the acts of persons to whom they are directed, but also from their intentions, motives and attitudes. More exactly, we become open to injury or benefit from their intentions, motives or attitudes towards us just because (*a*) they have them and (*b*) the intentions, motives and attitudes are what they are. Sometimes the injury or benefit comes directly from their intentions etc.; sometimes their intentions etc. merely add to or change the quality of an already-present injury or benefit. The feature of personal reactive attitudes and emotions just described might be called the 'special pleasure/pain (SPP) feature'. It is distinct from a second. Having each such attitude or emotion about someone makes us susceptible to having it augmented or diminished, or a cognate attitude evoked (e.g. anger in the case of feeling hatred), by his actions and intentions towards us. We might call this feature the 'special change-of-attitude (SCA) feature'. Of course, in having personal reactive attitudes or emotions, we need not actually experience either SPP or SCA. Also, we can experience one without the other, e.g. increased anger at a person (SCA) without injury or benefit from his intentions (SPP), or special benefit from the attitudes he adopts to me (SPP) without additional gratitude (SCA). If, however, we are *open* neither to SPP nor SCA from someone, then it is difficult to conceive that we have personal reactive attitudes to him at all.

Normally, in taking up personal reactive attitudes to someone we also take up certain expectations concerning him, and make certain demands on him. (We can, of course, have the expectations and demands without the attitudes, or vice versa.) If our demands are met with resentment, hostility or hatred, we are unhappy but do not, at least, complain of not being treated as persons. If, on the other hand, what we receive is simple indifference to all these expectations and demands – our interests as we see them – then we have grounds for the complaint. We demand, generally, more than personal reactive attitudes. We also demand various non-reactive attitudes special to persons, such as goodwill, consideration, respect and – a very important attitude – parity. The latter is the attitude that others are, if not exactly the same as us, at any rate equal to us in certain respects. (We shall describe it in greater detail later.) So at least some non-reactive attitudes (and emotions) feature in principles of s-person-ness.

Attitudes, reactive or otherwise, are not usually central, and could never by themselves be sufficient, to s-person-ness, because s-person-ness is a way of *treating* people. However the kind of treatment, i.e. the kind of actions which a person is giving or receiving, is determined largely by the motive behind the actions. The nature of the motives is, in turn, often criterially tied to the attitudes of the actor. The precise structures of these ties are intricate and endlessly intriguing. However, these ties are not importantly s-personal by themselves. Some kinds of motives, on the other hand, are, at least when they are expressed in actions.

Perhaps the most promising motive, or rather kind of motive, is acting for the sake of another. The phrase, 'for the sake of another', and its cognates (such as 'for his sake'), is curious and difficult to analyse. It makes sense to speak of acting 'for his sake' in the case of a person, but not 'for its sake' in the case of a thing. Yet many plausible translations of the phrases apply sensibly to both : 'for its benefit', 'for the sake of bettering it,' etc. Two plausible candidates do not apply sensibly other than to persons : 'in his interest' and 'because he wants (or "would want") me to'; but then they are neither of them complete translations of 'for his sake'. If I do something for the sake of someone, I need not be doing something in his interest (let alone doing it *because* it is in his interest), nor even more clearly because he wants, or would want, me to. Nor need I be doing it because it pleases him or would please him if he knew. However, if I claim to be doing something for his sake, but deny that I am doing it for any of these three reasons, what can I mean? Not that I am doing it for his sake; these three are each sufficient and seem to be, together, disjunctively necessary.

It is interesting that if I do something for the sake of a person, I must always aim at getting something valuable to him – that is, something which at least *I* believe to be valuable to him. (Acts which we do for the sake of children or people of whom we disapprove are often and emotionally considered by *them not* to be valuable.) As a consequence, acting for the sake of others cannot be a complete account of s-person-ness because it cannot account for what we called earlier the unpleasant s-personal attitudes and acts, such as resentment, hostility, hate, anger and acts of enmity.

Indeed, it is possible that we cannot act even simply to *damage* someone (which, if it were possible, would be a close cousin of acting for his sake). Difficulties in deciding what is true here will arise later, but it seems that to act to damage someone may always be also to act to satisfy a desire to damage him; whereas clearly, to act for the sake of someone need not be to act to satisfy a desire to benefit him. In acting for his sake I may, in fact, satisfy a desire to act for his sake. But to say that from this it follows that I acted to satisfy such a desire is to confuse the reason for an act with the results of an act.

This lack of parallel between the pleasant and the unpleasant may lead us to question anew the placing of the latter. Our answer must be the same as before. Though not entirely similar in character to the pleasant s-personal attitudes and acts, the unpleasant ones are tied so closely to the pleasant ones that they belong in the same class. First, all the unpleasant attitudes and acts contain an implicit or explicit demand for change in their object. A necessary condition of such a demand being intelligible is that the person making the demand believe that its object has the ability to choose – in general, what we usually mean by 'free will'. Someone will, undoubtedly, object that it makes perfect sense to hate the weather. Such hatred does indeed contain a demand, or at any rate, a wish, that the weather change. However, hating the weather is not on all fours with hating persons: 'strongly dislike' adequately translates 'hate' in 'I hate the weather' (on some Canadian mornings I doubt that!); it does not adequately translate 'hate' in 'I hate Nazis'. Second, unpleasant attitudes and acts are usually (perhaps must be) a response to what is believed to be some failure of s-person-ness in their object. When they are first felt or done, feeling or doing them usually disposes us to change other attitudes to their object: if we are indignant or contemptuous or disapproving, our degree of respect tends to diminish, and so on. (Here, too, many intriguing relationships offer themselves for our investigation.) Hate does not dispose us to change other attitudes: perhaps the reason is that hate is something we feel only after a long, or at any rate intense, history of feeling other unpleasant attitudes and emotions. And finally, our unpleasant s-personal attitudes and acts towards someone often contain an implicit threat that we will stop treating him s-personally, if unpleasantly, and adopt objective attitudes and do objective acts to him. The threat backs up our demand that he change what we dislike. For something to be used as a threat, it must be something that the threatened dislikes even more than, or at least differently from, what he is receiving. The distinction which makes our threat possible gives good grounds for reaffirming our classification.

One objection to our claim that acting for the sake of another is a principle of treating him s-personally is that it cannot account for unpleasant s-person-ness. It is a sound objection. One other objection is, though not so sound, worth noticing. We can act for the sake of another out of a sense of duty, it might be claimed, and acting merely to do our duty to someone is compatible with treating him quite objectively. To rebut this objection, observe that acting out of a sense of duty is *not* acting for the sake of another. It is acting to do our duty – which, perhaps, dictates acting as if for the sake of another, e.g. acting with his interests in mind. In acting truly for the sake of another we may do our duty; but that is not acting *to do* it. Recall the distinction between reasons and results.

I can act for the sake of something only if that thing is a person (or, perhaps, a higher mammal). Only persons (and, probably, the higher mammals) have interests, or can want something from me just because I am who I am, or can be pleased by something I do just because it is me who has done it. One cannot act for the sake of inanimate objects. One can, for example, paint a house for the sake of *improving* the house; but not simply for the

F

sake of the house. To act 'for the sake of the house' can only mean to act 'for the sake of its value' (implicitly 'to someone'). In general, we can treat s-personally only those things which have intentions. On the other hand, that something has intentions is not a necessary condition of treating it objectively.

The above observations suggest two more principles of s-personness. They also hint at a very important general feature of s-personal principles. The two principles are what we might call the 'special status principle' and, closely related to it, the 'unique status principle'. We generally value, as s-personal, attitudes and actions towards us which cannot intelligibly be directed towards anything but persons (and, often, higher mammals). We also generally value, as s-personal, others' viewing us as unique among persons. (The latter principle is, of course, the contradictory of the replaceability feature of objective attitudes and actions.) So the s-person-ness of acting for the sake of another consists in part of the fact that we cannot act for the sake of inanimate objects.

Attitudes, actions and relations which we can intelligibly aim only at persons and higher mammals will be, then, good hunting ground for principles of s-person-ness. We make better progress in finding such attitudes, etc., if we think of persons acting on one another, rather than contemplating or perceiving one another. The reasons why are not easy to find, but an example illustrates the point. When we think of perceiving something just out of interest in what it is (something very close to aesthetic perception), people and dogs and houses and paintings are on all fours. This is the most disinterested form of perception. But when we think of acting for the sake of another, the most disinterested form of action, we find a clear distinction between what is possible towards the inanimate and what is possible towards people.

In fact, most s-personal principles can be used only on *human* action and interaction. This is a point of some importance about the concept of s-person-ness. Buber failed to notice this feature of s-person-ness, partly because he did not pay much attention to the difference between contemplation and action. As a result, the class of objects with which he claimed we can enter I–thou relationships is implausibly large.

When we think of different sorts of human action and interaction from the standpoint of the special status principle, some new principles of s-person-ness readily appear. To take just one example, we can force or persuade creatures whom we cannot advise. Advising is a principle of s-person-ness, forcing, as we have seen, of objectivity. A characteristic of advising, the adviser's necessary intention to have the advisee freely make up his mind, might well be another principle of s-person-ness. This intention is, incidentally, a central part of what it is to be considerate. Other examples will present themselves when we turn to discuss s-personal principles in personal relationships.

Before we do, we might consider briefly a primarily contemplative motive which, though not a principle of s-person-ness itself, is of fundamental utility in achieving satisfactory s-personal relationships. It is also an example, indeed the finest example, of the unique status principle. The motive is to see things as others see them.

If 'acting for the sake of another' was slippery and difficult to tie down, 'seeing things as another sees them' is more so. When we have a vicarious experience we do not, of course, *have* the other person's experience. The very thought is probably incoherent. Rather, the behavioural signs of the experience he is having give us sufficient insight into what and how he is experiencing to lead us to say such things as 'I know just how you feel', or, more modestly and often more honestly, to believe that something in his way of seeing what we both see before us is interestingly different from my way of seeing it. We can be more or less clear about what is the difference. However, it is seldom transparent to us – if it were, perhaps intimations of others' ways of seeing things would not excite us so.

The above sort of vicarious experience is to be distinguished from being pleased at another's pleasure, or delighted at his improvement or the advancement of his interests. It is also to be distinguished from vicariously experiencing the effects, especially the pleasant or painful or beneficial or damaging effects, of one's actions. (This sort of vicarious experience also seems to add to the s-person-ness of our actions.) In these other cases what we experience is something in the other, but usually we do not intimate a way of experiencing different from our own.

The meaning of the notion 'way of experiencing' above is by no means clear. An analogy might help. What we gain when we intimate the way another sees things can perhaps be compared to what we gain when we first learn how to hear beauty, or even perhaps, order, in music which was previously just noise. (Learning to listen to atonal music is, for some, an example.) We hear the same noises in the same sequence. But something is added. Partly we gain the insight into relationships among the noises. But only partly. Another, less analysable, part of what we gain is a sense that what we are hearing is unified, 'hangs together', and that certain noises are inevitable, 'just right', or belong where they are. Similarly with gaining insight into the way another sees things. We intimate a way of unifying a personality different from our way. Partly we intimate new ways of associating experiences. Sometimes we gain insight into ways of toning experiences emotionally, different from our ways : another fears what we do not, and these fears colour his experience differently from ours. But often what is different is as difficult to analyse as beauty or unity in music. Think of the ways of experiencing of the innocent, of those who have a sense of wonder, or of the ironically world-weary. These people can experience all the same objects and events as we do. But something is different – and the differences are repulsive, attractive, compelling, delightful, exciting, boring, etc.

Whatever it is precisely, a person's way of experiencing is as unique to him as his face – and may indeed be one reason why his face is unique. It is also uniquely him, the most important element of his being the person he is, having the personality he has. If our interest in him is in his way of seeing, in vicariously experiencing what he experiences in the way he experiences it, he will usually be flattered. We are interested in him, to use one idiom, 'as a person'.

Such interest, and especially motives and actions arising from such interest, is a large part of many people's notion of s-personness. Nor, if the unique status principle is sound, should this surprise us. We act towards him in a way not only impossible with other than persons, but in a way impossible with anyone but him. Contrast this with the replaceability feature of objectivity. Nevertheless, such interest does not seem importantly s-personal by itself. Some support for this can be derived from the fact that such interest is entirely compatible with both sorts of objectivity : detachment, and using another for our ends. Selfish interest in another's way of seeing things may well be the most s-personal form of misusing someone, but it is still misuse. But the main support is simply our conviction that such interest is not part of what it is to treat persons in a way uniquely appropriate to persons. However, interest in another's way of seeing things is one of the most important *vehicles* for achieving satisfactory s-personal relationships with him.

Personal relationships contain some of the most central principles of s-person-ness. Not all relations between persons are personal relations. 'Being bigger than' is not. We save the phrase 'personal relationship' for a fairly restricted class of relations among persons. Only these relations contain additional principles of s-person-ness.

An analysis of the notion, 'personal relationship', as it is commonly used, yields the following criteria. A personal relationship :

(1) need have no converse. If A is bigger than B, then B is smaller than A. But if A is an enemy of B, B may be almost anything at all to A. (But see (7) and (8).) This is a purely grammatical criterion.

(2) entails that at least one term of the relationship has attitudes or emotions or intentions towards the other. (He need not know that he has them.) Thus 'bigger', 'older', 'richer', etc., do not name personal relations. This criterion explains the first, since, for any A, A's intentions to B seldom entail anything concerning B's intentions to A.

(3) entails, from (2), that one term of the relationship must know of the other term(s) under some description.

(4) must be possible independently of the existence of social, legal, or political institutions. Thus colleague-colleague, or teacher-pupil, or foreman-worker relationships are not inherently personal relationships, though their terms may also enjoy personal relationships.

All four of these are clearly criteria. All of them are also true of all the principles of objectivity. All personal relations have one additional criterion, many have two, and a few have four more, none of which is compatible with objectivity of treatment.

(5) In a personal relation, not only must one term take up an attitude, emotion, desire or intention to the other(s), but the other(s) must respond. The response may be to take up the same attitude etc. (a mutual relationship), it may be to disapprove of, refuse to satisfy or in other ways reject the attitude etc., or it may

even be a studied and partly genuine indifference (e.g. 'he bores me').

(6) In at least a large number of cases, the response must be one which encourages or at least allows a developing pattern of exchanges of some sort – of actions, attitudes, objects, etc. For in these cases, if the response leaves no room for further exchange, we say that no relationship has been formed.

Finally (7) with some relationships, the response must be the same as the approach : if I offer him friendship, he must respond with friendship for a relation of friendship to exist between us.

(8) The grammatical criterion in these cases is reversibility : if A r's B, B must also r A. (7) and (8) do not contradict (1), but for the few personal relationships to which they apply, they do impose a restriction on the kinds of asymmetrical relationships possible.

Since the satisfaction of (5), and perhaps also (6), is a necessary condition of the presence of a personal relationship, it is clear that we do not use the phrase for both objective and s-personal relationships between persons but restrict it to the latter.

So much for the criteria of a personal relationship. None of them, not even (5) or (6), constitutes the s-person-ness of an s-personal relationship. Such s-person-ness could, of course, consist in some or all of the principles already discovered. However, some characteristics of the relationships themselves are s-personal.

Most of us would include, among personal relationships, sycophancy and servility. These relationships do not seem to be, precisely, objective, yet we hesitate to call them s-personal either. Examining them will uncover some s-personal features of relationships. Both are master-servant relationships which can occur outside the context of institutions. We hesitate to call them objective because they are relations possible only with persons (and, perhaps, God); they often include a desire to see things as another sees them (on the part of at least one party to the relationship); they are often aimed at a person because he is the person he is; they often contain a developing pattern of exchanges; they frequently include a heavy emotional involvement; and finally, they are chosen by one party and often at least acceded to by the other. (This last is itself a principle of s-person-ness.)

We hesitate to call them objective. Yet we also hesitate to call them s-personal. Something is missing. When we try to say what, we use words such as 'imbalance', 'asymmetry', 'lack of equality' and 'lack of parity'. To expose what is in fact missing, compare them with unpleasant but clearly s-personal relationships, such as hate/pity relationships. Neither of them need satisfy the grammatical criterion of reversibility. On the other hand, both can contain mutually satisfying exchanges. (This latter, though not a principle of s-person-ness, is a condition of satisfactory s-personal relationships.) The difference between the two is this: nothing in even an unpleasant s-personal relationship, but something in every relationship of the class containing servility, *must* be asymmetrical. Usually one party must have a power over the other which is not reciprocal. The presence of such asymmetry is the absence of parity, a most important principle of s-person-ness. The possibility of parity in what we have called the unpleasant s-personal is the best support so far for so naming it.

This distinction between, e.g. hate and, e.g. servility offers one explanation of why it is held by many to be more s-personal to express honest hatred or anger than to suppress it and instead treat its object with 'tolerance' or 'understanding'. Hatred contains no suggestion that the object of hatred lacks anything the hater has. Such 'understanding' does; in particular, that its object lacks one's ability to guide one's actions for the best. Of course, such suppression is to be sharply contrasted with true suspension of such emotions as hate and anger when we sincerely believe that the person we are inclined to hate could do no other than he did. Ground for such suspension is an element in much tragedy.

Parity can consist in mutual feelings or actions, in my allowing the other, and acting as though he has, every significant power, quality and ability which I have (especially the power to choose, and to control his own behaviour), in my granting him no powers over me which I do not have over him or vice versa, and perhaps in other things. Achieving parity is necessary to achieve any of the inherently reversible relationships. Parity adds to the s-person-ness of both pleasant and unpleasant s-personal relationships.

Earlier, in the course of commenting on what the s-personal and the objective have in common, personal relations were mentioned in which neither party to the relation has a goal. Personal relations of this sort are important for a number of reasons. They are examples of parity, indeed of mutually satisfying parity. They show the way antecedents of action can affect the quality of re-lationships – an important point. And, finally, they contain yet another principle of s-person-ness.

In addition to being able to act for our own sake, and for the sake of another, we can also act for the sake of no one at all, or more accurately, with no motive, goal or plan to which to attach the concept, 'for the sake of', at all. Many of the purest examples of s-personal relations have this characteristic. It is a principle of s-person-ness. Think of a father playing with his child. He need have no motive, desire, goal or plan. He need not play with his child for his sake, the child's sake, for the sake of duty or even for the sake of enjoying the play (though he un-doubtedly does enjoy it, as does the child). Similarly with, for example, hugging one's wife. The act may fit into a long-term project of making a happy marriage. But clearly one need not have this project in mind, nor need it be a reason for the action. An objection to this view holds that one must do these actions, play with the child or hug the wife, because of something, e.g. in this case, love; for if, in this case, no love, then no actions. The answer to the objection is that so long as 'because' in the last sentence is parsed in a counter-factual such as 'If no love, then no actions', then no objection has been raised. Such a 'because' is not used in stating a *reason* for an action. Rather, it states a condition. Such actions, devoid of any reason, and the relations they create are what we call 'spontaneous', 'immediate', 'natural', 'direct' or 'pure'. Love is one of their commonest backgrounds. Indeed, love might be described in part as the doing of things, which give love's object pleasure, for no reason at all. An often delightful (or, if the love affair is chancy, quite anxious) impulse towards the other is all we need find when we look into our store of motives or reasons for actions.

We might ask whether any of the unpleasant s-personal atti-tudes, acts, or relations are covered by the principle just discussed. Here the answer is much less clear. A difficulty is inherent in trying to settle, both in the case of particular examples, and in general, whether any apparent cases, either pleasant or un-pleasant, are acts of persons aware of what they are doing, yet appropriately free of desires, motives, goals or projects. The difficulty is that we know only too well that often people act from unconscious motives and as often from motives which they have suppressed and about which they are deceiving themselves. This is the difficulty to which we alluded when last we turned to the unpleasant s-personal. It does not affect answering a question, however, as to whether such cases are possible. It is easy to imagine them in pleasant contexts. Indeed, many of us, hopefully, will have experienced sufficiently convincing examples to have few doubts remaining on the issue. But unpleasant contexts are less clear. Hating someone, feeling contempt for him, acting with hostility towards him : these seem not to be things we have or do spontaneously. We seem to require a reason. However, I can see no way of eliminating the bare possibility that we might have or do them without a reason, at least sometimes. One thing *is* clear : such cases are so rare that the notion of acting from no reason could not be a significant part of our idea of unpleasant s-person-ness.

Acting for our own sake, for the sake of another, and with no goal, plan, motive or desire at all: the first two can be aiming at a purely personal end, a common end or a joint end, and the third, though it has no *end*, can be action whose successful conclusion would be a purely personal, or common, or joint achievement. The last two members of this new class of characteristics of actions and their antecedents are two further principles of s-person-ness in a relationship. Common ends are ends which, though held in common by two or more people, can be achieved by any one of them, in principle, without being achieved by any other. Joint ends, on the other hand, must be obtained for more than one to be achieved by one. For example, if two people desire mutual friendship, they have a joint end : to be someone's friend, he must also be mine. A second example is contained in a desire to build a fully developed community. A soldier's desire to protect the liberty of his countrymen has a third : securing his own liberty will not satisfy him unless in so doing he has secured the liberty of his countrymen, too. This defining characteristic of joint ends can be found in ends held only by one. For example, A desires to be a friend of B, but B has no desire whatsoever with respect to A. None the less, A can achieve his end, become B's friend, only if B becomes his friend, too. We shall call any ends having this characteristic, whether held by one person or more than one, joint ends.

We may or may not, in desiring a joint end, have its jointness in mind. Whether we do is not important. More important, from the point of view of s-person-ness, is whether someone desires a joint end (*a*) merely for himself, or (*b*) for the other person(s) necessarily involved. Since (*a*) is selfishness, it seems that relations such as friendship are, in principle, compatible with selfishness. On the other hand, (*b*) is clearly a principle of s-person-ness, since acting on (*b*) would be acting for the sake of another.

That the *end* in (*b*) is joint adds, however, something new to its s-person-ness. Let us ignore the motive for seeking the end and concentrate on the end itself. To do so, we must remove an ambiguity. *All* ends in acting for the sake of another are joint ends; for they must be obtained in another to be obtained for oneself. So in order to convince ourselves that the jointness of joint ends adds to s-person-ness, we should make clear that some joint ends are possible in which the jointness is compatible with *not* acting, with respect to that end, for the sake of another. Among such joint ends are those, e.g. friendship, where what is obtained by oneself is the *same* as what is obtained by the other(s).

Against the claim that this restriction picks out a class of ends which adds to s-person-ness, someone might point to a desire that everyone be rich. It is a desire for a joint end, yet is hardly what most people call s-personal. To meet this suggestion, we might divide the class of joint ends, calling ends, such as the present one, where *desiring* something for more than oneself is a necessary condition of *having* a joint end, x-ends, and calling the rest y-ends. With y-ends, the necessary tie to the other is not in the fact that the desire is a desire ranging over more than one person (x-ends), but in the nature of what is desired without reference to the person(s) for whom it is desired (y-ends). In fact, only relationships could be y-ends: only relationships contain a necessary tie to another. Some examples are friendship, comradeship and reciprocal love. When obtained, y-ends, no matter what the motive for obtaining them, are strongly s-personal; they are close to being a sufficient condition of s-person-ness in one principle. However, they could not, because they cover so few cases, be a central principle.

We now have a considerable collection of s-personal principles.

We might wonder if any of them or any set of them is sufficient to guarantee that an action or relationship is s-personal. Complicated questions need to be discussed before we could settle this issue decisively, but I suspect that the answer is that no list short of all the principles which have been emphasized will do the job. Or rather, since some of these principles are mutually exclusive, no list will do the job which does not contain all the logically independent principles and at least one of the pairs of mutually exclusive principles. Treating persons appropriately is not a single sort of treatment, nor is it composed of elements which are logically tied to one another.

Of course, our present list is not exhaustive (indeed, it is hard to imagine what criteria of exhaustiveness might be in this context). Nor have we discussed the very interesting ways in which principles of the objective are compatible and incompatible with principles of the s-personal.

Our discussion has two practical goals of some importance. Some people emphasize as central to s-person-ness principles quite different from those emphasized by others. Not noticing this fact is a prime source of the jarring confusions which often infect controversy about moral judgments of personal relationships. Helping to remove or at least attenuate these confusions is the first practical goal of this paper.

The second is to oppose a tendency, very powerful in our culture at present, to think that the notion of treating persons appropriately, and the closely related notion of satisfactory personal relationships, are conceptually simple, though perhaps a bit difficult to achieve in practice. Buber's theory of I–thou relationships is a prime example of a philosophically sophisticated version of this tendency. For a Buberian, s-personal relationships, no matter how difficult they may be to achieve, have a single, common characterizing feature – and for that reason, it is possible to be certain about having achieved one of them. (Is it ever possible on our theory?) A very crude version of this Buberian sort of theory might be found in the drug sub-culture's belief that s-personal relationships are a matter of the right 'vibrations'.

Notes

1 Peter Winch makes this observation in the context of a discussion of Kantian theories of ethics. (Peter Winch, 'Moral Integrity', Inaugural

Lecture in the Chair of Philosophy delivered at King's College, London, 9 May 1968; Oxford, Blackwell, 1968.

2 P. F. Strawson, 'Freedom and Resentment', *Studies in the Philosophy of Thought and Action*, London, Oxford University Press, 1968, pp. 74–80.

3 Immanuel Kant, *Foundations of the Metaphysics of Morals*, New York, Library of the Liberal Arts, 1959, pp. 46–8.

4 Martin Buber, *I and Thou*, Edinburgh, T. & T. Clark, 1958.

5 Our concern with others

M. W. Hughes

I

Introduction

Thinking about minutiae of usage and inventing lines of demarcation between different applications of the same term are helpful activities : from either of them, one may come to notice shades and distinctions in ordinary thought which ordinarily, perhaps, are only half-understood. Where understanding is not complete there may be real problems whose problematic nature we do not fully realize because of the familiarity of our ways of talking about them. So linguistic philosophy may reveal them. To adopt Austin's metaphor in 'A Plea for Excuses',[1] purely linguistic philosophy is like probing with specially sharpened surgical instruments.

No one undertakes surgery without some prior diagnostic understanding, however vague. Otherwise he would not know when the malady was cured. Just so linguistic philosophy needs to be undertaken in the light of some prior conception of where the real problems lie. In ethics we need examples of moral attitudes to criticize and of moral doubts to discuss. Then we can hope to expose any underlying problems as clearly as possible and in terms as general as possible.

This work of exposition and exposure may be *purely* linguistic. But the solution of a real problem cannot come merely from stating that problem, however clearly. Sometimes it is possible to knock out a particular opinion by showing that it involves an unsuspected contradiction. Otherwise the only possible way of working to a conclusion is by agreed moral or empirical premises, if there are any. What makes the arguing not just a matter of pure moralizing or amateur science, but of philosophy, is the readiness to use moral, logical and empirical premises together in the same general argument, and to look for the relevance of particular considerations beyond their customary context. Of course, the linguistic mode of presentation of the case, the use of particular empirical premises and the philosophic attempt to find general relevance may occur in one passage of argument together rather than successively. For instance, I try in a linguistically presented argument in section III to suggest from what I believe to be agreed empirical premises certain conclusions about mental causes, which themselves interest me as part of a problem in morals.

But where no agreed premises are to hand, we repeatedly find fundamental problems whose solutions are either non-philosophical or nonexistent. There the philosopher's only advantage should be that in taking sides for non-philosophical reasons he can see what he is doing.

So my enquiry is linguistically constructed : it aims to expose one of these intractable problems (in morals) by contrast with some tractable ones (in morals and the philosophy of mind).

II

Some common opinions adumbrated

J. S. Mill[2] suggested that pagan self-assertion is possibly as good as Christian self-denial. If we take Christian self-denial as being self-denial in the interest of others – 'laying down one's life for one's friends' – I think Mill's view is that of a small minority. Shakespeare probably evokes more response when he presents Richard III[3] as a man who '*is himself alone*', and thus as repulsive to others as he is careless of them, a desperate blackguard who finally discovers that because he is all men's enemy, he has no peace with himself. On the other hand, when we read Hume's presentation in the *Enquiry concerning the Principles of Morals* of man as naturally generous, naturally responsive to the needs of others, we may think the idea unrealistic, but most of us would at least wish that its correspondence to reality were greater. By 'we' I mean primarily people with an upbringing like my own : perhaps people with a suburban and Anglican background are morally peculiar. But there is a section of humanity, even if only a restricted section, brought up not only to a view different from Mill's, but to regard selfishness as a vice, and its opposite – known by a strange variety of terms, such as service, compassion, public spirit, generosity – as good; and, therefore, who might be persuaded to express our vague moral convictions in the philosophical form of the belief that a man is good, or is really human, just so far as he is unselfish; that there can be no excess of unselfishness; that he must do as much as he can to show his unselfishness; and that this whole business of the expression of unselfishness in his life must be genuine and heartfelt, involving real feelings as well as a public front or image.

In reality I think 'our' social class is not very peculiar in this respect, except perhaps in its suspicious ability to assimilate unselfishness and conformity : I think the tendency to this belief is much more widespread and perennial. Sheridan, writing about aristocratic society, about men like himself with no bourgeois convictions about the sanctity of contracts and the payment of debts, nevertheless attracts sympathy for a character whose motto is 'While I have I'll give'.[4] St Matthew, writing for a group very remote culturally from 'ours', divides the Sheep from the Goats as those concerned with others from those neglectful of them.

The belief to which I suggest 'our' avowed morality of unselfishness tends is one that seems to fit very well into the scheme of modern ethics with its stress on universalizability. It seems to follow from the acceptance of universalizability that our reaction to injury or need should follow the same moral rules whether the injury is our own or someone else's. So if I am mildly annoyed when I burn my finger, I should feel pain and grief *in proportion* for the miserable fellow human being who has had most of his flesh scorched off by napalm in Vietnam. And since every man has his entitlement, my emotions in respect of each individual's injury should be heaped up.

Christianity has been able to add its own aesthetic force and its own theoretical justifications to this kind of humanitarianism. It is a common view among Christians that such secular humanitarianism as there is is really just a remnant or shred of the full Christian conviction. That conviction is that all men everywhere receive unconditionally and without merit on their part the unforgetting devotion of their God to the extent of his undergoing incarnation, humiliation, agony and death : he is the Good Shepherd, who will concern himself for one of his sheep as well as for a hundred. We are commanded to share his holiness and so to devote not only our concern, but also our love to each and to all impartially with ourselves.

Unfortunately, we cannot do it. Roughly speaking, our concern seems to fall into three circles, the innermost of concern with and for ourselves, the middle of concern with and for those about us, and the outermost full of shifting and weak interests in things and people more distant. If there is an air crash and a hundred people are killed, I will probably think vaguely that there may be a need for tighter regulations or something and forget the matter in a minute; if someone I know is killed, I say the matter is brought home to me, meaning that the impression on my emotions is stronger and not so soon forgettable; if I were in an aeroplane I thought was about to crash, the intensity and absorption of my interest would be, to say the least, on a quite different scale.

But, of course, it is possible for a matter to be distant, yet for a man to feel more concern about it than he does for those he meets every day. I have known people in Oxford who felt like that about Vietnam. It is also possible to feel shattering grief for the death or pain of another. The former possibility shows the power of what I call intellectual commitment, something I shall discuss presently. The latter possibility suggests to me not merely that there are exceptions and borderline cases within my first rough classification of the degrees of our concern, but that the classification is mistaken because it obscures an important fact, that there is some coincidence between generosity and self-interest.

Of course, there is very much more to be said at the sight of shattering grief than this, but it is one truth about the matter which seems to me very often to stand out. The person stricken has lost the self-fulfilment which he hoped to have with or in what is lost. Great personal love for someone dead, one of the most considerable sources of such grief, seems almost always to involve hopes of a shared future (sexual love is a clear example, so is the situation of a middle-aged person who lives for the service he or she can render to an aged parent) or else hopes that the person lost would have fulfilled us or some aspiration of ours (children are the best example of that). A very similar emotion might arise from outraged patriotism or partisan loyalty, which are always highly important examples of our concern with others. Someone whose country or whose cause is trampled on may well feel that the whole framework of his aspirations has been destroyed.

It is noteworthy that these emotions most often (not always) arise in their extremest form as a reaction to the annihilation of the person or institution to which we are committed rather than to misfortunes which though painful, do not threaten annihilation. Most Christians, indeed, would rather have the assurance that a sick person with whom they hope for a shared future would live and be restored to them than that they would rapidly die and be eternally happy. And if assurances of the happiness of the person lost do not console us, our concern is partly for ourselves.

Electra[5] spoke in inconsolable rather than modified grief when she said 'My longing is to die and never to leave your grave. For I do not see that the dead have any place for sorrow.' I see no way to deny that such emotion is strongly self-interested and yet concerned with another. The same feeling later manifested itself – when Electra found Orestes was not dead – in her undergoing hardship and danger that sheer selfishness would certainly have refused. Her loyalty to him was mirrored in extreme ferocity to those who opposed his cause. We recognize a similar mixture in patriotism, which can drive people to desperate extremes of cruelty without altogether losing its character as a generous emotion.

If I am right in thinking that many examples, even of the extreme commitment of our concern to others, are not fully selfless and that many people for much of the time are not capable of anything but an even more obvious selfishness, we might feel led towards the admission of the Christian claim that man is totally depraved, persecuted by the consciousness of being bound to a law he cannot fulfil. A less harsh claim would be that we are merely bound to move as close as we can to the state of concern for each and for all impartially. But if we accept even this, we shall never have peace. For this duty has an emotional side. We shall be committed to a series of emotional efforts which we know we cannot permanently maintain and from which we are likely to fall back with an exhausted sense of failure. And whatever state of success we achieve, we are only called to make our way yet further along the same endless road.

G

III

Compassion: is it a mental cause?

Perhaps we shall see this moral attitude and its claims to justification in a clearer light if we ask what variety of relations may be covered by such labels as 'commitment' and 'concern'. I shall concentrate on the latter term.

Concern divides into two elements at first glance. There is the passive element which appears when we say we *feel* concerned for others. And there is the active element which appears when we say we are *actively* concerned with something or that our concern shows itself in our labours.

I take the passive element, which I call compassion, first. I hope to show that it is advantageous for the study of the active element to know what compassion is. I define it as an emotional dislike for the harm of others quite irrespective of any harm to oneself. It is naturally associated with the ability to rejoice in the good fortune of others even when one has no such good fortune oneself, though this is not normally treated as a vital part of the emotions relevant to concern, since it has not the same relation with practicalities; fortunate people, in the respect that they are fortunate, do not need help. It is logically dissociated from what it is in practice often accompanied by or mingled with, aesthetic revulsion from the effects of cruelty. But the disposition to be sick at the sight of blood is different from the disposition profoundly to regret that it should be shed; we can see this when we consider that the former disposition is compatible with the disposition to applaud ruthlessness and to regard oneself as a weakling in need of a cure, or with a morbid enjoyment of the whole business. Of real, though vain, compassion, Augustine's weeping for Dido is a famous and clear example.

It would follow from my definition that no special relation to oneself is necessary in order to qualify for compassion and that someone, whoever he is, is entitled to it solely on the ground of having taken harm. It would follow from the law of universalizability that if you are going to claim compassion on such grounds, you should accord it on the same grounds. Here I think my definition coincides with the common moral opinion that there is such a thing as compassion or kindness, preferable to its opposite, which is unrestricted in its range and to which anyone in trouble can confidently turn, and whose results are vital for keeping the world a human place.

Here I must explain that this essay is written in the belief that there are real mental causes, mental states and events apart from overt bodily events, which can stand in the relation of cause and effect with those bodily events. But, of course, anyone who thinks this must take account of Ryle's classic arguments that talk of mental causation involves us in infinite regress, and that to talk of mental states apart from bodily events is to talk of single human actions as if they were two.

This is not the place to enter into lengthy consideration of Ryle's views, however; it is enough to point out that no infinite regress is implied by saying simply that for an overt bodily event to have a mental cause is not impossible. Nor does this involve flouting common sense by saying that there are two actions in many cases where common sense would say that there is just one. As Hume remarks, the least knowledge of anatomy (something common sense does not reject) informs us that several bodily parts of whose movement we are not conscious often participate in simple actions or movements of the human body. And as Berkeley[6] explained, it is arbitrary whether we talk about the totality of movements as one or about the series as multiplex. The procedures are compatible and innocuous, as the same thing can always be one whole and many parts. The controversy about the existence of mental causes is not about abolishing the series in favour of an atomic unity, because that would abolish the physiological as well as the psychological analysis of actions; it is not necessarily about reducing the length of the series, as some chains with alleged mental constituents may be shorter than some without; it is about admitting into the series elements of a certain kind. But the multiplex series will still be the same entity as the unitary totality, even if elements of this kind are admitted; and that common sense treats certain actions as units says nothing about the existence of the series or its nature.

I now offer reasons for adopting mental causes of this kind into the series. These reasons are that certain forms of discourse exist which we would have to abolish or regard as artificial (in the same way that some scientists regard talk of electrons as artificial, that is useful for empirical discourse, but not part of it), if elements of this kind did not sometimes exist in the series making up human actions. But we know empirically that they are neither artificial nor abolishable.

First there is discourse concerning hypocrisy. The hypocrite pretends he has motives that he really lacks and dissembles the motives that he has. What we need in practice to discover is just those motives which his overt behaviour is designed to conceal.

Some hypocrites are detected. But consider the difference between the detected hypocrite and the morally lapsed man. Both are similar in that their actions at an earlier time led us to believe that they were constantly committed to high moral standards, but their later actions can no longer support such a belief. But in the case of the hypocrite we now think that our belief was false always, even at times when all the evidence we could then have discovered would have supported it.

Not all hypocrites are detected. Perhaps if the man had died last year, we would never have suspected him. But now we must admit that the ascriptions to him of characteristics – such as low moral standards, or no moral standards, and certainly constant pretence – that would have falsified our belief about him, would have been justified even then. So some truths about a man may be unknown from his overt behaviour throughout his life.

But we can search for these truths, and if we discover them, we can use them effectively within our theories for the prediction of human behaviour. Provided the theories we use satisfy our standards for fruitfulness in prediction and elegance in use, why should we hesitate to admit that this search is a search for causal laws?[7]

One reason for hesitation might be that theories for the prediction of human behaviour are not yet developed to a satisfactory state. I agree they may not be developed well enough to support a complete determinism. But I want to avoid that complex subject and merely say that it seems a matter of the plainest common sense that we can only live our lives on the basis of some practical understanding of how other people can be expected to behave. This understanding is sufficiently subtle to resist exact and comprehensive formulation in words, but this does not prevent our being able to foresee the outcome of several very different situations, and able to marshal our knowledge quite effectively at short notice. It is the sort of knowledge we can expect to expand or refine with wider experience and with clearer reflection. Adults do better, on the basis of their experience, than children. People used to the customs of a place do better than strangers.

So here we have a kind of thought which is empirically based, predictive, fruitful, usable and worth trying to improve. I accept as causal kinds of thought which satisfy these standards – subject to the provision that any such thought would be vitiated if the alleged causes were not satisfactorily identifiable. (I discuss the identification of compassion in the next section.) Anyone who disagrees with me over the use of the word 'causal' may find that his disagreement with me is merely verbal. Nothing in this essay depends on taking 'causal' in any stronger sense. Given the sense I have mentioned, I can treat as fully causal such statements as 'Compassion is the cause of socially useful actions : let us encourage it if we can' or 'His trusting nature makes him gullible : he should train himself to be less credulous.' What is important for this essay is that I can treat emotions and states of mind as important for ethics, at least because of their effects on our moral life. Later, I shall suggest that they actually constitute part of our moral life.

A second reason for hesitation would be the belief that hypocrisy should be explained in terms of reasons, which are, of course, not causes. I agree at least that no account of hypocrisy would be complete without reference to reasons. But I reply to the objection that it merely shows that if my arguments are correct, reasons should so be introduced that reference to them harmonizes with causal analysis, where causal analysis is appropriate. This is most easily done by saying that reasons may not be causes, but states of mind, characterized by having accepted certain reasons as good, are.[8]

So I argue that to deny even the possibility of treating mental states or events as causes of bodily states or events is to assert that common sense talk about hypocrisy has nonsensical presuppositions.

Next, there is discourse concerning emotional frustration. A man who is frustrated is prevented from acting according to motives that really are present. Lancelot loved Guinevere, but for many years had to dissemble. I am sure he never doubted that he was subject to, but fighting against, a very powerful cause. Anyone who knew his state of mind could predict that his correct behaviour towards the Queen could not continue without a struggle, and therefore might not in the end continue at all. Once again, here is the discovery of cause affording grounds for a prediction. Once again what is discovered is *ex hypothesi* something hidden, not part of bodily behaviour.

We may also note that most people feel that those of their efforts directed to psychological control are as much causes as those directed to the production of some change in the material world. Both kinds of effort, of pushing a weight like Sisyphus or of restraining lust like Lancelot, seem to pass the Humean test of regular conjunction and we could theorize about them in ways that would be causal by our standards. Now, these efforts may be accepted as causal, but still be interpreted as nothing but certain episodes in bodily life, during which we act in a certain way – grit our teeth and so on. But we have then accepted at least that they *are* causal, and to describe an efficient cause C as operative on an object O is to admit that O displays to a significant extent a difference D when C is present, and that O displays D to a significantly lesser extent where C is not present. Hence O has causal properties of its own such that, other things being equal, it resists entry into the condition where D is displayed. If this were not true of O, then O might display D as often without C as in C's presence, and there would be no reason to formulate the causal law that C is operative on O – which is contrary to hypothesis.

So, just as the stone resists Sisyphus because it has the causal property of inertia (that is, it is in a state such that it can be predicted that it will not move without impact), Lancelot resists his own efforts at self-control because he has what must, *pari ratione*, be admitted to be the causal property of lustfulness – that is, he is in a state such that he can be predicted to be less likely to refrain from adultery than another man whom Guinevere leaves cold. So if the effort (even behaviouristically interpreted) is a cause, then the state characterized by lustfulness is a cause. And to say 'the state characterized by lustfulness' differs only by being a circumlocution from saying 'lustfulness' according to common speech. Emotion-describing words have precisely the function of discriminating one state of the person from another; in this discrimination they may refer to hidden properties, by my previous argument. And the analysis is in any case causal, not dispositional or Rylean.

Some may say that efforts of will cannot be regarded as causal because they cannot be regarded as episodic, that is, able to begin and end at points in time. But they can; Lancelot may not be considering visiting Guinevere in the morning, may be struggling to restrain himself at noon and may have yielded by midnight to his great love.

Some may say that these 'causal' laws admit of exceptions, or that causal analysis is impossible because mental 'causes' are 'logically' and therefore not in truth causally, connected with their results. The first suggestion is true, but is what on a causal analysis should be expected. It is always possible for a cause to be overborne by a stronger countervailing cause.

The second objection may look momentarily plausible. In certain cases intentions are customarily identified by words that refer to their achievement, and so are analytically connected with the words that describe that achievement: 'My intention to enter politics,' for example. But even if there exists no way of identification other than of this kind, that does not mean that the connection between the intention and the achievement themselves (as distinct from that between the words that describe them) is analytic or necessary in any way. What it does mean is that we cannot understand what the intention is unless we can understand what it would be for the state of affairs in which that intention was achieved, to come about. We have to understand what success would be like; but we have equally to understand what failure would be like, and that failure is always possible.[9]

As an example, consider that many people in the ancient world presumably intended to pass an immortal existence in the Elysian Fields, and the imagination of poets has given us a picture of such an existence that few people have found it difficult to understand. The people involved no doubt thought they knew the instruments – observance of moral codes, sacrifices – to achieve their intentions efficiently. Few of us would now doubt that all these intentions were from beginning to end frustrated.

Because there is an analytic connection between the words describing the intention and *both* the words describing the achievement *and* the words describing its failure, no mere identification of the intention in the sort of terms we are discussing – 'the intention to enter politics', 'the intention to commit murder' – can rule out either success or failure.

If there is a connection between an intention and its achievement, it must therefore be non-analytic. There can then be no objection to our asking whether experience allows us to formulate rules for such connections which can be organized within the theoretical structure of our explanations and predictions of behaviour. The answer must empirically be 'yes'. If so, there seems no reason to reject or reinterpret the common sense view that intentions succeed according as they are stronger and the circumstances are less difficult, and fail as they are weaker and the circumstantial difficulties greater. And this view in its obvious interpretation is quite recognizably a causal theory making customary allowance for the effect of countervailing causes.

There are, of course, many accounts of mental states in which conflict is all-important, with the result in terms of outward behaviour dependent on the result of the conflict. The mental states, such as Lancelot's love, and the outward results such as his adultery, must therefore be specifiable without *logical* connections that would restrict *causal* analysis. For there is no conflict without countervailing forces; and on any view that connected the mental state *logically* with one outcome alone, not merely with the alternative of the achievement or prevention of this outcome, countervailing forces could not exist.

IV

Identification of compassion

Even if it is sensible to suppose that compassion exists as a real mental cause, talk of it would still be otiose if there did not exist a way of identifying it. I think ways do exist, and ways that tell against the suggestion that talk of compassion as causal may be as artificial as talk of electrons.

However we understand the word 'compassion', most of us would agree that there may be difficulties because what appear to be compassionate acts can be spurious because of an ulterior purpose, or because the agent's real aim is self-advertisement. How are we to tell the difference?

It has traditionally been regarded as plausible to say that in our own minds we can discern one emotion from another by intuition or introspection. Few modern philosophers would go that far; I would go further, and say that it is not contradictory to suppose that we can intuit the mental states of others and indeed that we sometimes do. Without any such intuition, even of ourselves, it is hard to think that the language of mental states could ever have arisen, let alone have come to seem so intuitive and plausible.

This argument would have little force if mental-state language were just a set of ways of speaking, all reducible to physical observation language. But if the argument of the last section was right, this is not so. Mental states can be regarded as existences distinct from any physical state; they have causal properties and therefore should be so regarded.

Now it is another feature of the language in which these things are discussed that they are often said to be felt. This clearly does not mean simply that we feel the somatic sensations associated with the emotion. If I weep with grief for Dido, that is a different experience from weeping because of onion fumes, even though my tear-ducts are doing the same thing and the nerves making the same reports of their doing it. And this is not a difference we work out from the context; we experience it, without working anything out.

If this is so, then the specific nature of a mental state can be decided by experience as 'direct' as that of seeing or hearing. To say that it is not so is additionally implausible because it would mean that such expressions as 'I felt great grief' would be metaphorical or elliptical or false. Most people do not take them as such. But language is surely what most language-users make it, and it seems very high-handed to insist for the sake of theory that such a persistent claim to experience is false.

For other people, the claim to intuition is much shakier, both in particular and in general. But once again I doubt if the 'insights' we think we have, in life or in literature (where interest often seems to centre on the 'presentation of character'), are all false, or are present only in a metaphorical sense, or are all arrived at by a process of working out, either by analogy in the Cartesian or by linguistic context in the Wittgensteinian manner.

I should emphasize that not even in our own case need such intuition be infallible. It may need correction by further inspection; at any rate the reports of intuition, like the reports of sense in the case of an illusion, are only one item among many. If analogy and general experience tell us differently, we do not have to accept the report of intuition any more than we have to believe the reports of our eyes that the twig sticking out of the water is bent.

This corresponds to the customary fact that we can be more or less perceptive, more or less gullible, about our own psychological states. There is a distinction, now part of common speech, between reason and rationalization; every psychiatrist must know the difference between people who can honestly appreciate the reasons for their actions and those who cannot, those who habitually indulge in rationalization about themselves. Every salesman and confidence trickster must know an important difference between those who can easily be gulled about the motives of the person to whom they are talking and those who cannot.

Geach[10] pours great philosophic scorn on the assertion of this obvious fact. He says, probably rightly, that if mental perception is possible, it should have defects analogous to those of visual perception, such as colour blindness. (Of course, this could only be right if 'analogous' be taken in a loose sense; it might presumably be an even less close analogy than between sight and touch, where there is nothing that I know of precisely corresponding to colour blindness.) In fact, persistent imperceptiveness or gullibility is closer to colour blindness (Geach's chosen example) than any defect of the sense of touch. It is a habit of mistake in certain critical situations set against a background of success in ordinary situations. Colour-blind persons are not usually, as Geach assumes, persons with a bad habit of linguistic mistakes; they learn so well to cope with ordinary language-use that colour blindness was not diagnosed until 1784 when Dalton detected it in himself in the unusually difficult circumstances of work in a chemical laboratory.[11] Just so, the gullible man does not blunder through life, but fails when confronted with a clever trickster. At this rate, compassion is identifiable by observation, and entities that are observable and causal do not belong to an artificial form of speech, but are as empirical as tables and chairs.

But in addition to direct identification, there are other things we can do, such as look for slips in unguarded moments, or devise special tests, such as that devised for Joseph Surface in *The School for Scandal*, to reveal hypocrisy or inconsistency. We know the form of life characteristic of really compassionate, or courageous, or persistent men. We want to assure ourselves that a person really has adopted that form of life. As Hume said, much of the point of moral enquiry into someone's character is to assure ourselves about his future conduct. That is why the enquiry into what form of life is really his is a predictive and causal matter.

Now even if we are doubtful about direct identification of mental states, we can be confident that they are identifiable if we can form causal hypotheses which predict particular future actions on the basis of characteristics, recognizable by tests prior to the occurrence of some of those actions, and taken to be stable, because they can be referred to constantly amid any variety of particular situations. The predictions are different as these characteristics differ. In that case we must admit that they behave in causal laws just as the most uncontroversially empirical entities do. The descriptions we use of them give rise to no contradictions. So that the suggestion that all talk of mental states is artificial, as Berkeley[12] regarded some of Newton's theories (contradictory but useful, in his opinion) or as some moderns regard talk of (say) electrons, seems pointless and unevidenced.

v

Practical forms of concern

What does the compassionate man do? I distinguish three practical forms of concern which I call by the artificial names of concern-about, concern-for, and concern-with.[13]

Concern-about is the intellectual or investigative side of the matter. The wish to do something about the existing state of affairs can indeed lead to a mere wild lashing out against injustice, but it can equally naturally lead to careful investigation and planning, particularly as without these precautions attempts tend to fail. We wish to know for the present what means will be effective and how like evils to those we now oppose can be prevented from arising. So this disposition to intellectual enquiry should both give our present actions effectiveness and help us to put present problems in perspective. It would be opposite not only to the kind of complacency which cannot see need when it is pretty obvious, but also to that which will not look for need when it is not pretty obvious; the concerned person goes beyond the consistent person in always looking for new applications of his value-judgments and theories.

The virtue of concern-about comes from the vice of its opposite : both kinds of complacency seem to be standing temptations of happy individuals or prosperous societies. The objectionability of concern-about arises when the habit of thought about many situations does not engender a critical attitude, when there is failure to take the increased opportunity, which should come from the wide range of information that wide-ranging thought should consider, of falsifying mistaken large-scale theories or of discovering unacceptable consequences of existing principles and when wider thought produces nothing but wider arena for prejudice and fanaticism to display themselves. It is a standing temptation for concerned men to become prejudiced : we find that they may be very well informed, may look at many things, but look at them all with a kind of mental squint like Lewis Carroll's poet. Many active and intelligent members of political parties show signs of succumbing to this weakness.

But complacency has just the same tendency. Though its prejudices may be less fanatical than stolid, they can be just as infuriating and just as perverting to the judgment. There can be the same refusal to recognize as falsifications of theories what any impartial mind would take to be such, just as (for example) Mr Podsnap refused to listen to what people told him about starvation in the streets of London, when he was defending his thesis that England was perfect. Perhaps we may think the abolition of complacency and the encouragement of concern-about fairly important, if we consider that all social reform since Mr Podsnap's day would either not have happened or have happened only after revolution, if all middle-class people had been like Mr Podsnap.

Aristotle[14] said that the early occurrences of a practice that is or is becoming habitual in an individual's life make the latter occurrences come more naturally, that is, make the habit stronger. Here we have examples of a habit, incipient or established, of not caring, which produces a related habit of not being able to appreciate the truth. What Aristotle said is also important as indicating how someone can educate himself in the active habits of concern.

Concern-for is the disposition to respond to need practically and with kindness or sympathy. The response need not be very effective for the disposition to be genuinely shown. It can co-exist with anything short of total helplessness. The response may be general or unspecific or peripheral, like that of persons genuinely concerned for immigrants in Wolverhampton, who demonstrate in Oxford against Enoch Powell – which is to attack the problem, if at all, only generally; or who write letters to the press – an activity which might uninsultingly be called peripheral. But it is all genuine concern.

Concern-for might be described as a primary sign of the acknowledgment of the humanity of the person for whom you are concerned. (I suggest that we apply it to animals in so far as we consider them anthropomorphically.) That is why it is so important. People in need often desire it as much as they do more tangible benefits. Complaints of the impersonality of the social services have at least some reality and are based on this fact, that people want a concern which is sympathy without condescension. It is interesting to compare the expression of this kind of need as one might meet it in someone old and lonely (to take a set of our citizens whose needs are now much talked about) with the expression they might give to other needs, say for money. The latter kind of need only extreme necessity would drive them to express at all. It is, of course, common for them actively to resent the provisions made for them by the state, which are thought to resemble cold charity. Yet in my experience requests bearing on the former kind of need are made quite freely, requests, for instance, for company and conversation (the minimum expression of concern for those near you; if you just write to the press *about* them you are a detached and perhaps an unfeeling man). The money such people are glad to accept is money to which they think they have a right: products of contributory pension schemes, for example. I conjecture that they think that concern is something to which, merely by being human and capable of worry and loneliness, they have a right of some kind. I make this point in order to suggest that an investigation of the conceptual links between my subject of concern and another closely related aspect of personal relations, respect for others, may be fruitful. For we have a strong tendency to think that respect too is due by right to all persons.

Concern-with arises when we to any considerable extent[15]

Universitas
BIBLIOTHECA
Ottaviensis

identify our interests with those of others who are not, at any rate to start with, our natural associates. There is a difference between feeling sorry at someone's misfortunes and glad at their good fortune and feeling their victories and defeats as our own. For instance, in a situation like that of the recent Nigerian civil war, a person in a position like that of a British statesman or official might feel horrified at the suffering of the rebels, and do such small things as he could to have it relieved : that is, be concerned *for* the people on the other side. But he may nevertheless regard it as the other side, opposed to his side, and he may be totally committed to securing a government victory. He may feel every setback to the rebel cause, even if it involves the suffering he hates, as a victory for his country and himself, and wish for it to happen. He is concerned *with* his own side. His position may be uncomfortable or even deplorable but, I think, consistent.

Sometimes the outsider may be more sensitive to the victories and defeats of those he 'adopts' than they are themselves. The professional revolutionary probably feels the defeat of a movement he organizes for the sake of the oppressed more than the oppressed, used to being trodden on, do themselves. His reaction may well be stronger than theirs, determined where theirs is re-signed. St Paul expresses clearly how he regarded his followers' difficulties as his own. 'There is that which presseth upon me daily, anxiety for all the churches. Who is weak and I am not weak? Who is made to stumble and I burn not?' [16] Precisely because he was 'strong' Christian, successful in cutting other ties and in dedicating himself to the cause, he felt as his own the failure of weaker men to live up to the demands of Christianity. Perhaps he felt it more acutely than they did themselves, being men of lesser dedication.

Paul is an example of one who identified his interests with those of a certain group voluntarily and not as a result of interests he already had. He acted under a strictly religious impulse, but it is fully possible for people to make a similar identification of their interests with those of others as a result of their compassion for those others' sufferings.

This sort of commitment does not make us different people immediately; among the people to whom we are now committed we may for some time continue to wear the aspect of a benevolent outsider. But our situation has something new about it, in that we now feel as our own the triumphs and failures of the cause. This is not just the feeling of the leader who stands to gain by the success of the cause some reward such as office or fame for himself, but something more widespread and profound – the sheer satisfaction at being associated with victory, the strengthening of self-respect that comes with success and above all success in a morally justified cause.

People to whom this feeling of moral justification is important for their happiness have an interest in adopting causes they can accept as moral. If promoting the good of others is a serious part of their morality, they will display the kind of extended self-interest I mentioned in section II, which is also a sincere interest in the good of others, or some others.

So often, in our concerns-with others, we can support a cause with all the tenacity of one defending a vital personal interest, and with the complete assurance that we are not being narrowly selfish. This combination of altruism and selfishness is obviously a source of great strength. But it is also the source of a major moral difficulty for concern-with. Under this considered pressure we may so much want to advance the cause that we listen very readily to the suggestion that any dubious or even atrocious means is justified so long as the cause is advanced.

So commitment may make us radically different people over a time. The man who renounced narrow selfishness under the impulse of compassion to take up a difficult cause and to identify his interests with those of others may face serious internal conflict; his general feelings of compassion and the interests he has made his own, which have been in harmony, now conflict. If he decides that brutal action is justified, then he will find that compassion has led him to take up a cause within which he is led to abandon the values of the compassionate man for those of the warrior. For example, at the foundation of democracy in ancient Greece it seems that many of the leaders were people who would have done quite well under an oligarchy; so perhaps some of them were democrats out of high ideals. Nevertheless, Thucydides[17] commented on an example of civil strife that the democrats, just like the oligarchs, eventually forgot their principles and just fought to win.

VI

Proposed moral rules for practical concern

So much for the existence and importance of these forms of concern; now for their conflict. I want to trace this conflict and then ask what moral rules should regulate them and decide between them. It may be helpful to begin by stating their different relations to the emotion of compassion.

Concern-about and compassion are related (usually) as mutual reinforcements. Increasing knowledge of the scope of a problem increases the degree to which we regard it as serious and thus care about it. And the more we care about it, the more we want to know about its causes and hence its possible cure. The only restraint we might reasonably want to impose on it is in situations when we think that compassion itself needs to be restrained, or when we think it is leading us to interest ourselves too much in matters which are too remote for us to be able to influence them seriously, and distracting us from matters we could deal with usefully.

Given my definition of concern-for, it follows that, other things being equal, compassion will result in concern for whoever is in need. Thus in normal human circumstances, where other things are fairly equal, the presence of concern-for will become the primary test by which compassion is recognized, and it will be held in esteem by any society which esteems compassion. Then how, if at all, should concern-for be limited? The Golden Rule will certainly apply here; if these are situations in which we would demand help solely on the ground of being human and being in need, then we must extend help to others in any of those situations and on the same ground. If, as I suggested we should, we treat concern-for as accorded by right of their humanity to human beings, it cannot matter who the human being is.

He might be one who had committed a grave crime, whom it was our natural wish to punish. This attitude does not necessarily mean that we cease to be concerned for him, or to wish his good. Some kinds of punishment, like some kinds of medical treatment, can without hypocrisy or implausibility be regarded as cruelty for the sake of kindness. A parent may smack a child for going too near the fire and, however great the child's momentary resentment, the parent can be reasonably sure that the child will be better off for the warning. Concern-for does not imply weakness towards other people's faults: the reverse indeed.

But there are punishments and inflictions which are unaccompanied by any treatment of the person hurt as a reasonable and redeemable being; inflictions which cause degeneration, not improvement, and inflictions in which any good to the sufferer is totally disregarded. When you act like this to someone, you are unconcerned for him.

There is logical escape from the Golden Rule simply by adding an exception clause, applying potentially even to yourself, to the effect that anybody who has done such-and-such a thing or is of such-and-such a kind, no longer merits treatment as a human being. Many decent people make such exceptions against (say) murderers, child-molesters, fascists, imperialists or racialists. Often enough such exceptions are justified by reference to a cause; if the communists do not slaughter the capitalists, the proletariat cannot be saved from oppression; if the catholics do not burn the heretics, the heretics will damn the souls of the weaker brethren.

Can the philosopher say anything here, faced with these arguments which have never lacked plausibility and which, if accepted, lead to unconcerned (in effect brutal) action, or at any rate the readiness to take it? Conversely, can he say anything against those who maintain that to touch pitch is to be defiled, or that to think brutality justified is to misunderstand morality – a view I call purism?

Professor Bennett[18] has recently suggested against Professor Anscombe that we can, as philosophers, dismiss purism. If this were possible, it would at least be a start. The argument, in short, is that purism demands that rather than perpetrate a brutal deed, however small in comparison, we must take decisions whose effect is the actual infliction of brutality, however great in comparison that may be. So we are to decide in favour of great brutality in order to prevent the small brutality we might have committed in the first place. So purism insists on what it sets out to denounce, and is worse than its opposite in that it sacrifices the greater, not the smaller good; it is both contradictory and immoral.

H

But I think that this argument simply misunderstands the base on which purism rests. Normally the base is religious and I shall try to explain it as such. Fundamentally it is connected to concern-with and to loyalty.

Religious morality rests on a supposed divine law. A law, human or divine, normally has what we might call, following St Paul, a fulfilment. That is to say, we can see that there could be a situation which would be equivalent to the result of total obedience to the law by everybody. If everyone obeyed the command 'Thou shalt not kill', nobody would ever die by deliberate violence. New Testament writers correctly observe that fulfilment is a kind of transformation. After a time, at least, the situation achieved by complete obedience will come to feel like – indeed really will be, providing there is no tendency to backsliding – a state of willing co-operation in which the law no longer exercises any pressure. This transformation into liberty has still left something the same, for our excellence and our joy still consist in obedience to the divine will; but now this is achieved in a state more like union than subordination.

The reason why this theory turns into a consistent version of purism is that on this side of death – on the other side is the new life – the requirement for our transformation is not that we seek the state of fulfilment or whatever approximation to it comes to hand, but simply that we obey *cum caritate*. Compared with the eternal reality of our relation to God which this obedience sets up, the good and bad things of this world are minor or even illusory. Our aim should not be to bring these supposedly good things about except as the divine law requires – and certainly not to bring them about against the divine law. The fundamental points are that the value of the situation, even when produced by obedience, is of little or no importance compared with the value of the act of obedience itself, and that since every soul is responsible for itself, no act of obedience or disobedience is the cause of any consequence other than those of little or no importance and other than the redefinition of the soul's relationship to God. Hence it seems reasonable for God to persist in his demand to the point of the utmost sacrifice not only of our self-interest, but of our independent judgment; only so, as in the rightly much-stressed story of Abraham and Isaac, can perfect loyalty be expressed.

The morality which is opposite to purism is like it in that both are ready to bring about consequences to human beings which those concerned for those human beings would not wish to have happened. There is a morality thoroughly opposed to purism, which is ready to do this for the simple reason that it thinks certain states of affairs so important that they must be brought about at any cost. It talks in terms of an unquestionably supreme loyalty. Hence it is opposed, along with purism, to what I call common morality (of which utilitarianism is one version) which takes states of affairs to be important, but which thinks the moral value of any action always recalculable in the light of new information about what its cost will be. But calculation of costs is pointless when a certain end is declared to be worth any cost, and the habit of exercising independent judgment in this way suggests doubt of the very fundamentals of the loyalist system. So to the loyalist as well as to the purist, though for very different reasons, independent judgment is something to be sacrificed. That is why political systems with an overriding end and with no fastidiousness of means make a virtue of the submission of the individual will to the accepted repository of political wisdom – the party or the chairman's thoughts.

Loyalism is a form of concern with others that acknowledges *no* moral restriction. Among sane people it is not likely to appear unless in the service of a serious, perhaps a great, cause or movement. Often enough it is a strong and developed sense of compassion reinforced with much careful thought and concern about the ills of the world that leads people to adopt great causes – by 'great' I mean those that seek to affect or protect all or very many aspects of life by promoting or resisting great changes in the world. Since the world is a violent place, this sort of cause will often enough commit us to utterly uncompassionate action against our opponents. For them, we may believe, we cannot be concerned. It follows that either our concern-for must be limited so that it does not prevent concern-with from reaching its fullest extent at least sometimes; or concern-with must be limited so that it does not reach this extent. But if I am right about their relations with compassion, compassion itself is likely to lead us to resist both kinds of limitation.

Emotion and expression

Philosophical treatment of this problem might begin by noticing that it is irrational to demand support for a cause on compassionate grounds and at the same time to pursue the ends of that cause with any extreme of brutality that appears convenient, because brutality repels the kind of support you seek. With any step of brutality beyond the stage where severity can be justified as designed to improve the situation of whoever suffers it, the cause must be justified in spite of, rather than with the support of, compassion.

In the extreme case compassion is murdered by its offspring; it is no use inviting people on compassionate grounds to bring about such a murder. The extreme case may be rare, but it seems to me equally contradictory to appeal on compassionate grounds to let compassion be merely mutilated : to ask someone to accept a significant shift within his own mind towards the repression of compassion, or to enter a society biased against it. And repression would ensue if compassion is to be denied any of its normal results. Compassion tending to arise in response to *any* need will, of course, be seriously denied if confined to 'Us' rather than 'Them'.

For instance, if hardness of heart is to become habitual and concern-for correspondingly rare, compassion will either be seriously frustrated or seriously reduced (the former situation would soon produce the latter). Also if concern-about is not to be allowed in anything but its uncritical form in which independent judgment is sacrificed, the compassion of anyone to whom that kind of critical judgment, rather than its fanatical counterpart, is natural, will be frustrated or denatured.

So extreme loyalist morality, which would repel compassion on both these counts, should give up seeking support on compassionate grounds. Yet without any kind of compassionate ground, any kind of feeling that one is serving the needs of the human race, the commitment of loyalty necessary to great causes will not often be forthcoming.

I can perhaps bring out what I mean by the *denial* of compassion by contrasting the *discipline* of compassion with it. Sometimes people need to devote themselves to an organized effort to achieve what compassion would wish done, and sometimes the situation is such that final victory or defeat for the cause is not in question. The task may be rather the endless one of coping with a series of problems or disasters of which we cannot foresee a final end; for instance, a hospital may face an indefinitely continuing stream of casualties, or a school a comparable stream of subnormal children. What matters then is efficiency; any sense of victory or defeat for a person conscientious in understanding such a task will be associated with the maintenance or relaxation of that efficiency. But this kind of victory, and sensitivity to it, is important to an organization; so we have here a form of concern-with.

What we do not have here is a continuous stream of compassion. What efficiency requires is smooth working, independent of all the normal variations of individual psychology; so someone whose operation depended on upsurges of compassion would be unreliable. This attempt continually to feel such upsurges would provoke a terrible sense of failure and reduce the person concerned to an emotionally exhausted heap. Efficiency requires the reverse of this, that people be not more than ordinarily strained emotionally, and that they be strengthened for their work by access to the normal enjoyment of life, which endless dwelling on the suffering of others would spoil. This may require some restriction of compassion, but ultimately for compassionate reasons; we would expect a good nurse (say) to be less sensitive to the misfortunes of particular patients than outsiders and more sensitive to the need for effectiveness in the organization. This is why it is very hard to think of compassion's being offered on a professional basis, why outsiders can often usefully supplement the efforts of professionals in these contexts, and why complaints of the 'impersonality of the social services' are often misguided. But they are justified if the restriction of compassion goes beyond what compassionate reasons can justify; or if professional people become so hardened that they have no nerve of compassion that can ever be touched. Then they cease to be trustworthy, because their moral responses no longer give them any ability to judge what compassion requires, what compassionate reasons do or do not justify. In sum, the activity need not always express, but should not ever suppress the emotion.

This example is one of the familiar Humean[19] kind in which someone's trustworthiness for future overt activity is assessed by their inner state; but we should notice that to believe in inner mental causes and to believe that all the characteristics of man with any bearing on his conduct can genuinely be assessed from a moral point of view is to believe that it is part of man's moral task to improve (as far as he can) his inner state as well as to regulate his outward conduct. Plato believed that inner moral life was supremely important for happiness, outweighing all external considerations, so that the murderous King Archelaus would not be compensated for a depraved character by all his power and glory.[20] The Christian purist believes something similar. I think them right to this extent, that the perversion of the inner moral state brought about by brutality is an independent reason for avoiding it.

I think this problem tractable because it can be shown that loyalist morality, prepared to be brutal, would commit itself to a contradiction by appealing to and denying compassion, and that there is no plausible suggestion of an escape that will give the loyalist the moral licence he wants. The problem is tractable because either I am right or I can be shown to be wrong by the production of such a plausible suggestion.

VIII

Conclusion

There is another side to the argument against loyalism, one that would support common morality in an unrigorous form. If we are not to appeal on compassionate grounds for action that would deny compassion its natural results, we must not press it to the point beyond which it makes us incapable of any happiness in the world; for then we have no self-interest, either in a narrow or extended form, there being nothing which can make us happy; so we are incapable of concern-with others based on compassion, which would frustrate all those to whom concern with others was a natural expression of their compassion. Once again compassion could be mutilated or seriously reduced without being destroyed and once again it seems contradictory to embark for compassionate reasons on a serious reduction of compassion.

Also the whole point of concern-for and concern-with is the relief of need and the improvement of human life by moving it away from suffering and misery and towards happiness. If this activity is not to be self-stultifying, then either we must be utopian in the sense that we believe that a practically misery-free society will emerge after a finite effort, or we must believe that it is permissible for us to be happy to some significant extent even in a world where others are forced by circumstances to enjoy very little happiness. Otherwise all concern can offer is a doubtful promotion from one unhappiness to another.

At this rate our universalized rule about the emotions which arise in reaction to our compassionate contemplation of other people's pain (itself usually unpleasant to us in a sense, especially as a distraction from our own happiness) in comparison to our own pain should be : compassionate emotion should be encouraged to that extent and in that way which will enable it to have its full range of natural results. If weakness, temporary generosity or self-centredness cause upsurges of emotion, then that is to be tolerated, but we need not regard it as any kind of obligation, to ourselves or to others. To work up compassion beyond what is necessary to produce its full range of desirable results, so that it tends to reduce happiness, would then be morally undesirable.

But this case against the position I initially adumbrated, that there can be no excess of unselfishness, is not so strong as the case against brutality for the good of a cause. It may well be that neither our compassion nor its natural results could survive under a system where we had to consent to brutality, but it might under a system where we denied ourselves happiness on the grounds of a utopian expectation of some kind. I find it hard to say that all utopian beliefs (in the sense in which I have defined the word) are implausible, considering that they are so popular : in Marxism, which thinks of such a huge part of human misery as simply the result of a doomed system of exploitation, in purist Christianity with its belief in transformation and new life, or in Kantian Christianity with its belief in a God who adjusts consequences, in the end, to favour morality.

Even apart from this there is the simple evaluative question of whether we think that moral self-satisfaction is a permissible part of happiness. If we limit compassion at the point where it does not seriously reduce our happiness, we may find ourselves, particularly if we are in a position where no difficult or risky action is required of us or even open to us, sitting back and congratulating ourselves on having done all that morality requires of us. Some may argue that there is no danger of efforts to increase compassion reducing happiness so completely that compassionate action becomes pointless – no danger because our stubborn natures would in any case not respond sufficiently. But there is, they would say, a great danger in allowing ourselves to take a rosy view of our moral attainments, because the rosiness will gradually infect our view of the world. So at the cost of some damage to happiness moral efforts to increase compassion beyond whatever point we have attained should always be undertaken, and people can be exhorted to do this on the grounds of compassion. To say that there can be an excess of compassion or unselfishness is at best to say something pointless in this world.

Behind this view of self-satisfaction as dangerous lies the value-judgment that it is unfitting for a man to be compassionate towards others and thus be dissatisfied with the general state of the world and humanity while accepting a satisfied view of his own nature and morality. This is a judgment characteristic of those seriously influenced by Christian theology, and forms an interesting contrast with the apparently patronizing conviction that Christians often seem in practice to display – that they are privileged persons with nothing to worry about on their own account, kindly coming to pluck brands from the burning. On this view we are, as I have said, to travel an endless road and we are not entitled to any final peace while we belong to a wicked world. The moral task of the compassionate man is a quest after something always visible but always receding in this world. Again utopianism steps in to offer something better in the next.

The pagan or humanist dislikes anything that can tend or slide into a stultifying abolition of human happiness, and makes it *his* value-judgment that any such tendency is bad, because it goes against his ideal of the compassionate man. This is over and above his dispute over the extent of the threat to happiness from the effort to increase compassion. He has an ideal of the compassionate man as one who has established harmony within himself and is trying to raise others to this state. A pagan once replied to a Christian, who pressed him to accept divine redemption, that he did not need it because he had never sinned. Both parties to this dialogue were saying things inconceivable or incomprehensible to each other. They were working from different views of the obligations of a man trying to do this human duty in a bad world. There are some disputes in which the philosopher can be certain that even if he cannot prove one side's case, he can explain both clearly in the expectation that almost all impartial minds will concur in their judgments. This is not one of them. If any definitive treatment of this ancient and fundamental controversy is possible, I wait to hear of it.²¹

Notes

1 J. L. Austin, 'A Plea for Excuses', *Proceedings of the Aristotelian Society*, N.S. 57, 1956–7.
2 J. S. Mill, *On Liberty*, Dent, Everyman edition, p. 120.
3 W. Shakespeare, *King Henry VI Pt III*, Act V, sc. vi., l. 83.
4 R. B. Sheridan, *The School for Scandal*, Act IV, sc. i, ad fin. . . .
5 Sophocles, *Electra*, 1168–70.
6 G. Berkeley, *Essay towards a New Theory of Vision*, for example, para. 109.
7 I should explain that my view of cause is Humean with the reservation that Hume should have considered the importance of theoretical structures in prediction. Hence a causal law whose operation we cannot often observe (and so cannot build up a Humean *custom* of thought about it) can be accepted as a deduction within such a structure. And we may feel suspicious of a prediction made on the basis of regularly observed conjunctions, if that prediction is simply *ad hoc*, and cannot be fitted into a structure of satisfactory fruitfulness and elegance and and remains isolated from the general process of our thought.
8 Cf. D. Davidson, 'Action, Reason and Cause', *Journal of Philosophy*, 60, 23, 1963. This is admittedly a contentious view.
9 By 'understanding' here we mean simply something sufficient to guide us in our use of words. There is certainly no need for an intellectually or imaginatively complete understanding.
10 P. T. Geach, *Mental Acts*, London, Routledge & Kegan Paul, 1957, p. 107 ff.
11 I owe this information to Professor C. W. K. Mundle's interesting book, *Perception: Facts and Theories*, Oxford University Press, 1971.
12 Cf. K. Popper, *Conjectures and Refutations*, London, Routledge & Kegan Paul, 1963, ch. 6.
13 It has been put to me that in classifying concern as I do, I am playing a linguistic trick possible only in English. But for me what holds together the different 'forms of concern' is their connection with the emotion

of compassion. I was led to think this by reflection on the word 'concern' that began as an academic game; but words with no etymological connection, such as 'generosity' or 'partisanship' would express my meaning just as well.

14 Aristotle, *Nicomachean Ethics*, Book II, ch. I.

15 'To any considerable extent': this is possible only when the 'others' involved have interests sufficiently similar for there to be some practical programme of action to serve those interests. If those interests are dissimilar (even conflicting), or all programmes considered are impractical, we remain at the level of hopes and dreams for the future, rather than at that of real service to the interests of others. If there were a practical scheme for the service of all members of the human race who are in need, and it were pursued without resort to uncompassionate or brutal measures, concern-for and concern-with the human race would become identical.

16 2 Cor. 11: 28–9.

17 Thucydides, III, 82–8.

18 Jonathan Bennett, 'Whatever the Consequences', *Analysis*, 26, 3, January 1966. Cf. R. W. Beardsmore's perceptive reply, 'Consequences and Moral Worth', *Analysis*, 29, 6, June 1969.

19 D. Hume, *Enquiries concerning the Human Understanding and concerning the Principles of Morals*, para. 76.

20 Plato, Gorgias, 470 d ff.

21 Valuable suggestions for this essay came from Martin Holt and Gill Scholefield.

6 A conceptual investigation of love*

W. Newton-Smith

Concepts like love, which we use in describing, explaining and ordering the personal relations of ourselves and others, have received scant attention in the recent Anglo-American philosophical tradition. This contrasts decidedly with philosophical interests on the continent. The difference may be explained in part by the fact that here interests have lain in different areas. More interestingly, perhaps, this difference may reflect disagreement about the connection between such an account and more basic issues in epistemology and the philosophy of mind and about the import of a philosophical account of, say, love. For example, Sartre, when discussing relations with others in *Being and Nothingness*, concludes at the end of something bearing at least a family resemblance to an argument, that it follows from his account of the relation between mind and body that an attempt to love is bound to fail. The acceptance of Sartre's argument would have clear import for someone who regulated his or her sex life according to the principle that sex without love was not permissible. A person who accepted the argument and who was unwilling to adopt a chaste life would seem to be compelled either to violate or to revise his or her principles. Clearly, if one accepts that an account of the relation between mind and body might entail conclusions of this force, one would be interested, to say the least, in working out the entailments.

On a conception of philosophy which has had some currency in the recent Anglo-American tradition such conclusions would not be expected. For, on this view, philosophy is seen as a sort of second-order discipline, which seeks to give a descriptive, and possibly systematic, account of the concepts we employ in dealing with the world. Philosophy presupposes a linguistic practice which it describes and leaves untouched. Within this framework it is highly unlikely that someone would argue that something which we took, at the level of common sense, to be the case was not in fact the case. In the presence of Sartre's strong and counter-intuitive conclusion that love is not possible, it would be argued via paradigm cases that love is indeed possible and that consequently Sartre's account of the relation between mind and body is shown, by *reductio ad absurdum,* to be false. While these few remarks have done justice neither to Sartre nor to the practitioners of this linguistic conception of philosophy, they do suggest an important contrast between these traditions with regard to their expectations of the possible fruits of a philosophical account of concepts such as love.

In this paper I will seek both to provide an account of our concept of love and to explore the possible practical bearing of such an account for our thinking and acting in the context of personal relations. The first part of the paper will involve an attempt to determine some of the concepts analytically presupposed in the employment of the concept of love and to ascertain some of the features which mark the concept off from certain related concepts. Within the confines of this paper, this treatment can only be provided in detail sufficient to suggest the general structure of the concept. A more detailed tracing of the multifarious web of connections will, I hope, come later. In the second part of the paper a number of hypothetical situations in which the protagonists appear to be disagreeing about matters of love will be considered. This will allow us to test the adequacy of the philosophical account of love in terms of its power to account for these disputes. These cases will also be used to determine what relevance the philosophical account might have for us in our personal relations with others. That there may be some practical relevance is suggested by the following considerations.

Any complete account of the state of a relation between persons, as opposed to objects, must take account of what the persons involved take the state of the relationship to be. The state of a personal relationship between business colleagues, Smith and Jones, may be a function more of how Smith sees Jones (i.e. as dishonest) than of how Jones actually is (i.e. honest). Similarly, the practical course of a relationship between Joe and Joel, which they both see as one of love, might be in part a function of what they take love to be or to involve. A philosophical account of love which ruled out one of their ways of thinking of love would then be relevant. Whether this philosophical intervention was for the better is entirely another matter. Rather than defend or amplify this thesis here, it will be left until we consider some hypothetical personal relationships.

Before proceeding further it will be helpful to introduce the following methodological distinctions. As well as speaking of the concept of x, I will talk of someone's conception of x. Someone's conception of x refers to how that person uses the term 'x'. The concept of x refers to those features which anyone's conception of x must possess in order to count as a conception of *x* at all. This distinction is intended as a device to avoid prejudging the issue concerning the existence of a precise, determinate, public concept of x. That is, different persons might draw the boundaries of their concepts somewhat differently but not so differently that they cannot be said to be speaking of the same thing. For instance, two persons might be said to have the same concept of x in virtue of an agreement about paradigm cases of x but to have slightly different conceptions of x in virtue of making different decisions about borderline cases. I will also speak of someone's picture of x. By this I mean the answer the person would give to the question 'What is x?'. Roughly, then, someone's picture of x is the account he would offer of x. This is intended as a distinction between someone's possessing a certain concept where this is displayed through the correct application of the concept and the person's being able to say in virtue of what features he applies the concept. Someone may possess a concept, x, but have no picture of x at all. If we ask him 'What is x?' he draws a blank or can only point to examples. Someone's picture of x might be a full-blown philosophical analysis of x. It might also be incompatible with the actual use he makes of the concept.

Use will also be made of the following distinction between two sorts of non-contingent truth. If, for example, it should be a necessary truth that *all* cases of love must involve sexual desire, I will speak of a necessary connection between love and sexual desire. And if it should be a necessary truth that *generally* cases of love involve sexual desire I will speak of a g-necessary connection. A particular case lacking a g-necessary feature of x-hood, will count as a case of x only in the presence of some special explanation.

Obviously this paper is not the place to enter into a discussion of the nature of necessary truth, and I can here offer no defence of this distinction beyond an attempt to display its fruitfulness in application.

I

This study cannot deal with all our uses of 'love'. We speak of loving persons, food, countries, art, hypothetical divine beings, and so on. In this paper I will be interested only in cases where the object of a love is some one or more persons. It would seem fairly clear that this is, as it were, the home territory of the concept of love and that the use of 'love' in conjunction with objects other than persons is best understood as an extension of this use. Having distinguished a kind of love in terms of a kind of object, namely persons, of a love relation, it is necessary to narrow the field of investigation further. And so attention will be confined to cases of love which involve sexuality. For the balance of this paper then, 'love' is to be understood as implying this restriction. 'Sexuality' is used here as a generic term whose species are sexual feelings, desires, acts and so on. Thus the stipulation excludes from present consideration cases of fraternal love, paternal love, and other cases not involving sexuality.

While this restriction is not intended as a substantial point about love, neither is it purely arbitrary. Rather it is intended to reflect a rough distinction that we do make between kinds of love between persons. Cases of love between persons cluster around certain paradigms. On the one hand we have a group of paradigms which includes Romeo and Juliet, Abelard and Helöise, and Caesar and Cleopatra. Jules and Jim provide another set of paradigms; the heroine of Gorky's *Mother* and the father of the prodigal son still another. It would seem that sexuality can serve as a criterial mark for picking out those cases that cluster around our first set of paradigms. Thus for instance, given a parent that loves a child, the occurrence of a prolonged, active and intense desire for sexual relations with the child on the part of the parent would lead us to regard the love, all things being equal, as not purely maternal. Analogously, the absence of sexuality between two persons of the opposite sex whom we think of as loving each other may incline us to describe the love as platonic or aesthetic. Anyone who thinks that this requirement of sexuality does not capture what is the essential delimiting feature of the romantic paradigms, can regard the requirement as simply a device for selecting a more manageable set of cases for this preliminary investigation.

A brief word about the status of these paradigms is in order. One way of displaying in part what someone's conception of, say, Ø is, is by displaying what he would regard as paradigm instances of Ø. While the cases given above would be offered as paradigms by a large number of persons, there is no proper set of paradigms. By this I mean that while the conceptual features of love to be given below rule out certain things as not possibly being paradigms of love, it is possible for different individuals to have different paradigms. In what follows I hope to display what we must think of a relationship in order to think of it as a relationship of love at all. I will suggest that this leaves considerable range for the construction of competing paradigms. This divergence in paradigms leaves room for interesting psychological and sociological investigations in the variations in paradigms from person to person, for instance, or from class to class, or historical era to historical era. And, given the normative aspect of a conception of love, these paradigms take on the character not just of clear examples but of ideals. Some of the consequences of this will be seen in the second half of this paper.

It is not suggested that the sexuality requirement provides any precise distinction. It seems likely that there is not a precise distinction to be marked. For we might wish to allow some feelings of a sexual sort to enter into a case of basically maternal love. And we might allow some aspects of homosexual love in the close relationship between the officer and men of a marine platoon without the relationship ceasing to be basically a fraternal one. However, things are different if the officer is continually wanting to get to bed with one particular soldier. Thus while there may be no precise distinction here, there is nonetheless a distinction. To be any more definite than this would require an exploration of sexuality that cannot be undertaken here.[1]

It might be objected on the basis of certain psychoanalytic theories that all personal relations involve sexuality, and hence sexuality could not be used as the distinguishing feature of a kind of personal relation. The grounds on which such a claim would rest are not uncontroversial. In any event, their acceptance involves the hypothesizing of repressed sexual feelings. This in turn does not invalidate our distinction but rather requires us to draw it in terms of a contrast between repressed and unrepressed sexuality rather than in terms of a contrast between the presence and absence of sexuality. In fact, Freud, in *Civilization and its Discontents*, contrasted aim-inhibited love in which the sexual component is suppressed and sexual love in which it is not suppressed. Freud took this distinction to divide the field roughly as we have done. Thus acceptance of certain psychoanalytic theories would require only the recasting, and not the abandoning, of our sexuality requirement.

The preceding modification would be required if a psychoanalytic theory which claimed that *all* relations involve a form of sexuality was adopted. More plausibly perhaps, it might be argued that in some relationships with no apparent sexuality involved, some form of suppressed sexuality was present. That is, given a psychoanalytic theory of genuine explanatory power, we might want to hypothesize on the basis of, say, some form of aberrant behaviour, the presence of repressed sexuality in a relationship apparently devoid of sexuality. In this case we would have a non-analytic counter-factual to the effect that the removal of repression would lead to explicit sexuality. If such a theory is produced our sexuality requirement will have to be extended to include both explicit and repressed sexuality.

It might also be objected to my sexuality requirement that while instances of courtly love belong with our romantic paradigms, not only was sexuality absent in courtly love relations, it was thought to be incompatible with true (courtly) love. Now evidence of the chastity of courtly lovers is decidedly absent. But in any case, courtly lovers must be thought of as possessing sexual feelings which they set aside. This is implicit in their thinking of themselves as noble for not expressing sexual feelings. There would be no trick to it, and hence no nobility involved, if they simply did not have sexual feelings or inclinations at all.

Having defined the field of investigation, we can now sketch the concepts analytically presupposed in our use of 'love'. An idea of these concepts can be gained by sketching a sequence of relations, the members of which we take as relevant in deciding whether or not some given relationship between persons A and B is one of love. These are not relevant in the sense of being evidence for some further relation 'love' but as being, in part at least, the material of which love consists. The sequence would include at least the following:

(1) A knows B (or at least knows something of B)
(2) A cares (is concerned) about B
 A likes B
(3) A respects B
 A is attracted to B
 A feels affection for B
(4) A is committed to B
 A wishes to see B's welfare promoted

The connection between these relations which we will call 'love-comprising relations' or 'LCRs', is not, except for 'knowing about' and possibly 'feels affection for', as tight as strict entailment. While perhaps in certain paradigm cases of love these relations would all be satisfied to a high degree, they are not jointly necessary. In a particular case which we are inclined to regard as one of love, some LCRs may be satisfied to only a low degree or not satisfied at all. For there is no contradiction involved in speaking of, say, love without commitment or love without respect. There would of course be a contradiction involved in asserting that some relationship was one of love while denying that any of the LCRs were satisfied. Thus we have a g-necessary truth that love involves the satisfaction of the LCRs to an as yet unspecified degree.

That the LCRs listed are non-contingently involved in love seems fairly obviously and for that reason not particularly interesting. We would not countenance the claims of A to love B if A had neither met B nor knew anything about B. I will argue below when discussing the limitations of the sorts of reasons A can have for loving B in particular that there are certain sorts of things that A must know about B. The items in group 2 embody the fact that love involves having certain pro-attitudes to the object of the love. Group 3 embodies the condition that the lover sees the object of his love as having in his eyes at least meritorious features. In love it is not just the case that the lover holds the re-

I

lations of groups 2 and 3 to the object of his love, these relations are held to such a degree that the lover is inclined to act on behalf of his beloved in ways that he is not inclined to act for arbitrary strangers or the general run of the mill acquaintances. Suppose that someone has the unhappy choice of saving either his putative beloved or an arbitrary stranger from drowning. If the putative lover elects to save the stranger, then, all things being equal, the relation is not one of love. Acting out of panic or just after a quarrel, among other possibilities, might show that all things were not equal. This feature of love is captured by the items of group 4.

It may seem frivolous to have introduced this thought experiment to prove such an obvious point. However, that the element of commitment is important in marking off love from other related relations can be seen if we vary the parameters in the thought experiment. Suppose the putative lover has to choose between saving his beloved and a group of strangers. In the event of a choice between a single stranger or a large group of strangers, we clearly think that we should opt for the larger number. Does the commitment element entail that the lover place the welfare of his beloved above the welfare of a group of strangers? Or can he call across to her as he saves the strangers, 'I love you, but unfortunately there are more of them'?

A similar dilemma arises if we imagine a putative lover having to choose between his putative beloved and adherence to his ethical or political principles. In fiction anyway, lovers frequently test the devotion of one another by asking if they would steal etc. for their sake. In *Middlemarch*, for example, Rosamund thinks that if Lydgate does in fact love her, he ought to be willing to set aside his moral scruples for her sake. She wants him to withhold large debts owed to the tradesmen in order to sustain her luxurious standard of living. And in Moravia's *Bitter Honeymoon*, Giacome and Simona are portrayed as being in love and as thinking themselves in love. Simona is a committed communist. Giacome describes himself as an 'individualist'. The following interchange takes place:

> *Giacome*   'For instance, if a communist government comes to power and I say something against it, you'll inform on me. . . .'

It was true then, he thought to himself, since she didn't deny it, then she would inform on him. He gripped her arm tighter almost wishing to hurt her. 'The truth is that you don't love me.'

Simona 'I wouldn't have married you except for love.'

These examples are not meant to imply any thesis to the effect that in 'true' love, commitment to the beloved must take preference over all other commitments. The significant conceptual point of the examples is that in the case of love there are these tensions, and this displays the extent to which love involves a commitment. This marks off love from, for example, relations of just 'liking' or 'being attracted to', where these tensions do not arise. We would not, I think, be tempted to redescribe an apparent relation of liking or being attracted to as not being a relation of liking or being attracted to, just because the protagonists did not tend to place the other party on a par with political or ethical commitments.

It has been suggested that love involves holding the LCRs to the beloved. If someone holds these relations to another, he will hold them to the person under certain descriptions of the person. For a relation to count as one of love these descriptions must be of certain sorts. A's saving his putative beloved, B, from drowning only because she is wearing his watch or has just won the pools, may be incompatible with A's thinking of the relationship as being one of love. Of course motives on a particular isolated occasion are not necessarily conclusive determinants of the kind of relationship one way or the other. But there are general limitations on the sorts of ways in which A thinks of the object of his affections where the ways in question are the grounds of his affection for the person. Very roughly, A must, say, care about B for herself, A must be attracted to B on her own account. That is, not all properties which A sees B as possessing can serve as the grounds for loving B.

Of the descriptions which A sees as applying to B, I will call those which can be the grounds of A's loving B, intrinsic descriptions of B. Descriptions which cannot play this role will be called extrinsic descriptions. Clearly there are some extrinsic and some intrinsic descriptions. Suppose we have an apparent love relation between A and B where B is very wealthy. Suppose B's wealth suddenly evaporates. If A's interest in B should also evaporate, we conclude that, all things being equal, the relation had not been one of love. We might say that A loved not B but B's money. A was interested in B not for her own sake but for the sake of her money. A liked B-the-wealthy-woman and not B *per se*. Of course it is simplistic to speak as I have been doing, as if one isolated incident would lead us to revise our description of a particular personal relation. The complexity of these situations is such that no one incident is likely to be decisive one way or the other. All that is required for the argument is that these incidents give cause to reconsider the descriptions given.

Suppose on the other hand we have an apparent love relation between A and B. A claims to love B largely on account of certain features of her personality and character. But one day, perhaps as the result of some traumatic accident, B undergoes a radical personality transformation. B no longer has those attributes that A loved her for. A, realizing this, can, we suppose, no longer love B. Here we are not so inclined to revise our descriptions of the relation as we were in the case above. We might say that A had indeed loved B but that this was no longer the case as B is no longer the person she once was.

In attempting to draw this distinction I am assuming that it is not a necessary condition of a relationship's being one of love that the lover's attitude to the beloved remain unchanged through all possible changes in the beloved. This question of constancy in love will be taken up later in one of our case studies. The classification of features as extrinsic or intrinsic depends on our attitude to inconstancy, given that the feature in question changed. That is, if A claims to love B in part at least because of her being $\emptyset$, and if A's attitude to B would be negatively affected should B cease to be $\emptyset$ (or, should A cease to see B as being $\emptyset$) then, if we count this inconstancy as evidence against the relationship's having been one of love, $\emptyset$ is an extrinsic property of B; otherwise $\emptyset$ is an intrinsic property. This places no limitations whatsoever on the features which initially attracted A to B. B's money may have been the initial lure. But, if the relationship is to count as one of love, the money cannot be the sustaining feature. In some cases there may be an intimate causal relation between extrinsic and intrinsic factors. In our previous example, B may have been a dynamic capitalist entrepreneur whose personality is intimately bound up with the acquisition of wealth. Financial failure might bring about a personality change. However, only intrinsic factors matter for themselves. The extrinsic factors are relevant only in as much as they are evidence for intrinsic factors.

It was suggested that features of personality and character clearly count as intrinsic and that the state of someone's bank balance was clearly extrinsic. Not all features are so easily classified. Consider the details of the beloved's physical make-up. Traditionally lovers are enraptured with dainty ears, firm thighs and so on. The general acceptance of these sorts of features as grounds for loving suggests that they are to be counted as intrinsic. But, on the other hand, if the moment the ears thicken or the thighs soften the lover falters, we may well have doubts about his alleged love. This suggests that we consider physical features to be extrinsic ones. Perhaps the most that we can say is that someone might love another solely or chiefly because of his or her physical features but that such cases will not be as near to our paradigms of a love relation as cases in which the beloved is loved solely or chiefly for attributes of his or her personality and character. That is, while physical features can be offered as reasons for loving (indeed our sexuality requirement would entail this), we tend to consider relations, which are not also grounded on regard for aspects of the personality and character of the object of the relation, as lacking certain dimensions. A person having as his chief or only reasons for loving another, regard for their physical attributes, would seem to be regarding the object of his love as being less than a person. Persons are not just bodies, they are at least bodies which think and act.

Any attempt to distinguish between physical characteristics as more extrinsic than features of personality and character is complicated by the problematic status of the role of physical features in determining personality and character. Clearly we identify some personality features via physical features – the look of the eyes, the character of the smile. The possession of some, though certainly not all, personality traits may be tied to the possession of certain physical characteristics. Perhaps some properties, for instance, elegance, while not being entirely physical attributes, can only be possessed by someone with certain physical attributes. I mention this as a question of some interest requiring a detailed consideration which cannot be given here.

That someone might love another for certain of her features suggests a problem. Suppose someone else should appear who also instantiates these properties. If the possession of these properties is someone's reason for loving one, reasons being universalizable, he will have equal reason to love the other as well. Perhaps the second person more perfectly embodies those properties which the lover previously lauded in the first. According to Gellner,[2] if someone in this kind of context should divide his affection between the two persons, neither relationship can be counted as a relationship of love. (We will have reasons to challenge this assumption later.) In most actual cases the universalizability of reasons will not require a person, A, to extend his affection to cover both B and C where C is a second embodiment of those features which A lauded in B. For, often A's reasons for loving B will involve reference to what B has done for him, to what they have done together. If A has been socially interacting with B, he is likely to have reasons of this character and these reasons would not be grounds for loving C as well. However, suppose A falls in love with B from a distance and has no social contact with B. Even here, one of A's reasons for loving B may be that it was B that first excited this passion in him. A might recognize that C would have done the same, if he had first known of C. But, A first met B and B generated the passion. A may now love B for having been the generator of the passion.

Of course it is possible that reasons of this sort are not among A's reasons for loving B and that either A does not love B for the reasons he thought he did, or that A will transfer his affection. I shall argue (part II) that if A extends his affection in this way, he may nonetheless love both B and C. If A does not think of himself as having any reasons for loving B that do not equally apply to C, and if A does not have any inclination to extend his affection to C, this provides us with the grounds for supposing that A is simply mistaken about his reasons for loving. That is, we would, I think, suppose that there is some present feature of B, or some feature of B's history or their history together, that was important to A and was part of A's reasons for loving B whereas the feature in question is not shared by C.

There are two sorts of intriguing and subtle kinds of cases

which might seem to suggest that we have been assuming too readily that there is no problem in identifying who the object of a love is. The first relates to the suggestion, to be found in Stendhal, that one never really loves another person but one loves rather some creation of one's imagination based on, but usually bearing little resemblance to, the actual person one appears to love. Following Stendhal, I will refer to this theory as the 'crystallization' theory of love. Stendhal thought of the actual object of a love as an imaginary creation built on and transforming a few true perceptions of the apparent object of the love, in a manner analogous to the growth of crystals on a branch placed in the Salzburg salt mines. Lawrence Durrell, in *Clea*, provides a model of what I take Stendhal to have in mind. Here Darley is presented as suddenly realizing that he never loved Justine. He concludes that he loved some 'illusory creation' of his own based on Justine. The revelation comes to him on Justine's informing him that it was pointless for her to return to him after their separation, for it was not *her* Darley loved. As the case is presented, Darley thinks of himself as loving Justine because of certain intrinsic features. But the features do not apply to Justine.

Darley thinks of himself as loving Justine for a sequence $\emptyset_1, \ldots, \emptyset_n$ of features which he takes to apply to Justine. If the following counter-factual is true, the case is easily dealt with. If Darley would feel as strongly about Justine should he come to see that she does not possess the properties in question, he does in fact, all things being equal, love her. He has simply been radically mistaken about her. Perhaps when he discovers what she is really like his attraction for her will actually increase. Suppose on the other hand, Darley would not think of himself as loving Justine if he came to realize his mistake. In this case he never loved anyone at all and to speak of having loved an 'illusory creation' is, at best, a metaphorical way of saying that he mistakenly thought of himself as loving someone as a result of radically misunderstanding the sort of person she was.

The 'crystallization' theory draws our attention to the notorious fact that we often misapprehend the properties of persons and often act in personal relationships on the basis of our beliefs about persons which are wrong and sometimes radically so. But as a theory to the effect that we never love other persons, it is just wrong. We are not always mistaken about other persons. In many cases the beloved will in fact have some of the properties on the basis of which the lover loves. Even in cases of grave error, the lover may, as I argued above, be said to love in spite of being mistaken.

The other intriguing case concerning the real object of a love arises in psychoanalytic theory. Aberrant behaviour on the part of a person A, who appears to love person B, might be thought explicable in some contexts on the hypothesis that A does not in fact love B but really loves, say, a parental figure. B is a sort of stand-in in an elaborate fantasy. This seems like a misleading description of the case. For, it is towards B and not towards, say, his mother, that A performs the action appropriate in a context of love. Perhaps it is therefore best to say that A does love B while admitting the existence of a causal connection between his attitude towards his mother and his attitude towards B. Perhaps A would not care for B at all if he had not had a certain attitude towards his mother. Or, perhaps A's loving B depends on his thinking of B in ways appropriate to thinking of a mother.

It has been argued that love involves having certain kinds of relations (the LCRs) to some person, and that it also involves thinking of the object of these relations in certain ways. In addition love is essentially reciprocal. Stendhal reports André le Chapelain as writing in his twelfth-century Code of Love 'No one can love unless bidden by the hope of being loved'. It does seem to be a g-necessary truth that if A loves B, A wishes to be loved by B. We can see that this is a conceptual fact and not just a matter of fact about lovers, by seeing what would be involved in imagining a case where A loves B but does not wish to be loved in return. The following situation, drawn with adaptation, from Dickens' *Little Dorrit* seems to provide the sort of case we want. A loves B who is already married to another. A is particularly concerned for the welfare and happiness of B. A knows that B would not be happy loving him. For, if B loved A in return B would suffer extreme guilt feelings at taking on another affection while committed in marriage to another. B has, let us suppose, a loving husband and children. A, being magnanimous, does not reveal his love for B, for fear that the mere revelation would precipitate reciprocated love and subsequent unhappiness for B. In one sense the lover does wish for reciprocated love. He would wish it if all things were equal. But given the circumstances as they are, he does not wish it. No doubt we would countenance the lover's denial of any wish for reciprocated love in the circumstances. But to render this plausible we had to imagine a case where the reciprocated love would be an unhappy love. Other cases can be provided if the lover is imagined to be masochistic or to be involved in some form of self-abasement. In the absence of such a background we would simply fail to understand a denial of a wish for reciprocated love. If someone claims to love another, we understand him as wishing to be loved in return. We do not have to ask, 'And do you wish her to love you?' The inference to a wish for reciprocated love is blocked only if the background is filled out in certain ways. Loving entails, *ceterus paribus*, the desire for reciprocated love.

This essential reciprocity interestingly delimits love from many other concepts used in describing personal relations. A clear case in point is that of worship. A's worshipping B does not, *ceterus paribus*, entail that A wishes to be worshipped by B. Quite the contrary in fact. For, in wishing to be worshipped by B, A would be demeaning B from the elevated position relative to himself, that A accords to B, in thinking of B as an object of worship. Perhaps 'liking' is a more pertinent example for our present purposes. We do not take someone's claim to like another as implying a wish on his part to be liked by the other person. He may or may not. Perhaps we do take him as wishing not to be disliked but this is not the same as wishing to be liked. The reciprocal factor is similarly absent in the case of a commitment outside the context of a love relation (except possibly in the context of a contractual relation). A claim to be committed to my party leader does not imply a wish that he commit himself to me (I may think of myself as a lowly pawn not deserving such a commitment) in the way that a claim to be committed to my beloved does.

It is not suggested that the features of the concept of love which have been given provide anything like a calculus for deciding, objectively, whether or not any given relationship is one of love. The term 'love' has undeniable emotive force. Different individuals may require that the LCRs be satisfied to different degrees before awarding the epithet love to a relationship. It is not uncommon[3] to find the requirements placed so high as to make relationships that count as relationships of love a very rare commodity. The account of love given is intended to display only what one must think of as involved in thinking of a relationship as love. For instance, it is g-necessary that a case of love involves concern. The person who thinks of himself as loving another, and who at some time sees himself as having failed to act as concern requires, must (g-necessarily) think of himself as having failed. He must see himself as being under a *prima facie* obligation to make excuse. If the person does not see the relation as one of love, he may not see his failure to display concern as anything for which excuse need be made. One does not have an obligation to display to just any acquaintance the sort of concern that loving involves. While we can thus display what is involved in thinking of a relationship under the concept of love, we have no criterial test for 'love' simply because there are not public, objective standards as to the degree of concern, respect, etc., that is required to constitute love. In the case studies that follow we will see something of the consequences of this fact.

II

Case one: love and responsibility

This first case will be constructed around conflicting theories or 'pictures' of love. On one picture of love, a picture most prominent in the romantic tradition, love is seen as a feeling or emotion which simply overcomes one with an all-conquering force. The lover is held to be a victim of his passion. And, if the lover can avoid giving in to his passion, it is not genuine. This picture will be called the involuntaristic one.

I have referred to the above as a 'picture' of love. The reason for so doing is to avoid begging the question that the term is used or could consistently be used by those who would offer this picture in a manner consistent with the picture. For instance, someone might claim that 'red' is the name of a kind of purely private mental impression. It might be argued that no one uses the term in this way and that no one could use a term in this way. In my terminology this could be summed up by saying that this person has an erroneous picture of the concept he in fact possesses.

According to another picture, call this one the 'voluntaristic' picture, love is seen as a deliberate, volitional commitment to another. It is this sort of picture that has at times been appealed to in justifying arranged marriage. The partners once selected and brought together will, it is felt, come to love one another if they make a sincere exercise of will.

We can see how subscribing to one of these pictures can have a practical impact on one's personal relationship. For, on the involuntaristic picture, to be in love is to be in a state of diminished responsibility. Once one is in the grip of love, one may act out of passion in ways that one cannot help. The picture is rarely held in this categorical form. Most commonly on this picture, love is taken as a force, difficult to resist, which comes not of the agent's choice and brings not total absence of responsibility but the diminishing of culpability for acts done out of love. This picture is to be found in the writings of George Sand. Interesting illustrations of the effects of adopting it can be found in the far from simple relations of the Herzens to the Herweghs (and others). Under the sway of George Sand, the protagonists, in what can only be described as an eternal polygon, followed courses of action which they themselves regarded as *prima facie* undesirable, involving as they did considerable unpleasantness for other parties. But acting out of love and seeing love in terms of the involuntaristic picture, they saw themselves as not culpable for these consequences. Or, more accurately, they saw themselves as less culpable than they would have seen themselves if the acts had not been done in the throes of love.

One possible impact of the voluntaristic picture is seen in the context of unobtainable love. In the merry-go-round of relationships in Iris Murdoch's *Bruno's Dream*, one of the protagonists, Lisa, is smitten with love for Miles who is unobtainable. Danby, who is presented as seeing love in an involuntaristic manner, loves Lisa. Lisa emphatically does not love him. However, Lisa, presented as subscribing to a voluntaristic picture, simply decides, when it becomes clear that Miles is indeed unobtainable, to cure herself by taking up with Danby and by coming to love Danby. Of course, when she reveals this to Danby, with his rather more romantic picture of things, he is, to say the least, puzzled and sceptical. Danby thinks that either she loves Miles, and if so cannot volitionally pull off what she is attempting, or that she can pull this off and hence does not love Miles. Lisa thinks of herself as both genuinely and passionately loving Miles and as capable of transferring this sort of affection volitionally to another.

Both of these pictures have some basis in the conceptual facts about love as a look at the LCRs will reveal. For instance, among the LCRs are the relations of respect, affection and attraction. The involuntaristic picture calls attention to these. One may identify the presence of affection, attraction and respect in terms partly of patterns of volitions. A crude example of this would be concluding that someone is attracted to another because he regularly does things with the intent of being in the presence of this person. But there is a sense in which these feelings are not subject to volitions. For, I cannot here and now decide to feel or not to feel attraction for some given person. I can decide to try and see the girl next door, I cannot decide to be attracted to her. Of course, my deciding to go and see her may be evidence of a degree of attraction. Being attracted involves wanting. I do not decide my wants, I have them and decide on the basis of them to do or not to do various actions. I might decide to give these sorts of feelings the best chance of developing. I focus my attention on the given person, I get to know them intimately, I try to dwell on their good points, and so on. Whether this will lead to attraction, only time will tell. Similarly, I can attempt to put myself in the worst position for the continuation of current feelings of attraction. I join the foreign legion, I associate intimately with other persons, I focus on the given person's worst characteristics and so on. Time and effort may bring success.

Attention to other of the LCRs will bring out the conceptual basis of the voluntaristic picture. For instance, consider commitment. A commitment is something that I can here and now decide to take up. I can promise to commit myself for ever to another, I can promise always to be concerned. I cannot, in the same way, promise to be always attracted to another.

On the basis of the account given of love, we can reject any 'picture' which allows only voluntaristic elements or only involuntaristic elements. But granted this, different individuals are free to give different stress to the importance of different LCRs in their conception of love. Someone can give more prominence to the aspects of love involving attraction, than to commitment. This is likely to reveal itself in the selection of paradigms this person would offer. Someone else can give more importance to commitment. There is no conceptual resolution of the question as to which features are more important. The concept is not determinate in this way. We can uncover the features which anyone's conception of love must have in order to be a conception of love at all. However, within these confines one is free to stress passion or commitment.

Case two: constancy of love

Suppose that Jude and Jan are two persons of the same or opposite sex who have been having an intense affair over a period of time. Mutual declarations of love have been made and all concerned regard the relationship as entirely satisfactory. Until, that is, Jude announces the demise of his love for Jan. The following dialogue ensues:

> *Jan* 'What do you mean, you don't love me anymore!
> Have I done anything, said anything?'
> *Jude* 'No, it's just that my feelings for you have changed.'
> *Jan* 'Why? I don't understand. Have I changed in your
> eyes? Have you changed? What is it?'
> *Jude* 'No. It's not anything like that. We're still the same
> people. It's just that . . . well, the old intensity of
> feeling just isn't there anymore, that's all.'
> *Jan* 'You flirt! You never really loved me at all. It's just
> been an adventure. Look, read this, this is what love
> is: "Love is not a feeling. Love is put to the test, pain
> not. One does not say: 'That was not true pain or it
> would not have gone off so quickly.' " '[4]

To this Jude replies with a recitation of 'A Woman's Constancy' and 'The Broken Heart' in which Donne describes 'true' love which flourishes and passes in a single day. Jude adds: 'You admit that there was nothing in my former behaviour and attitude to suggest a lack of love. What has time got to do with it? Love isn't any less true for having been short-lived.'

It may make a difference to Jan whether she(he) decides that Jude did or did not love her. Deciding that it was love may incline her to view the current situation just with regret for the passing of Jude's love. Deciding that Jude never loved may incline her to think of Jude as having operated under false pretences and to see herself as having been trifled with. As we shall see, the various LCRs differ in their temporal aspects. Thus it may be that Jude and Jan are in a sense disagreeing at cross purposes in that they may be operating with conceptions of love that give different stress to the importance of particular LCRs. Some LCRs, like respect and affection, may be imagined to flourish and pass in a relatively short period of time. Some act or feature of a person might call forth feelings of respect or affection. Some later revelations may reveal that things are not as they appeared, thus ending the respect or affection. If the time span is sufficiently long, I think we would allow that affection can simply fade away without there being any particular occurrence which is seen as ending the affection. Perhaps Jude found some things about Jan intriguing which lose their mystery on constant exposure. However, if the time span during which affection is thought to be involved is short enough, we have to think of some things having happened, some realization having occurred, which can be described as the reason for the withdrawal of affection. If an apparent affection begins in the evening and evaporates in the morning and if the person involved cannot point to something real or imagined which serves as a reason for the withdrawal of affection, we would be inclined to view the affection as merely apparent.

Concern and commitment, on the other hand, seem significantly different in this respect from respect and affection. For it would seem that genuine concern or commitment cannot be terminated simply by some revelation about or change in the object of that concern or commitment. We are inclined to accept : 'I felt affection for her so long as I thought she was pure and innocent' but not, 'I was really concerned for her welfare so long as I thought she was pure and innocent'. Being genuinely concerned or committed seems to involve a willingness on my part to extend that concern or commitment to the person even if I have been mistaken about that person with regard to some feature of her that led to the concern, and even if that person ceases to have those features that led me to be concerned or committed to her. I do not want to suggest that there is a total asymmetry between these pairs of relations. But to some extent, one measure of the degree of concern or commitment at a time, is the time it extends and its constancy in the face of alteration. And the measure of affection at a time is more the way it disposes me to act at that time and not through some period of time.

To return to Jude and Jan. It may be that Jude has a picture of love which construes love as just a feeling which can come and go. In declaring his love he did not think of himself as taking on any commitments. If the account of love provided in this paper is at all near the mark, we see that he has failed to see what the concept involves and has possibly misled Jan in his declarations. Or, it may be the case that while Jude and Jan both see that love involves the satisfaction of the LCRs they have different conceptions, Jude giving less stress to affection than commitment than Jan does. As we saw in case 1, there is no conceptual resolution of this sort of difference. Allowing this freedom to legislate within certain bounds does not mean that each conception is equally appropriate. Concepts are tied to forms of life. Just as our concept of love is tied to the fact that we are sexual beings, it is also tied to general facts about social organization. Thus, someone like Donne in opting for a short-range conception of love would appear to be opting for a form of life in which personal relations are diverse, changing and not closely tied to long-term responsiblities. In a society which institutionalizes personal relations and attempts to tie them to long-term responsibilities in the form of children, it is not surprising that many opt for long-range conceptions of love which lay stress on commitment.

Case three: multiple person love

Much is made of the particularity of love. It seems commonly felt that if A is in intimate relations with both B and C, whatever the state of that relationship is, it is not one of love. We have this on authority as diverse as André le Chapelain and E. A. Gellner.[5] Apparently proposition 3 of le Chapelain's code of love was : no one can give himself to two loves. I want to consider whether anything in the concept of love rules out multiple person love relations. By a multiple person love relation, or MPLR, I mean some social set-up in which a person is in intimate relations with more than one person, each of whom he *claims* to love. According to Fromm, Jaspers and other moralists, MPLRs are ruled out as relations of love by the 'very nature (or essence) of love'. This seems rather strong, What we have here in fact is an attempt for normative purposes to enforce a range of paradigms, i.e. those which do not involve MPLRs. I will suggest that there is nothing in the concept of love which rules out MPLRs as relations of love. Any move to rule out the MPLRs will be a legislative one.

No doubt there are severe practical difficulties involved in staging a MPLR. The protagonist in such a situation is apt to find himself spread a little thin if he attempts to provide the sort of concern, interest, commitment and so on which we take love to involve. In his paper on sexual perversion Nagel has elaborated on some of the complexities involved in staging a multiple person sexual relationship that would approach the paradigms of non-multiple person sexual relations. Such complexities are bound to increase dramatically in any MPLR. But, that it will be difficult to bring off does not show that it is in principle impossible. And there may be those like the carpenter in Agnes Varda's film *Le Bonheur* who find it as easy to do for two persons as for one, what love requires.

Difficulties are most apt to arise if the set-up is not mutual all round. By being mutual all round I mean that each person in the set-up claims to love each other person involved. Suppose Jude thinks of himself as loving both Jan and Joe. Jude, Jan and Joe may be of the same or different sex. Jan and Joe not only loathe each other, they are most unhappy about Jude's divided affection. We may feel that Jude cannot be really concerned for both Jan and Joe if he continues this relationship in a manner which clearly distresses them. But probably all that is required for Jude to be thought of as loving both Jan and Joe is that he be thought of as distressed at their distress. Jude may think, say, that more happiness is to be had all around by this shared affection than by one of them having his whole concern and affection. In any event, to show that love is not so exclusive as to rule out multiple love relationships we need only imagine a set-up that is mutual all round.

For those like Jaspers, who claims in his *Philosophie* that 'He only does love at all who loves one specific person', we might suggest the following thought experiment. Consider that all factors involved in loving, excepting any reference to numbers, are satisfied to a high degree by the pair of persons, A and B, and by the pair, C and D. What grounds could one have for retracting a description of these cases as cases of love when it is discovered that

B and D are the same person? The only grounds for ruling out such a case would seem to be an *ad hoc* rule that love is necessarily a one to one relationship. While Jaspers and Fromm are entitled to make up their own rule here, should they wish, it cannot be presented as a fact about the nature or essence of love. Of course, the desirability of multiple love does not follow from its possibility.

I have tried in this paper to sketch some conceptual features of love and to illustrate the role these features, and pictures of these features, play in judgments about personal relations. And if my account of the case studies is at all plausible, coming to accept a philosophical analysis of the concept of love may bear on how we think about our personal relations and may, in affecting how we think about them, affect the state of the relationship itself, though the affects are unlikely to be of a Sartrian magnitude. The variability in possible conceptions of love has ruled out the sort of precise and determinate conceptual relations that philosophers are prone to seek. Because of this indeterminacy, how one must (conceptually) think about love drifts imperceptibly into how one does generally think about love. Crossing this boundary can give rise to the worst sort of arm-chair psychology. But then to shy away from the boundary for fear of crossing is not entirely satisfactory either.

One final, and perhaps pessimistic, note. To show that an analysis of love is relevant to practical dealings in personal relations, would not in any way demonstrate that beneficial results would accrue for the lover or the beloved from the utilization of such knowledge. Ibsenian life lies may be productive of the greater happiness.[6]

Notes

* An obvious debt of gratitude is owed to all those who participated in the discussions that led to this volume. I would like especially to thank Derek Parfit, Alan Montefiore and my wife for many stimulating discussions.

1 Some beginnings towards such an explication can be found in Thomas Nagel's paper, 'Sexual Perversion', *Journal of Philosophy*, 66, 1969, pp. 5–17.

2 E. A. Gellner, 'Ethics and Logic', *Proceedings of the Aristotelian Society*, 55, 1955, pp. 157–78.

3 In this regard see Erich Fromm's *The Art of Loving*, London, Allen & Unwin, 1957 and José Ortega y Gasset's *On Love. . . . Aspects of a Single Theme*, trans. Toby Talbot, London, Jonathan Cape, 1967.
4 L. Wittgenstein, *Zettel*, Berkeley, University of California Press, 1967, p. 89e.
5 Gellner, op. cit., p. 159.
6 Since this paper was written I have come to regard this account of love as in many ways too simplistic.

7 Later selves and moral principles*

Derek Parfit

I shall first sketch different views about the nature of personal identity, then suggest that the views support different moral claims.

I

Most of us seem to have certain beliefs about our own identity. We seem for instance to believe that, whatever happens, any future person must be either us, or someone else.

These beliefs are like those that some of us have about a simpler fact. Most of us now think that to be a person, as opposed to a mere animal, is just to have certain more specific properties, such as rationality. These are matters of degree. So we might say that the fact of personhood is just the fact of having certain other properties, which are had to different degrees.

There is a different view. Some of us believe that personhood is a further, deep, fact, and cannot hold to different degrees.

This second view may be confused with some trivial claims. Personhood is, in a sense, a further fact. And there is a sense in which all persons are equally persons.

Let us first show how these claims may be trivial. We can use a different example. There is a sense in which all our relatives are equally our relatives. We can use the phrase 'related to' so that what it means has no degrees; on this use, parents and remote cousins are as much relatives. It is obvious, though, that kinship has degrees. This is shown in the phrase 'closely related to' : remote cousins are, as relatives, less close. I shall summarize such remarks in the following way. On the above use, the fact of being someone's relative has in its *logic* no degrees. But in its

137

nature – in what it involves – it does have degrees. So the fact's logic hides its nature. Hence the triviality of the claim that all our relatives are equally our relatives. (The last few sentences may be wrongly worded,[1] but I hope that the example suggests what I mean.)

To return to the claims about personhood. These were : that it is a further fact, and that all persons are equally persons. As claims about the fact's logic, these are trivial. Certain people think the claims profound. They believe them to be true of the fact's nature.

The difference here can be shown in many ways. Take the question, 'When precisely does an embryo become a person?' If we merely make the claims about the fact's logic, we shall not believe that this question must have a precise answer.[2] Certain people do believe this. They believe that any embryo must either be, or not be, a complete person. Their view goes beyond the 'logical claims'. It concerns the nature of personhood.

We can now return to the main argument. About the facts of both personhood and personal identity, there are two views. According to the first, these facts have a special nature. They are further facts, independent of certain more specific facts; and in every case they must either hold completely, or completely fail to hold. According to the second view, these facts are not of this nature. They consist in the holding of the more specific facts; and they are matters of degree.

Let us name such opposing views. I shall call the first kind 'Simple' and the second 'Complex'.

Such views may affect our moral principles, in the following way. If we change from a Simple to a Complex View, we acquire two beliefs: we decide that a certain fact is in its nature less deep, and that it sometimes holds to reduced degrees. These beliefs may have two effects: the first belief may weaken certain principles, and the second give the principles a new scope.

Take the views about personhood. An ancient principle gives to the welfare of people absolute precedence over that of mere animals. If the difference between people and mere animals is in its nature less deep, this principle can be more plausibly denied. And if embryos are not people, and become them only by degrees, the principle forbidding murder can be more plausibly given less scope.[3]

I have not defended these claims. They are meant to parallel what I shall defend in the case of the two views about personal identity.

II

We must first sketch these views. It will help to revive a comparison. What is involved in the survival of a nation are just certain continuities, such as those of a people and a political system. When there is a weakening of these continuities, as there was, say, in the Norman Conquest, it may be unclear whether a nation survives. But there is here no problem. And the reason is that the survival of a nation just involves these continuities. Once we know how the continuities were weakened, we need not ask, as a question about an independent fact, 'Did a nation cease to exist?' There is nothing left to know.

We can add the following remarks. Though identity has no degrees,[4] these continuities are matters of degree. So the identity of nations over time is only in its logic 'all-or-nothing'; in its nature it has degrees.

The identity of people over time is, according to the 'Complex View', comparable.[5] It consists in bodily and psychological continuity. These, too, are matters of degree. So we can add the comparable remark. The identity of people over time is only in its logic 'all-or-nothing'; in its nature it has degrees.

How do the continuities of bodies and minds have degrees? We can first dismiss bodies, since they are morally trivial.[6] Let us next call 'direct' the psychological relations which hold between: the memory of an experience and this experience, the intention to perform some later action and this action, and different expressions of some lasting character-trait. We can now name two general features of a person's life. One, 'connectedness', is the holding, over time, of particular 'direct' relations. The other, 'continuity', is the holding of a chain of such relations. If, say, I cannot now remember some earlier day, there are no 'connections of memory' between me now and myself on that day. But there may be 'continuity of memory'. This there is if, on every day between, I remembered the previous day.

Of these two general relations, I define 'continuous with' so that, in its logic, it has no degrees. It is like 'related to' in the use on which all our relatives are equally our relatives. But 'connectedness' has degrees. Between different parts of a person's life, the connections of memory, character, and intention are – in strength and number – more or less. ('Connected to' is like 'closely related to'; different relatives can be more or less close.)

We can now restate the Complex View. What is important in personal identity are the two relations we have just sketched. One of these, continuity, is in its logic all-or-nothing. But it just involves connectedness, which clearly has degrees. In its nature, therefore, continuity holds to different degrees. So the fact of personal identity also, in its nature, has degrees.

To turn to the Simple View. Here the fact is believed to be, in its nature, all-or-nothing. This it can only be if it does not just consist in (bodily and) psychological continuity – if it is, in its nature, a further fact. To suggest why : These continuities hold, over time, to different degrees. This is true in actual cases, but is most clearly true in some imaginary cases. We can imagine cases where the continuities between each of us and a future person hold to every possible degree.[7] Suppose we think, in imagining these cases, 'Such a future person must be either, and quite simply, *me*, or *someone else*'. (Suppose we think, 'Whatever happens, any future experience must be either *wholly* mine, or *not* mine *at all*'.) If the continuities can hold to every degree, but the fact of our identity must hold completely or not at all, then this fact cannot consist in these continuities. It must be a further, independent, fact.

It is worth repeating that the Simple View is about the nature of personal identity, not its logic. This is shown by the reactions most of us have to various so-called 'problem cases'.[8] These reactions also show that even if, on the surface, we reject the Simple View, at a deeper level we assume it to be true.[9]

We can add this – rough – test of our assumptions. Nations are in many ways unlike people; for example, they are not organisms. But if we take the Complex View, we shall accept this particular comparison : the survival of a person, like that of a nation, is a matter of degree. If instead we reject this comparison, we take the Simple View.

One last preliminary. We can use 'I', and the other pronouns, so that they cover only the part of our lives to which, when speaking, we have the strongest psychological connections. We assign the rest of our lives to what we call our 'other selves'. When, for instance, we have undergone any marked change in character, or conviction, or style of life, we might say, 'It was not *I* who did that, but an earlier self'.

Such talk can become natural. To quote three passages:

> Our dread of a future in which we must forego the sight of faces, the sound of voices, that we love, friends from whom we derive today our keenest joys, this dread, far from being dissipated, is intensified, if to the grief of such a privation we reflect that there will be added what seems to us now in anticipation an even more cruel grief : not to feel it as a grief at all – to remain indifferent : for if that should occur, our self would then have changed. It would be in a real sense the death of ourself, a death followed, it is true, by a resurrection, but in a different self, the life, the love of which are beyond the reach of those elements of the existing self that are doomed to die. . . .[10]

> It is not because other people are dead that our affection for them grows faint, it is because we ourself are dying. Albertine had no cause to rebuke her friend. The man who was usurping his name had merely inherited it. . . . My new self, while it grew up in the shadow of the old, had often heard the other speak of Albertine; through that other self . . . it thought that it knew her, it found her attractive . . . but this was merely an affection at second hand.[11]

> Nadya had written in her letter : 'When you return. . . .' But that was the whole horror : that there would be no *return*. . . . A new, unfamiliar person would walk in bearing the name of her husband, and she would see that the man, her beloved, for whom she had shut herself up to wait for fourteen years, no longer existed. . . .[12]

Whether we are inclined to use such talk will depend upon our view about the nature of personal identity. If we take the Simple View, we shall not be so inclined, for we shall think it deeply true that all the parts of a person's life are as much parts of his life. If we take the Complex View, we shall be less impressed by this truth.

It will seem like the truth that all the parts of a nation's history are as much parts of its history. Because this latter truth is superficial, we at times subdivide such a history into that of a series of successive nations, such as Anglo-Saxon, Medieval, or Post-Imperial England.[13] The connections between these, though similar in kind, differ in degree. If we take the Complex View, we may also redescribe a person's life as the history of a series of successive selves. And the connections between these we shall also claim to be similar in kind, different in degree.[14]

III

We can now turn to our question. Do the different views tend to support different moral claims?

I have space to consider only three subjects: desert, commitment, and distributive justice. And I am forced to oversimplify, and to distort. So it may help to start with some general remarks.

My suggestions are of this form: 'The Complex View supports certain claims.' By 'supports' I mean both 'makes more plausible' and 'helps to explain'. My suggestions thus mean: 'If the true view is the Complex, not the Simple, View, certain claims are more plausible.[15] We may therefore[16] be, on the Complex View, more inclined to make these claims.'

I shall be discussing two kinds of case: those in which the psychological connections are as strong as they ever are, and those in which they are markedly weak. I choose these kinds of case for the following reason. If we change from the Simple to the Complex View, we believe (I shall claim) that our identity is in its nature less deep, and that it sometimes holds to reduced degrees. The first of these beliefs covers every case, even those where there are the strongest connections. But the second of the two beliefs only covers cases where there are weak connections. So the two kinds of case provide separate testing-grounds for the two beliefs.

Let us start with the cases of weak connection. And our first principle can be that we deserve to be punished for certain crimes.

We can suppose that, between some convict now and himself when he committed some crime, there are only weak psychological connections. (This will usually be when conviction takes place after many years.) We can imply the weakness of these connections by calling the convict, not the criminal, but his later self.[17]

Two grounds for detaining him would be unaffected. Whether a convict should be either reformed, or preventively detained, turns upon his present state, not his relation to the criminal. A third ground, deterrence, turns upon a different question. Do potential criminals care about their later selves? Do they care, for instance, if they do not expect to be caught for many years? If they do, then detaining their later selves could perhaps deter.

Would it be deserved? Locke thought that if we forget our crimes we deserve no punishment.[18] Geach considers this view 'morally repugnant'.[19] Mere loss of memory does seem to be insufficient. Changes of character would appear to be more relevant. The subject is, though, extremely difficult. Claims about desert can be plausibly supported with a great variety of arguments. According to some of these loss of memory would be important. And according to most the nature and cause of any change in character would need to be known.

I have no space to consider these details, but I shall make one suggestion. This appeals to the following assumption. When some morally important fact holds to a lesser degree, it can be more plausibly claimed to have less importance – even, in extreme cases, none.

I shall not here defend this assumption. I shall only say that most of us apply the assumption to many kinds of principle. Take, for example, the two principles that we have special duties to help our relatives, or friends. On the assumption, we might claim that we have less of a special duty to help our less close relatives, or friends, and, to those who are very distant, none at all.

My suggestion is this. If the assumption is acceptable, and the Complex View correct, it becomes more plausible to make the following claim: when the connections between convicts and their past criminal selves are less, they deserve less punishment; if they are very weak, they perhaps deserve none. This claim extends the idea of 'diminished responsibility'. It does not appeal to mental illness, but instead treats a later self like a sane accomplice. Just as a man's deserts correspond to the degree of his complicity with some criminal, so his deserts, now, for some past crime correspond to the degree of connectedness between himself now and himself when committing that crime.[20]

If we add the further assumption that psychological connections are, in general, weaker over longer periods,[21] the claim provides a ground for Statutes of Limitations. (They of course have other grounds.)

IV

We can next consider promises. There are here two identities involved. The first is that of the person who, once, made a promise. Let us suppose that between this person now and himself then there are only weak connections. Would this wipe away his commitment? Does a later self start with a clean slate?

On the assumption that I gave, the Complex View supports the answer, 'yes'. Certain people think that only short-term promises carry moral weight. This belief becomes more plausible on the Complex View.

The second relevant identity is that of the person who received the promise. There is here an asymmetry. The possible effect of the Complex View could be deliberately blocked. We could ask for promises of this form : 'I shall help you, and all your later selves.' If the promises that I *receive* take this form, they cannot be plausibly held to be later undermined by any change in *my* character, or by any other weakening, over the rest of *my* life, in connectedness.

The asymmetry is this : similar forms cannot so obviously stay binding on the *maker* of a promise. I might say, 'I, and all my later selves, shall help you'. But it is plausible to reply that I can only bind my present self. This is plausible because it is like the claim that I can only bind myself. No one, though, denies that I can promise you that I shall help someone else. So I can clearly promise you that I shall help your later selves.

Such a promise may indeed seem especially binding. Suppose that you change faster than I do. I may then regard myself as committed, not to you, but to your earlier self. I may therefore think that you cannot waive my commitment. (It would be like a commitment, to someone now dead, to help his children. We cannot be released from such commitments.)

Such a case would be rare. But an example may help the argument. Let us take a nineteenth-century Russian who, in several years, should inherit vast estates. Because he has socialist ideals, he intends, now, to give the land to the peasants. But he knows that in time his ideals may fade. To guard against this possibility, he does two things. He first signs a legal document, which will automatically give away the land, and which can only be revoked with his wife's consent. He then says to his wife, 'If I ever change my mind, and ask you to revoke the document, promise me that you will not consent'. He might add, 'I regard my ideals as essential to me. If I lose these ideals, I want you to think that *I* cease to exist. I want you to regard your husband, then, not as me, the man who asks you for this promise, but only as his later self. Promise me that you would not do what he asks.'

This plea seems understandable.[22] And if his wife made this promise, and he later asked her to revoke the document, she might well regard herself as in no way released from her commitment. It might seem to her as if she has obligations to two different people. She might think that to do what her husband now asks would be to betray the young man whom she loved and married. And she might regard what her husband now says as unable to acquit her of disloyalty to this young man – of disloyalty to her husband's earlier self.

Such an example may seem not to require the distinction between successive selves. Suppose that I ask you to promise me never to give me cigarettes, even if I beg you for them. You might think that I cannot, in begging you, simply release you from this commitment. And to think this you need not deny that it is I to whom you are committed.

This seems correct. But the reason is that addiction clouds judgment. Similar examples might involve extreme stress or pain, or (as with Odysseus, tied to the mast) extraordinary temptation. When, though, nothing clouds a person's judgment, most of us believe that the person to whom we are committed can always release us. He can always, if in sound mind, waive our commitment. We believe this whatever the commitment may be. So (on this view) the content of a commitment cannot stop its being waived.

To return to the Russian couple. The man's ideals fade, and he asks his wife to revoke the document. Though she promised him to refuse, he declares that he now releases her from this commitment. We have sketched two ways in which she might think that she is not released. She might, first, take her husband's change of mind as proof that he cannot now make considered judgments. But we can suppose that she has no such thought. We can also suppose that she shares our view about commitment. If so, she will only believe that her husband is unable to release her if she thinks that it is, in some sense, not *he* to whom she is committed. We have sketched such a sense. She may regard the young man's loss of his ideals as involving his replacement by a later self.

The example is of a quite general possibility. We may regard some events within a person's life as, in certain ways, like birth or death. Not in all ways, for beyond these events the person has earlier or later selves. But it may be only one out of the series of selves which is the object of some of our emotions, and to which we apply some of our principles.[23]

The young Russian socialist regards his ideals as essential to his present self. He asks his wife to promise to this present self not to act against these ideals. And, on this way of thinking, she can never be released from her commitment. For the self to whom she is committed would, in trying to release her, cease to exist.

The way of thinking may seem to be within our range of choice. We can indeed choose when to *speak* of a new self, just as we can choose when to speak of the end of Medieval England. But the way of speaking would express beliefs. And the wife in our example cannot choose her beliefs. That the young man whom she loved and married has, in a sense, ceased to exist, that her middle-aged and cynical husband is at most the later self of this young man – these claims may seem to her to express more of the truth than the simple claim, 'but they are the same person'. Just as we can give a more accurate description if we divide the history of Russia into that of the Empire and of the Soviet Union, so it may be more accurate to divide her husband's life into that of two successive selves.[24]

V

I have suggested that the Complex View supports certain claims. It is worth repeating that these claims are at most more plausible on the Complex View (more, that is, than on the Simple View). They are not entailed by the Complex View.

We can sometimes show this in the following way. Some claims make sense when applied to successive generations. Such claims can obviously be applied to successive selves. For example, it perhaps makes sense to believe that we inherit the commitments of our parents. If so, we can obviously believe that commitments are inherited by later selves.

Other claims may be senseless when applied to generations. Perhaps we cannot intelligibly think that we deserve to be punished for all our parents' crimes. But even if this is so, it should still make sense to have the comparable thought about successive selves. No similarity in the form of two relations could force us to admit that they are morally equivalent, for we can always appeal to the difference in their content.

There are, then, no entailments. But there seldom are in moral reasoning. So the Complex View may still support certain claims. Most of us think that our children are neither bound by our commitments, nor responsible for all we do. If we take the Complex View, we may be more inclined to think the same about our later selves. And the correctness of the view might make such beliefs more defensible.

VI

What, next, of our present selves? What of the other kind of case, where there are the strongest psychological connections? Here it makes no difference to believe that our identity has, in its nature, degrees, for there is here the strongest degree. But in the change to the Complex View we acquire a second new belief. We decide that our identity is in its nature less deep, or involves less. This belief applies to every case, even those where there are the strongest connections.

It is worth suggesting why there must be this second difference between the two views. On the Complex View, our identity over time just involves bodily and psychological continuity. On the Simple View, it does not just involve these continuities; it is in its nature a further fact. If we stop believing that it is a further fact, then (by arithmetic) we believe that it involves less. There is still the bare possibility that we thought the further fact superficial.[25] But it seems to most of us peculiarly deep.[26] This is why, if we change to the Complex View, we believe that our identity is in its nature less deep.

Would this belief affect our principles? If it has effects, they would not be confined to the special cases where there are only weak psychological connections. They would hold in every case. The effects would not be that we give certain principles a different scope. They would be that we give the principles a different weight.

Such effects could be defended on the following assumption. When some morally important fact is seen to be less deep, it can be plausibly claimed to be less important. As the limiting case, it becomes more plausible to claim that it has no importance. (This assumption is a variant of the one I used earlier.) The implications are obvious. The principles of desert and commitment presuppose that personal identity is morally important. On the assumption I have just sketched, the Complex View supports the claim that it is – because less deep – less important. So it may tend to weaken these principles.

I shall not here discuss these possible effects. I shall only say that the principle of commitment seems to be the less threatened by this weakening effect. The reason may be that, unlike the principle of desert, it is a conventional or 'artificial' principle. This may shield it from a change of view about the facts.[27]

I shall now turn to my last subject, distributive justice. Here the consequences of a change to the Complex View seem harder to assess. The reason is this : in the case of the principles of desert and commitment, both the possible effects, the weakening and the change in scope, are in theory pro-utilitarian. (Since these principles compete with the principle of utility, it is obviously in theory pro-utilitarian if they are weakened.[28] And their new scope would be a reduced scope. This should also be pro-utilitarian.[29]) Since both the possible effects would be in the same direction, we can make this general claim : if the change of view has effects upon these principles, these effects would be pro-utilitarian. In the case of distributive justice, things are different. Here, as I shall argue, the two possible effects seem to be in opposite directions. So there is a new question : which is the more plausible combined effect? My reply will again be: pro-utilitarian.

VII

Before defending this claim, I shall mention two related claims. These can be introduced in the following way.

Utilitarians reject distributive principles. They aim for the greatest net sum of benefits minus burdens, whatever its distribution. Let us say they 'maximize'.

There is, here, a well-known parallel. When we can affect only one person, we accept maximization. We do not believe that we ought to give a person fewer happy days so as to be more fair in the way we spread them out over the parts of his life. There are, of course, arguments for spreading out enjoyments. We remain fresh, and have more to look forward to. But these arguments do not count against maximization; they remind us how to achieve it.

When we can affect several people, utilitarians make similar claims. They admit new arguments for spreading out enjoyments, such as that which appeals to relative deprivation. But they treat equality as a mere means, not a separate aim.

Since their attitude to sets of lives is like ours to single lives, utilitarians disregard the boundaries between lives. We may ask, 'Why?'

Here are three suggestions. – Their approach to morality leads them to overlook these boundaries. – They believe that the boundaries are unimportant, because they think that sets of lives are like single lives. – They take the Complex View.

The first suggestion has been made by Rawls. It can be summarized like this. Utilitarians tend to approach moral questions as if they were impartial observers. When they ask themselves, as observers, what is right, or what they prefer, they tend to *identify* with *all* the affected people. This leads them to ignore the fact that *different* people are affected, and so to reject the claims of justice.[30]

In the case of some utilitarians, Rawls's explanation seems sufficient.[31] Let us call these the 'identifying observers'. But there are others who in contrast always seem '*detached* observers'. These utilitarians do not seem to overlook the distinction between people.[32] And, as Rawls remarks, there is no obvious reason why observers who remain *detached* cannot adopt the principles of justice. If we approach morality in a quite detached way – if we do not think of ourselves as potentially involved[33] – we may, I think, be somewhat more inclined to reject these principles.[34] But this particular approach to moral questions does not itself seem a sufficient explanation for utilitarian beliefs.

The Complex View may provide a different explanation. These two are quite compatible. Utilitarians may both approach morality as observers, and take the Complex View. (The explanations may indeed be mutually supporting.)

To turn to the remaining explanation. Utilitarians treat sets of lives in the way that we treat single lives. It has been suggested, not that they ignore the difference between people, but that they actually believe that a group of people is like a super-person. This suggestion is, in a sense, the reverse of mine. It imputes a different view about the facts. And it can seem the more plausible.

Let us start with an example. Suppose that we must choose whether to let some child undergo some hardship. If he does, this will either be for his own greater benefit in adult life, or for the similar benefit of someone else. Does it matter which?

Most of us would answer : 'Yes. If it is for the child's own benefit, there can at least be no unfairness.' We might draw the general conclusion that failure to relieve useful burdens is more likely to be justified if they are for a person's *own* good.

Utilitarians, confusingly, could accept this conclusion. They would explain it in a different way. They might, for instance, point out that such burdens are in general easier to bear.

To block this reply, we can suppose that the child in our example cannot be cheered up in this way. Let us next ignore other such arguments.[35] This simplifies the disagreement. Utilitarians would say : 'Whether it is right to let the child bear the burden only depends upon how great the benefit will be. It does not depend upon who benefits. It would make no moral difference if the benefit comes, not to the child himself, but to someone else.' Non-utilitarians might reply : 'On the contrary, if it comes to the child himself this helps to justify the burden. If it comes to someone else, that is unfair.'

We can now ask : do the two views about the nature of personal identity tend to support different sides in this debate?

Part of the answer seems clear. Non-utilitarians think it a morally important fact that it be the child himself who, as an adult, benefits. This fact, if it seems more important on one of the views, ought to do so on the Simple View, for it is on this view that the identity between the child and the adult is in its nature deeper. On the Complex View, it is less deep, and holds, over adolescence, to reduced degrees. If we take the Complex View, we may compare the lack of connections between the child and his adult self to the lack of connections between different people. That it will be *he* who receives the benefit may thus seem less important. We might say, 'It will not be *he*. It will only be his adult self.'

The Simple View seems, then, to support the non-utilitarian reply. Does it follow that the Complex View tends to support utilitarian beliefs? Not directly. For we might say, 'Just as it would be unfair if it is someone else who benefits, so if it won't be he, but only his adult self, that would also be unfair.'

The point is a general one. If we take the Complex View, we may regard the (rough) subdivisions within lives as, in certain ways, like the divisions between lives. We may therefore come to treat alike two kinds of distribution : within lives, and between lives. But there are two ways of treating these alike. We can apply distributive principles to both, or to neither.

Which of these might we do? I claim that we may abandon these principles. Someone might object : 'If we do add, to the divisions between lives, subdivisions within lives, the effects could only be these. The principles that we now apply to the divisions we come to apply to the sub-divisions. (If, to use your own example, we believe that our sons do not inherit our commitments, we may come to think the same about our later selves.)

'The comparable effect would now be this. We demand fairness to later selves. We *extend* distributive principles. You instead claim that we may abandon these principles. Since this is *not* the comparable effect, your claim must be wrong.'

The objection might be pressed. We might add : "If we did abandon these principles, we should be moving in reverse. We should not be treating parts of one life as we now treat different lives, but be treating different lives as we now treat one life. This, the reverse effect, could only come from the reverse comparison. Rather than thinking that a person's life is like the history of a nation, we must be thinking that a nation – or indeed any group – is like a person.'

L

To review the argument so far. Treating alike single people and groups may come from accepting some comparison between them. But there are two ways of treating them alike. We can demand fairness even within single lives, or reject this demand in the case of groups. And there are two ways of taking this comparison. We can accept the Complex View and compare a person's life to the history of a group, or accept the reverse view and compare groups to single people.

Of these four positions, I had matched the Complex View with the abandonment of fairness. The objection was that it seemed to be better matched with the demand for fairness even within lives. And the rejection of this demand, in the case of groups, seemed to require what I shall call 'the Reverse View'.

My reply will be this. Disregard for the principles of fairness could perhaps be supported by the Reverse View. But it does not have to be. And in seeing why we shall see how it may be supported by the Complex View.

Many thinkers have believed that a society, or nation, is like a person. This belief seems to weaken the demand for fairness. When we are thought to be mere parts of a social organism, it can seem to matter less how we are each treated.[36]

If the rejection of fairness has to be supported in this way, utilitarians can be justly ignored. This belief is at best superficially true when held about societies. And to support utilitarian views it would have to be held about the whole of mankind, where it is absurd.

Does the rejection of fairness need such support? Certain writers think that it does. Gauthier, for instance, suggests that to suppose that we should maximize for mankind 'is to suppose that mankind is a super-person'.[37] This suggestion seems to rest on the following argument. 'We are free to maximize within one life only because it is *one* life.[38] So we could only be free to maximize over different lives if they are like parts of a single life.'

Given this argument, utilitarians would, I think, deny the premise. They would deny that it is the unity of a life which, within this life, justifies maximization. They can then think this justified over different lives without assuming mankind to be a super-person.

The connection with the Complex View is, I think, this. It is on this view, rather than the Simple View, that the premise is more plausibly denied. That is how the Complex View may support utilitarian beliefs.

To expand these remarks. There are two kinds of distribution : within lives, and between lives. And there are two ways of treating these alike. We can apply distributive principles to both, or to neither.

Utilitarians apply them to neither. I suggest that this may be (in part) because they take the Complex View. An incompatible suggestion is that they take the Reverse View.

My suggestion may seem clearly wrong if we overlook the following fact. There are two routes to the abandonment of distributive principles. We may give them no scope, or instead give them no weight.

Suppose we assume that the only route is the change in scope.[39] Then it may indeed seem that utilitarians must either be assuming that any group of people is like a single person (Gauthier's suggestion), or at least be forgetting that it is not (Rawls's suggestion).

I shall sketch the other route. Utilitarians may not be denying that distributive principles have scope. They may be denying that they have weight. This, the second of the kinds of effect that I earlier distinguished, *may* be supported by the Complex View.

The situation, more precisely, may be this. If the Complex View supports a change in the scope of distributive principles, it perhaps supports giving them more scope. It perhaps supports their extension even within single lives. But the other possible effect, the weakening of these principles, may be the more strongly supported. That is how the net effect may be pro-utilitarian.

This suggestion differs from the other two in the following way. Rawls remarks that the utilitarian attitude seems to involve 'conflating all persons into one'.[40] This remark also covers Gauthier's suggestion. But the attitude may derive, not from the conflation of persons, but from their (partial) disintegration. It may rest upon the view that a person's life is less deeply integrated than we mostly think. Utilitarians may be treating benefits and burdens, not as if they all came within the same life, but as if it made no moral difference where they came. This belief may be supported by the view that the unity of each life, and hence the difference between lives, is in its nature less deep.[41]

VIII

I shall next sketch a brief defence of this suggestion. And I shall start with a new distributive principle. Utilitarians believe that benefits and burdens can be freely weighed against each other, even if they come to different people. This is frequently denied. We must first distinguish two kinds of weighing. The claim that a certain burden 'factually outweighs' another is the claim that it is greater. The claim that it 'morally outweighs' the other is the claim that we should relieve it even at the cost of failing to relieve the other. Similar remarks apply to the weighing of benefits against burdens, and against each other.

Certain people claim that burdens cannot even *factually* outweigh each other if they come to different people. (They claim that the sense of 'greater than' can only be provided by a single person's preferences.) I am here concerned with a different claim.[42] At its boldest this is that the burdens and benefits of different people cannot be *morally* weighed. I shall consider one part of this claim. This goes: 'Someone's burden cannot be morally outweighed by mere benefits to someone else.' I say 'mere' benefits, because the claim is not intended to deny that it *can* be right to let a person bear a burden so as to benefit another. Such acts may, for instance, be required by justice. What the claim denies is that such acts can be justified solely upon utilitarian grounds. It denies that a person's burden can be morally outweighed by *mere* benefits to someone else.

This claim often takes qualified forms. It can be restricted to great burdens, or be made to require that the net benefit be proportionately great.[43] I shall here discuss the simplest form, for my remarks could be adapted to the other forms. Rawls puts the claim as follows: 'The reasoning which balances the gains and losses of different persons . . . is excluded.'[44] So I shall call this the 'objection to balancing'.

This objection rests in part on a different claim. This goes: 'Someone's burden cannot be *compensated* by benefits to someone else.' This second claim is, with qualifications,[45] clearly true. We cannot say, 'On the contrary, our burdens can be compensated by benefits to anyone else, even a total stranger'.

Not only is this second claim clearly true; its denial is in no way supported by the Complex View. So if the change to this view has effects upon this claim, they would be these. We might, first, extend the claim even within single lives. We might say, in the example that I gave, 'The child's burden cannot be compensated by benefits to his adult self.' This claim would be like the claims that we are sometimes not responsible for, nor bound by, our earlier selves. It would apply to certain parts of one life what we now believe about different lives. It would therefore seem to be, as a change in scope, in the right direction.[46]

We might, next, give the claim less weight. Our ground would be the one that I earlier gave. Compensation presupposes personal identity. On the Complex View, we may think that our identity is, because less deep, less morally important. We may therefore think that the fact of compensation is itself less morally important. Though it cannot be denied, the claim about compensation may thus be given less weight.[47]

If we now return to the objection to balancing, things are different. The concept of 'greater moral weight' does not presuppose personal identity.[48] So this objection can be denied; and the Complex View seems to support this denial.

The denial might be put like this : 'Our burdens cannot indeed be *compensated* by mere benefits to someone else. But they may be *morally outweighed* by such benefits. It may still be right to give the benefits rather than relieve the burdens. Burdens are morally outweighed by benefits if they are factually outweighed by these benefits. All that is needed is that the benefits be greater than the burdens. It is unimportant, in itself, to whom both come.'

This is the utilitarian reply.[49] I shall next suggest why the Complex View seems, more than the Simple View, to support this reply.

The objection to balancing rests in part on the claim about compensation. On the Complex View, this claim can more plausibly be thought less important. If we take this view, we may (we saw) think both that there is less scope for compensation and that it has less moral weight. If the possibilities of compensation are, in these two ways, less morally important, there would then be less support for the objection to balancing. It would be more plausible to make the utilitarian reply.

The point can be made in a different way. Even those who

object to balancing think it justified to let us bear burdens for our own good. So their claim must be that a person's burden, while it can be morally outweighed by benefits to him, cannot ever be outweighed by mere benefits to others. This is held to be so even if the benefits are far greater than the burden. The claim thus gives to the boundaries between lives – or to the fact of non-identity – overwhelming significance. It allows within the same life what, for different lives, it totally forbids.

This claim seems to be more plausible on the Simple View. Since identity is, here, thought to involve more, non-identity could plausibly seem more important. On the Simple View, we are impressed by the truth that all of a person's life is as much his life. If we are impressed by this truth – by the unity of each life – the boundaries between lives will seem to be deeper. This supports the claim that, in the moral calculus, these boundaries cannot be crossed. On the Complex View, we are less impressed by this truth. We regard the unity of each life as in its nature less deep, and as a matter of degree. We may therefore think the boundaries between lives to be less like those between, say, the squares on a chess-board,[50] and to be more like those between different countries. They may then seem less morally decisive.[51]

IX

We can now turn to different principles, for example that of equal distribution. Most of us give such principles only *some* weight. We think, for instance, that unequal distribution can be justified if it brings an overall gain in social welfare. But we may insist that the gain be proportionately great.[52]

We do not, in making such claims, forbid utilitarian policies. We allow that every gain in welfare has moral value. But we do restrain these policies. We insist that it also matters *who* gains. Certain distributions are, we claim, morally preferable. We thus claim that we ought to favour the worst off, and to incline towards equality.

Utilitarians would reply : 'These claims are of course plausible. But the policies they recommend are the very policies which tend to increase total welfare. This coincidence suggests[53] that we ought to change our view about the status of these claims. We should regard them, not as checks upon, but as guides to, utilitarian policy. We should indeed value equal distribution. But the value lies in its typical effects.'

This reply might be developed in the following way. Most of us believe that a mere difference in *when* something happens, if it does not affect the nature of what happens, cannot be morally significant. Certain answers to the question 'When?' are of course important. We cannot ignore the timing of events. And it is even plausible to claim that if, say, we are planning when to give or to receive benefits, we should aim for an equal distribution over time. But we aim for this only because of its effects. We do not believe that the equality of benefit at different times is, as such, morally important.

Utilitarians might say: 'If it does not, as such, matter *when* something happens, why does it matter *to whom* it happens? Both of these are mere differences in position. What is important is the nature of what happens. When we choose between social policies, we need only be concerned with how *great* the benefits will be. *Where* they come, whether in space, or in time, or as between people, has in itself no importance.'

Part of the disagreement is, then, this. Non-utilitarians take the question 'Who?' to be quite unlike the question 'When?' If they are asked for the simplest possible description of the morally relevant facts, they will sometimes give them in a form which is tenseless; but it will always be personal. They will say, 'Someone gains, the same person loses, someone else gains. . . .' Utilitarians would instead say, 'A gain, a loss, another gain. . . .'

There are many different arguments for and against these two positions. We are only asking: would a change to the Complex View tend to support either one?

It would seem so. On the Simple View, it is more plausible to insist upon the question 'Who?' On the Complex View, it is more plausible to compare this to the question 'When?', and to present the moral data in the second, or 'impersonal', form.[54]

It may help to return to our comparison. Most of us believe that the existence of a nation does not involve anything more than the existence of associated people. We do not deny the reality of nations. But we do deny that they are separately, or independently, real. They are entirely composed of associated people.[55]

This belief seems to support certain moral claims. If there is nothing to a nation but its citizens, it is less plausible to regard the nation as itself a (primary) object of duties, or possessor of rights. It is more plausible to focus upon the citizens, and to regard them less as citizens, more as people. We may therefore, on this view, think a person's nationality less morally important.[56]

On the Complex View, we hold similar beliefs. We regard the existence of a person as, in turn, involving nothing more than the occurrence of interrelated mental and physical events. We do not, of course, deny the reality of people (our own reality!). And we agree that we are not, strictly, series of events – that we are not thoughts, but thinkers, not actions, but agents. But we consider this a fact of grammar. And we do deny that we are not just conceptually distinct from our bodies, actions, and experiences, but also separately real. We deny that the identity of a person, of the so-called 'subject' of mental and physical events, is a further, deep, fact, independent of the facts about the interrelations between these events.[57]

This belief may support similar claims. We may, when thinking morally, focus less upon the person, the subject of experience, and instead focus more upon the experiences themselves. Just as we often ignore whether people come from the same or different nations, so we may more often ignore whether experiences come within the same or different lives.

Take, for example, the relief of suffering. Suppose that we can only help one of two people. We shall achieve more if we help the first; but it is the second who, in the past, suffered more.

Those who believe in fair shares may decide to help the second person. This will be less effective; so the amount of suffering in the two people's lives will, in sum, be greater; but the amounts in each life will be made more equal.

If we take the Complex View, we may reject this line of thought. We may decide to do the most we can to relieve suffering. To suggest why, we can vary the example. Suppose that we can only help one of two nations. Here again, the one that we can help most is the one whose history was, in earlier centuries, the more fortunate. Most of us would not believe that it could be right to allow mankind to suffer more, so that its suffering could be more equally divided between the histories of different nations.

On the Complex View, we compare the lives of people to the

histories of nations. We may therefore think the same about them too. We may again decide to aim for the least possible suffering, whatever its distribution.[58]

X

We can next explain what, earlier, may have seemed puzzling. Besides the Complex View, which compares people to nations, I mentioned a reverse view, which compares nations to people. How can these be different?

It will help to introduce two more terms. With respect to many types of thing, we may take one of two views. We may believe that the existence of this type of thing does not involve anything more than the existence of certain other (interrelated) things. Such a view can be called 'atomistic'. We may instead believe that the things in question have a quite separate existence, over and above that of these other things. Such a view can be called 'holistic'.

One example of an atomistic view is the one we mostly take about nations. Most of us do not (here and now) believe that there is more to nations than associated people. On the other hand, we mostly do seem to assume that there is more to us than a series of mental and physical events. We incline to what I call the Simple View. Most of us are therefore atomists about nations, holists about people.

It is the difference between these common views which explains the two comparisons. The claim that X is like Y typically assumes the common view of Y. We shall therefore say 'People are like nations' if we are atomists about both. We shall instead say 'Nations are like people' if we are holists about both. Either way, we assume one of the common views and deny the other.[59]

We can end by considering a remark in Rawls. There is, he writes, 'a curious anomaly':[60]

> It is customary to think of utilitarianism as individualistic, and certainly there are good reasons for this. The utilitarians ... held that the good of society is constituted by the advantages enjoyed by individuals. Yet utilitarianism is not individualistic ... in that ... it applies to society the principle of choice for one man.

Our account suggests an explanation. Individualists claim that the welfare of society only consists in the welfare of its members, and that the members have rights to fair shares.

Suppose that we are holists about society. We believe that the existence of society transcends that of its members. This belief threatens the first of the individualist claims. It supports the view that the welfare of society also transcends that of its members. This in turn threatens the second claim, for in the pursuit of a transcendent social goal, fair shares may seem less important. Social holists may thus reject both of the individualist claims.

Utilitarians reject the second claim, but accept the first. This would indeed be anomalous if their attitude to these claims rested upon social holism. If this were their ground, we should expect them to reject *both* claims.

We have sketched a different ground. Rather than being holists about society, utilitarians may be atomists about people. This dissolves the anomaly. For they are also atomists about society, and this double atomism seems to support the two positions Rawls describes. If we are atomists about society, we can then more plausibly accept the first of the individualist claims, *viz.* that the welfare of society only consists in that of its members.[61] If we are also atomists about people, we can then more plausibly reject the second claim, the demand for fair shares. We may tend to focus less upon the person, the subject of experience, and instead focus more upon the experiences themselves. We may then decide that it is only the nature of what happens which is morally important, not to whom it happens. We may thus decide that it is always right to increase benefits and reduce burdens, whatever their distribution.[62]

'Utilitarianism,' Rawls remarks, 'does not take seriously the distinction between persons.'[63] If 'the separateness of persons . . . is *the* basic fact for morals',[64] this is a grave charge. I have tried to show how one view about the nature of persons may provide *some* defence.[65]

Notes

* I have been helped in writing this by T. Nagel; also by S. Blackburn, E. Borowitz, S. Clark, L. Francis, H. Frankfurt, J. Griffin, R. M. Hare, S. Lukes, J. Mackie, A. Orenstein, C. Peacocke, A. Rorty, A. Ryan, S. Shoemaker, D. Thomas, R. Walker, and others.

1 But compare *'de dicto'* versus *'de re'*.

2 We might say, 'The concept of a person is too vague to yield such an answer'.

3 Here is another example. Some of those who dislike all Jews seem to take Jewishness to be a special, deep property, equally possessed by all Jews. If they lose this belief, their attitude may be both weakened and reduced in scope. They may dislike 'typical Jews' less, and untypical Jews not at all.

4 The thing of which X is true can only be, or not be, the thing of which Y is true.

5 Cf. Hume: 'I cannot compare the soul more properly to anything than to a republic or commonwealth.' (Hume, Book I, Part IV, Section 6, p. 261.)

6 They cannot be so dismissed in a full account. The Complex View is not identical to Hume's view. It is even compatible with physicalism. See, for example, Quinton (1962), and Quinton (1972), pp. 88–102.

7 Here are two (crude) ranges of cases. In the first, different proportions of the cells in our brains and bodies will be replaced by exact duplicates. At the start of this range, where there is no replacement, there is full bodily continuity; at the end, where there is complete (simultaneous) 'replacement', there is no bodily continuity. In the second range, the duplication is progressively less accurate. At the start of this range, where there are perfect duplicates, there is full psychological continuity; at the end, where there are no duplicates, there is none. In the first case of the first range there is clearly personal identity. In the last case of the second range there is clearly no identity. But the two ranges can be super-imposed to form a smooth spectrum. It is unbelievable that, at a precise point on the spectrum, identity would suddenly disappear. If we grant its psycho-physical assumptions, the spectrum seems to show that our identity over time could *imaginably* hold to any degree. This prepares the ground for the claim that it *actually* holds to reduced degrees.

8 The main such reaction is the belief that these cases pose problems. (Cf. our reaction to the question, 'When, precisely, does an embryo become a person?') Among the 'problem' cases would be those described in note 7, or in Williams.

9 That we are inclined to this view is shown in Williams. That the view is false I began to argue in Parfit (1971).

10 Proust (1967), p. 349. (I have slightly altered the translation.)

11 Proust (1949), p. 249.

12 Solzhenitsyn, p. 232. (Curiously, Solzhenitsyn, like Keats (p. 322), seems to attach weight not just to psychological but to *cellular* change. Cf. Hume.)

13 Someone might say, 'These are not successive nations. They are just stages of a single nation.' What about Prussia, Germany, and West Germany? We *decide* what counts as the same nation.

14 Talk about successive selves can be easily misunderstood. It is intended

only to imply the weakening of psychological connections. It does *not* report the discovery of a new type of thing. We should take the question, 'When did that self end?' as like the question, 'What marked the end of medieval England?' Cf. note 24. (There is of course another use of 'earlier self' which, because it equates 'self' and 'person', does not distinguish successive selves.)

15 I do not mean 'more plausible than their denials'; I mean 'than they would be if the Simple View were true'.

16 The implied factual assumption surely holds for *some* of us.

17 Talk about successive selves can be used, like this, merely to imply the weakness of psychological connections. It can also be used to assign moral or emotional significance to such a weakness. This 'evaluative' use I have sketched elsewhere, in Parfit (1972). It is the 'descriptive' use which I need here. On this use, if a convict says, 'It was only my past self', all that he implies is the weakening in connections. On the 'evaluative' use, his claim suggests that, because of this weakening, he does not now deserve to be punished for his crime. Since the questions I am asking here all concern whether such a weakening *does* have such significance, it is the 'descriptive' use which I here employ. The 'evaluative' use begs these questions.

18 Locke, Book II, chapter XXVII, section 26. (Cf. also the 'Defence of Mr. Locke's Opinion' in certain editions of Locke's *Works* (e.g. 11th edn, vol. 3).)

19 Geach, p. 4.

20 If we are tempted to protest, 'But it was just as much *his* crime', we seems to be taking the Simple View. The comparable claim, 'Every accomplice is just as much an accomplice' is, in the sense in which it is true, clearly trivial. (See Parfit (1972).) (It is perhaps worth repeating that the Complex View deals with our relations at certain times, to ourselves at other times. The convict and criminal are, time-lessly, the same person. But the convict's present self and his past self are not the same, any more than Roman and Victorian Britain are the same.)

21 This is only generally true. Old men, for instance, can be closer to themselves in childhood than to themselves in youth.

22 It involves the new use of pronouns, and of the word 'man', to refer to one out of a series of selves.

23 I have here moved from the use of talk about successive selves which is merely 'descriptive', which merely implies the weakening of connections, to the use which is also 'evaluative', which assigns to such a weakening certain kinds of significance. It may seem confusing to allow these different uses, but they cannot be sharply distinguished. The 'merely descriptive' use lies at the end-point of a spectrum.

24 If we take the Complex View, we might add: 'It would be even more accurate to abandon talk about "selves", and to describe actions, thoughts, and experiences in a quite "impersonal" way. (Cf. Strawson, pp. 81–4). If these are not ascribed to any "subject", their various inter-

connections can then be directly specified. But the concept of a "subject of experience", like that of a nation, is an abbreviatory device of enormous convenience. If we remember that it is just this, and nothing more, it can be safely used.' (Cf. Mill, p. 252. Those who disagree, see note 57). These remarks may *not* apply to the concept of a persisting object. This may be essential to the spatio-temporal framework. But observed objects do not require observers. They require observations.

Here is another way in which the move from 'person' to 'successive self' may help to express the truth. Suppose that, in middle age, the Russian wife asks herself, 'Do I love my husband?' If it is asked in this form, she may find the question baffling. She may then realize that there is someone she loves – her husband's earlier self. (The object of love can be in the past. We can love the dead.) Cf. Solzhenitsyn, p. 393:

> Innokenty felt sorry for her and agreed to come. . . . He felt sorry, not for the wife he lived with and yet did not live with these days, the wife he was going to leave again soon, but for the blond girl with the curls hanging down to her shoulders, the girl he had known in the tenth grade. . . .

Cf. also Nabokov, p. 64:

> They said the only thing this Englishman loved in the world was Russia. Many people could not understand why he had not remained there. Moon's reply to questions of that kind would invariably be: 'Ask Robertson' (the orientalist) 'why he did not stay in Babylon.' The perfectly reasonable objection would be raised that Babylon no longer existed. Moon would nod with a sly, silent smile. He saw in the Bolshevist insurrection a certain clear-cut finality. While he willingly allowed that, by-and-by, after the primitive phases, some civilization might develop in the 'Soviet Union', he nevertheless maintained that Russia was concluded and unrepeatable. . . .

25 As, for example, Leibniz may have done. See the remark that Shoemaker quotes in Care, p. 127. Locke sometimes held a similar view. (I refer to his claim that 'whether it be the same identical substance, which always thinks in the same person . . . matters not at all'.)

26 As Williams suggests. Cf. Bayle's reply to Leibniz quoted by Chisholm in Care, p. 139; and, for other statements, Geach, pp. 1–29, Penelhum, closing chapters (both implicit), Butler, pp. 385 ff., Reid, Essay III, chs 4 and 6, and Chisholm (more explicit).

27 We should perhaps add the obvious remark that the principle of desert seems itself to be more threatened by a change of view, not about personal identity, but about psychological causation.

28 That it may in practice be anti-utilitarian is, for instance, emphasized in Sidgwick (1901), Book IV, ch. V. (In Sidgwick (1902), p. 114, he writes, 'It may be – I think it is – true that Utilitarianism is only adapted for practical use by human beings at an advanced stage of intellectual development.')

29 There are some exceptions. If, for instance, we hold the principle

of desert in its 'negative' form (cf. Hart), its receiving less scope may in theory seem anti-utilitarian. Useful punishments might be ruled out on the ground that they are no longer deserved. But this would in practice be a minor point. (And there seems to be no corresponding point about commitment.)

30 Rawls, p. 27, and pp. 185–9.

31 Rawls mentions C. I. Lewis (Rawls, p. 188); but the explanation cannot hold for him, for he insists upon the claims of justice (Lewis, pp. 553–4). The explanation may seem to apply to Hare; see Hare (1963), p. 123; but p. 121 suggests that it does not. In Mackaye, pp. 129–30 and p. 189 seem to fit; but again, pp. 146–50 point the other way.

32 Among the many utilitarians who clearly remain detached is Sidgwick. To quote a typical sentence: 'I as a disengaged spectator should like him to sacrifice himself to the general good: but I do not expect him to do it, any more than I should do it myself in his place.' (Sidgwick (1901), pp. xvii–xviii.) Sidgwick ended the first edition of his book with the word 'failure' mostly because he assigned such weight to the distinction between people. (See, for example (1901), p. 404, or (1902), p. 67, or the remark in *Mind* (1889), pp. 483–4, 'The distinction between any one individual and another is real, and fundamental.' (Sidgwick's own view about personal identity is hard to judge. In (1901), pp. 418–19, he appears to disclaim one form of the Complex View. In *Mind* (1883), p. 326, he admits a Kantian claim about the necessity of the 'permanent, identical self'. Perhaps (like Kant himself?) he was torn between the two views.))

33 As we do if we are either contracting agents (Rawls), or universal prescribers (Hare).

34 As the contrast between the two halves of the first quotation in note 32 may suggest. For a different suggestion, see Hare (1972) and (1973).

35 Such as those which appeal to the undermining of the general sense of security, or to pessimism about the 'acceptance-utility' of utilitarian beliefs.

36 Cf. the claim of Espinas, that society 'is a living being like an individual' (Perry, p. 402). Good Hegelians do not argue in this way.

37 Gauthier, p. 126.

38 Someone might say: 'No. We are free, here, because it is not a moral matter what we do with our own lives.' This cannot be right, for we are allowed to maximize within the life of *someone else*. (Medicine provides examples. Doctors are allowed to maximize on behalf of their unconscious patients.)

39 As Rawls seems to do. Cf. his remark: 'the utilitarian extends to society the principle of choice for one man' (p. 28, and elsewhere, e.g. p. 141). The assumption here is that the route to utilitarianism is a change in the scope, not of distributive principles, but of their correlative: our freedom to ignore these principles.

40 p. 27; cf. p. 191; cf. also Nagel, p. 134.

41 The utilitarian attitude is *impersonal*. Rawls suggests that it 'mistakes

impersonality for impartiality' (p. 190). I suggest that it may in part derive from a view about the nature of persons. This suggestion, unlike his, may be no criticism. For as he writes 'the correct regulative principle for anything depends upon the nature of that thing' (p. 29).

42 The possibility of 'factual weighing' over different lives can, I think, be shown with an argument which appeals to the Complex View. But the argument would have to be long.

43 Cf. Perry, p. 674: 'We do not . . . balance one man's loss against a million's gain. We acknowledge that there are amounts or degrees of value associated with each party, between which it is impossible to discriminate.' This claim seems to be slightly qualified. (It is not wholly clear whether Perry is objecting *only* to *moral* weighing.)

44 p. 28. I omit the words 'as if they were one person', for I am asking whether this reasoning must involve this assumption.

45 The main such qualification is to exclude cases where the first person wants the second to receive the benefit.

46 It seems worth mentioning here an idea of Nagel's. Like Rawls, Nagel claims that if we imagine that we are going to *be* all of the affected parties, we may then ignore the claims of justice. He then suggests that this is only so if our future lives are to be had *seriatim*. 'We can [instead] imagine a person splitting into several persons. . . . . This provides a sense in which an individual might expect to become *each* of a number of different persons – not in series, but simultaneously.' (Nagel, pp. 141–2; cf. Rawls, pp. 190–1.) *This* model, he believes, 'renders plausible the extremely strict position that there can be no interpersonal compensation for sacrifice'. Why? How can it make a difference whether the person's future lives are to be lived in series, or concurrently? The relation between the person now and the future lives is, in either case, the same. (It is 'as good as survival'; see Parfit (1971), pp. 4–10.) Nagel suggests an answer: '*Each* of [the] lives would in a sense be his unique life, without deriving any compensatory or supplementary experiences, good or bad, by seepage from the other unique lives he is leading at the time.' This, of course, is the *utilitarian* answer. (Cf. p. 15 above.) It treats *pure* compensation as of no value. It suggests that compensation only matters when it actually has good effects (when it produces 'compensatory . . . supplementary experiences'). The disagreement seems to disappear!

47 This distinction bears on the 'Is-Ought' debate. That it is unjust to punish the innocent cannot be denied; but the claim can be given no weight. We might say, 'It is just as *bad* to punish the guilty'.

48 It might do so, indirectly, if we cannot even *factually* weigh over different lives, and adopt utility as our only principle. No one (that I know) holds this position.

49 It would be their reply to the many arguments in which the objection to balancing and the claim about compensation are intertwined. Cf. Rawls's phrase 'cannot be justified by, or compensated for, by . . .' (p. 61), and similar remarks on pp. 14–15, p. 287, and elsewhere. Perry

writes: 'The happiness of a million somehow fails utterly to compensate or even to mitigate the torture of one.' This undeniable remark he seems to equate with the objection to balancing (Perry, p. 671).

50 Cf: 'The difference between self and another is as plain as the difference between black and white.' (Hobhouse, p. 51.)

51 Someone might object: 'On the Complex View, we may claim that the parts of each life are less deeply unified; but we do not claim that there is more unity between lives. So the boundaries between lives are, on this view, just as deep.' We could answer: 'Not so. Take for comparison the fact of personhood. We may decide that to be a person, as opposed to a mere animal, is not in its nature a further fact, beyond the fact of having certain more specific properties, but that it just consists in this fact. This belief is not itself the belief that we are more like mere animals than we thought. But it still removes a believed difference. So it makes the boundaries between us and mere animals less deep. Similar remarks apply to the two views about personal identity.'

52 These are examples of what both Sidgwick and Rawls would call 'the intuitionism of Common Sense'. I cannot here discuss Rawls's principles, or his 'contractual' argument. (I should point out that a contractual argument for the principles of justice seems to be in no way weakened by the Complex View. But alongside the contractual argument, Rawls suggests another: that these principles are required by the *plurality* of persons (cf. p. 29). This is the argument which, however strong, seems to me less strong on the Complex View.)

53 See, for instance, Sidgwick (1901), p. 425 (or indeed pp. 199–457).

54 I am here claiming that the Complex View tends to weaken distributive principles. What of the other possible effect, the change in scope? Might we demand fair shares for successive selves? *Perhaps.* (Cf. Findlay, p. 239). But the demand would, I think (and for various reasons), be rare. And the argument in the text only requires the following claim: the weakening of distributive principles would be more supported than the widening in their scope. The effects of the former would outweigh the effects of the latter. As the limiting case, if we give distributive principles no weight, nothing follows from a change in their scope.

55 This is ontological reductionism. It may not require the truth of analytical reductionism (or 'methodological individualism'). See, for instance, Strawson, p. 201, Dummett, p. 242, and Kripke, p. 271. I have no space to pursue this point here.

56 We could, of course, still claim that the fact of being associated-in-a-nation has supreme importance. But this claim, though possible, may still be less supported by this view. This it will be if the independent reality, which this view denies would have helped to support the claim.

57 Someone might object: 'The comparison fails. The interrelations between citizens could in theory be described without mentioning nations. The interrelations between mental and physical events could *not* in theory be described without mentioning the "subject of experience".' This seems to me false. The difference is only one of

practical convenience. (See Parfit (1971), section III, for a very brief statement.) But even if the comparison *does* fail in this respect, it would still hold in the respects which are morally important.

58 Someone might object: 'This reasoning only applies to the demand for equal distribution as between entire lives. But we might make the demand in a form which ignores both the past and the future. We might value equal distribution as between people (or "successive selves") at any given time.' True. But this new demand seems, on reflection, implausible. Why the restriction to the *same* (given) time? How can simultaneity have intrinsic moral weight? (The new demand may, of of course, have good effects. This is here irrelevant.)

59 I am here forced (by lack of space) into gross oversimplification. There are many intermediate views. To give one example: if we are atomists about organisms, we shall find it easier to compare nations to organisms. For some of the complexities see Perry, p. 400 onwards and Hobhouse.

60 Rawls, p. 29.

61 Cf.: 'As the public body is every individual collected, so the public good is the collected good of those individuals' (Thomas Paine, quoted in Lukes, p. 49). Sidgwick remarks that while we commend 'one man dying for his country . . . it would be absurd that all should: there would be no country to die for.' (1902, p. 79.) We might still deny that 'the public good is merely a . . . collection of private goods' on the ground that 'men desire fo rtheir own sake' irreducibly public goods (Plamenatz, p. 251). But this claim still appeals to personal desires.

62 The Complex View seems also to support other utilitarian claims, such as that the welfare of a person just consists in the quality of his experiences, or (to give a variant) in the fulfilment of his various particular desires. Cf. the remark in Anschutz (pp. 19–20) that 'Bentham's principle of individualism', unlike Mill's, 'is entirely transitional', since 'Bentham is saying that . . . as a community is reducible to the individuals who are said to be its members, so also are the individuals reducible, at least for the purposes of morals and legislation, to the pleasures and pains which they are said to suffer.'

63 Rawls, p. 27; cf. Nagel, p. 134.

64 Findlay, p. 393; cf. p. 294.

65 I have not claimed that it could provide a sufficient defence.

Bibliography

ANSCHUTZ, R. P., *The Philosophy of J. S. Mill*, Oxford, Clarendon Press, 1953.

BUTLER, JOSEPH, 'Of Personal Identity', appendix to *The Analogy of Natural Religion*, vol. 1, ed. W. E. Gladstone, Oxford, Frowde, 1897.

CARE, N. and GRIMM, R. H., *Perception and Personal Identity*, Cleveland, Press of Case-Western Reserve University, 1967.

CHISHOLM, R., 'Problems of Identity', in *Identity and Individuation*, ed. M. K. Munitz, New York University Press, 1971.

M

DUMMETT, M., 'The Reality of the Past', *Proceedings of the Aristotelian Society*, 69, 1968–9.

FINDLAY, J., *Values and Intentions*, London, Allen & Unwin, 1961.

GAUTHIER, D., *Practical Reasoning*, Oxford, Clarendon Press, 1963.

GEACH, P. T., *God and the Soul*, London, Routledge & Kegan Paul, 1969.

HARE, R. M. (1963), *Freedom and Reason*, Oxford, Clarendon Press.

HARE, R. M. (1972), 'Rules of War and Moral Reasoning', *Philosophy and Public Affairs*, winter.

HARE, R. M. (1973), review of Rawls in *Philosophical Quarterly*.

HART, H. L. A., *Punishment and Responsibility*, Oxford, Clarendon Press, 1968.

HOBHOUSE, L. T., *The Metaphysical Theory of the State*, London, Allen & Unwin, 1918.

HUME, DAVID, 'A Treatise of Human Nature', 1740.

KEATS, JOHN, *Letters*, ed. R. Gittings, London, Oxford University Press, 1970.

KRIPKE, S., 'Naming and Necessity', in *Semantics of Natural Language*, eds. D. Davidson and G. Harman, Dordrecht, Reidel, 1972.

LEWIS, C. I., *An Analysis of Knowledge and Valuation*, La Salle, Illinois, Open Court, 1962.

LOCKE, JOHN, *Essay Concerning Human Understanding*, 1690.

LUKES, S., *Individualism*, Oxford, Blackwell, 1973.

MACKAYE, J., *The Economy of Happiness*, Boston, Little, Brown, 1906.

MILL, J. S., *An Examination of Sir William Hamilton's Philosophy*, London, Longmans, 1872.

NABOKOV, V., *Glory*, London, Weidenfeld & Nicolson, 1971.

NAGEL, T., *The Possibility of Altruism*, Oxford, Clarendon Press, 1970.

PARFIT, D. (1971), 'Personal Identity', *Philosophical Review*, January.

PARFIT, D. (1972), 'On "The Importance of Self-Identity"', *Journal of Philosophy*, 21 October.

PENELHUM, T., *Survival and Disembodied Existence*, London, Routledge & Kegan Paul, 1970.

PERRY, R., *General Theory of Value*, Cambridge, Mass., Harvard University Press, 1950.

PLAMENATZ, J., *Man and Society*, vol. 2, London, Longmans, 1963.

PROUST, MARCEL (1949), *The Sweet Cheat Gone*, trans. by C. K. Scott Moncrieff, London, Chatto & Windus.

PROUST, MARCEL (1967), *Within a Budding Grove*, vol. 1, trans. by C. K. Scott Moncrieff, London, Chatto & Windus.

QUINTON, A. M. (1962), 'The Soul', *Journal of Philosophy*, 59.

QUINTON, A. M. (1972), *On the Nature of Things*, London, Routledge & Kegan Paul.

RAWLS, J., *A Theory of Justice*, Cambridge, Mass., Harvard University Press, 1971.

REID, JOSEPH, *Essays on the Intellectual Powers of Man*, Essay III., chs IV and VI.

SIDGWICK, HENRY (1901), *Methods of Ethics*, sixth edition, London, Macmillan.

SIDGWICK, HENRY (1902), *The Ethics of Green, Spencer, and Martineau*, London, Macmillan.

SOLZHENITSYN, A., *The First Circle*, New York, Bantam Books, 1969.

STRAWSON, P. F., *Individuals*, London, Methuen, 1959.

WILLIAMS, B. A. O., 'The Self and the Future', *Philosophical Review*, 1970.

8   Psychological explanations and interpersonal relations

Michael Schleifer

Is there any legitimacy in the use of psychological explanations ('Ps-explanations' for short) in our ordinary interpersonal relations? In what way can Ps-explanations rationally affect our evaluations of what people do as well as what they say? P. F. Strawson's British Academy Lecture, 'Freedom and Resentment', has as a main theme the denial of the legitimacy of using Ps-explanations in our normal relations with people. I shall attempt to clarify the use of psychological explanations by considering two special kinds of relationships: that between an adult and a child, and that between a therapist and his client. I shall then argue that Strawson is wrong to depict these relationships as relevantly different from so-called 'normal' ones and consequently that Ps-explanations may affect our evaluations of what any person does or says.

In defending the last part of the thesis, namely, that we may legitimately make use of Ps-explanations in regard to what people say, I shall also consider very seriously the objections of philosophers like Sidney Hook and Raphael Demos,[1] who reject this view as *ad hominem*, and fallacious. In propounding my own view, I attempt to avoid the errors which would leave the present thesis open to the objections of these philosophers.

I

Whenever one is confronted with human behaviour it seems quite legitimate, and it is often necessary, to attempt to understand and explain it. We may be satisfied with a superficial question-
170

and-answer. However, it often seems appropriate and desirable to go beyond this and invoke generalizations about human behaviour. I propose to define a Ps-explanation as any explanation which goes beyond the immediately obtainable verbal answer by invoking general knowledge of behaviour. A Ps-explanation tries to take into consideration not just an immediately-present conscious awareness, but a great variety of relevant background conditions such as desires and dispositions, and specific environmental and physiological variables.[2] The expression 'knowledge of behaviour' is meant to include knowledge of what men do and say ('acts') as well as what the psychologist may re-describe more technically in terms of movements and glandular secretions.[3] It is perhaps mistaken to attempt any more precise definition for an admittedly vague term. It will perhaps suffice to note that smiles, tears and blushes, as well as speech and physical acts, should all be understood as 'behaviour' in the relevant sense.

Certain other features of the Ps-explanation may be clarified by considering its use in the paradigm cases of children's behaviour and psychopathology. For example, when a child cries or throws a tantrum one may want to know what has led to this. Asking the child is one way of getting an explanation. (He may answer: 'I don't like you!') However, one may use a Ps-explanation such as 'He has acted this way to get attention because he was being ignored' or 'He was frustrated earlier and this is the reaction'. These are Ps-explanations because they seek to go beyond question-and-answer and they employ generalizations concerning behaviour.

It is interesting to note that the Ps-explanation is often communicated to the child. One might simply rephrase the explanation in the second person, e.g. '*You* have acted this way to get attention because you were being ignored'. The reason for communicating the explanation is that one hopes thereby to change the behaviour in a more desirable direction. One may often judge that it is better to communicate the explanation in more suitable terms depending upon the age and comprehension of the child. One might even argue that there are times when communicating the explanation may do less good than harm. My own conviction is that it is most often better to communicate the explanation to the child using the same words that would appear in the corresponding third-person explanation. The justification for communicating the Ps-explanations is exactly the same, in my view, in the case of children as in the case of psychotherapeutic patients.

Let us take an example from psychopathology : a man has left his job and has begun drinking excessively; he is often violent and unreasonable at home with his family. In order to help this person one would want to understand his behaviour. If simply asked, he might say : 'I am fed up with the world.' A clinical psychologist would certainly go beyond this and attempt to isolate the active ingredients – past and present, environmental and physiological – which explain the man's behaviour. One Ps-explanation might be : 'You have built up a tolerance for alcohol which has given reinforcement as an anxiety-reducer when taken in the past.' Knowledge about behaviour in general is used to explain the individual case.

These examples may throw light on two important and related questions concerning Ps-explanations : Why are they used? How do they relate to what X can tell us about his own behaviour? One can begin to answer the second question by noting that a Ps-explanation can be given by someone other than X, although X can also invoke a Ps-explanation about his own behaviour. But why would one want to appeal to an explanation which uses general knowledge about behaviour? In what circumstances would this override the simple question-answer procedure? At this point the second question lapses into the first : viz, why use Ps-explanations? The short answer to *that* question has to be : because they are more adequate and satisfying as explanations. Surely it will be acknowledged that the Ps-explanations given by the clinician or parent *are* better explanations than those given by the child and patient? But this leaves the task of depicting the criteria that make one explanation more adequate, more satisfying – in short better – than another.

There is one type of philosophical characterization of Ps-explanations which I cannot accept. According to this view, Ps-explanations undermine the ordinary reasons that X might give about his own behaviour, and this is because all normal reasons are somehow bad ones (mere 'rationalizations').[4] If this view were correct, it would count against my claim that Ps-explanations have a general use. For there would be conceptual confusion in supposing that *all* reasons must be bad ones. Fortunately, this view is both false and irrelevant. It is irrelevant if it restricts the question to explanations of the psychoanalytic type – which many philosophers are prone to do.[5] For I must emphasize that the Ps-explanations characterized above are by no means restricted to explanations of any one school (although explanations using Freudian theory can certainly be included in my broader classification). For that matter, Ps-explanations may be relatively atheoretical. The explanation in terms of 'reinforcement' used above is considered by some psychologists to be *completely* atheoretical.[6]

The view that Ps-explanations must imply that all reasons are rationalizations is similarly irrelevant if it has restricted the discussion to so-called non-teleological ('causal') explanations. For there is nothing in the logic of an explanation of behaviour nor in the history of psychology which precludes Ps-explanations from being teleological.[7] In any case the view that psychologists must necessarily hold reasons to be 'rationalizations' is mistaken. No psychologist in attempting to explain behaviour (*even if using psychoanalytic notions*) is committed to any *particular* view about the everyday reasons people cite. Logic demands only that he be committed to *some* view about the relative inadequacy of these first-level explanations. But it is this very 'inadequacy' which must be characterized.

The question of the adequacy of explanations can be considered in two different ways – as a general problem in the philosophy of science or as a more specific philosophical problem related to moral and legal contexts. Seen as a general problem about scientific explanation, questions of laws, generalizations, and predictive value are relevant to the question of adequacy; whatever makes an explanation from physics (say) more adequate than common sense will hold for Ps-explanations as well. Ultimately one explanation is seen as more adequate than another upon appeal to the principles of simplicity and parsimony.

It is more fruitful for present purposes, however, to emphasize other features of explanations – those more relevant to the context of interpersonal relations. Here more pertinent analogies are provided by explanations in medicine, history, and law. These disciplines use explanations in a somewhat different way; however, it is unnecessary to assume some difference in kind between (say) natural science and human explanations. All forms of explanations have certain features in common; I am here concerned with the differences.

The first important feature of these explanations is their close association with an immediate practical need. Collingwood, talking of medical explanations, emphasized their close ties to our goals of prevention and control.[8] Ps-explanations – like medical ones – are tied to attempts at changing the behaviour in a direction which is considered better. They are more adequate, provided they give us this ability to handle, treat and change the behaviour in desired directions.

Philosophers of law have similarly underlined the practical nature of legal explanations – a feature they share with medical and historical explanations. Hart and Honoré make use of Collingwood's analysis up to a point : legal explanations are indeed 'practical', but they have a specific practical function; they are used in attributive contexts.[9] (In this respect legal explanations are somewhat like historical ones, but rather different from the medical example.) Now Ps-explanations – like legal explanations – are also often tied to attributive contexts. We may be concerned with an *evaluation* of the behaviour and with possible subsequent action.

With this general characterization in mind let us reconsider the use of Ps-explanations. They are invoked by the clinical psychologist as the first step in an attempt to change or 'treat' the behaviour : the Ps-explanation *is* part of the psychotherapy. With children, similarly, questions concerning how to alter their behaviour inevitably arise for parents. Concerned with teaching their children, as well as with the inevitable practical problems of discipline, parents invoke Ps-explanations as part of the first step towards some sort of action. We now have an answer to the question : why are Ps-explanations more adequate? They better serve the needs of the situation – either the need to help a person change as in therapy, or the need to make an evaluation concerning quesions of culpability and punishability.

These ends are clearest in the special cases discussed, but the same ends are part of normal personal relationships. This may seem less than obvious, but that may be because the processes and ends are usually less explicit. A parent sees himself quite clearly as involved in the forming of the life of the child. It is similarly obvious that a therapist is involved in changing the behaviour of a person; this is also made explicit at the beginning of therapy. Might it not be that Ps-explanations have the same legitimate role in our normal interpersonal relations – namely as part of the process of evaluating and changing the behaviour of the other and oneself?

II

Ps-explanations clearly make a difference in regard to our views concerning responsibility for undesirable acts. As pointed out above, we will often modify our views concerning blameworthiness and punishability as we make an attempt to understand the behaviour in question. Just as we do this in the case of children and people seeking treatment in psychological clinics, so we can and do maintain this attitude towards people in general. Can one *justify* this point of view in our interpersonal relations?

A demand for justification is ambiguous. It may be answered by showing the point of the practice and some good reasons. Or it may be that the question of justification lies deeper than this – a challenge to demonstrate that the practice does not conflict with other basic values and beliefs. I leave the deeper question of moral justification and legitimacy for the next section. For the present I will restrict myself to the justification which shows the point of the practice. I take it that the point of the practice will also indicate the beginnings of the moral justification – following a standard Benthamite procedure.[10]

The modifications of one's tendency to blame others with whom one has personal relations is done in the same way, and for the same reasons, as in the so-called 'special' cases. When confronted with undesirable behaviour it is better to eradicate this behaviour than to reinforce it with hostile reactions. For example, suppose we know a person with the habit of talking too much about his achievements. This behaviour might be explained as the result of pressures towards greater acceptance and affection by others, coupled with a paradoxical rejection. In this regard we are more likely to understand the larger significance of what the person is saying and doing – as an expression of that all-too-human trait which we know generally occurs in others and ourselves. If we did not attempt a Ps-explanation and rather contented ourselves with a superficial characterization of the behaviour, we would more than likely react with hostility and have the ironic effect of strengthening the very behaviour we wish to eliminate. However, in view of the Ps-explanation of this behaviour, it becomes *irrational* to react with hostility and blame. In the final analysis it is rational to employ Ps-explanations to alter our ascriptions of culpability because we will thereby help achieve the behaviour and relationships that we want.

Questions concerning blame and punishment represent one very important form of evaluation. These evaluations are usually labelled issues of 'responsibility' and arise where the behaviour is somehow unwanted. The concept of 'responsibility' need not be defined in terms of blame and punishment and can be given an independent analysis. Moreover, it is important to do so because of the implications for current philosophical and legal debates.[11]

'Responsibility' can be defined as the unique ability to give an account or make a response. One should rephrase the definition to take the inevitable prepositional context into account. Thus what is responsibility for something? It is the ability to give an account of (for) that thing. The 'thing' can best be characterized as a situation where this refers to any 'possible' (practically possible) state of affairs under a certain description. What makes one responsible, then, for a situation under a certain description is one's *unique* capacity to account for it. This unique capacity depends upon one's position *vis-à-vis* the situation in question. It may be in virtue of certain things one has done (e.g. if one paints a picture, or writes an examination, or drives a car which causes an accident) or in virtue of the things one is (e.g. a policeman, or a doctor or a philosopher or a German in the Nazi era). These examples help show how accounting for something does not necessarily involve either blame or punishment: perhaps the only ascriptive questions concern possible praiseworthiness or dispraiseworthiness – if that is a possible word! When one paints a picture clearly one is the person 'responsible', although no questions of blame or punishment need be involved. Although further argument may be needed, it can be shown that blame and praise are *not* polar opposites.

These kinds of evaluations are extremely central to our interpersonal relations and relate to almost everything a person says and does. Furthermore, there are issues of 'responsibility' (as defined above) in which questions of blame and punishment are *completely* irrelevant. One important example is the responsibility of a person for what he says regarding its truth and substantiation. We must make evaluations concerning truth and substantiation in order to decide to accept or reject what was said. Similarly we must evaluate the importance, relevance and significance of things said to us. These evaluations will affect our decision whether or not to accept what was said; at other times they will influence our decisions concerning possible action as a response to what was said. In regard to most of these sorts of explanations Ps-explanations may be directly relevant.

The applicability of Ps-explanations to evaluations differs depending upon the type of evaluation involved. In general, the more questions of truth and falsehood are directly at issue, the less legitimate is the use of a Ps-explanation in making the evaluation. Conversely, where the evaluations are less directly concerned with issues of truth, the applicability of Ps-explanations is greatest. It may be helpful at this point to list the types of evaluations:

(1) Punishment.
(2) Blame.
(3) Decision concerning possible action.
(4) Acceptance or rejection.

Questions of truth and falsehood are in some sense tied to all evaluations. Clearly, before questions of punishability (say) arise there are questions concerning what, if anything, happened? At *that* stage Ps-explanations have little application. When questions of causation arise the ascriptive nature of the enterprise make Ps-explanations more relevant. Finally, when evaluations are concerned with whether or not to punish, Ps-explanations can have an important bearing on the outcome – as I have argued above. I turn now to consider the third and fourth types of evaluations listed above.

When a child says something we should be aware that he may be attempting to express much more than simply the content of his utterance. If he reports: 'I played with the *boys*' toys at school today!' one should realize that there may be more than the simple report of an unimportant activity at school. One may want to evaluate what action one might take as a consequence of hearing this statement. What difference ought the hearing of these words to make in one's behaviour? Without this kind of sensitivity one will inevitably lose something in the understanding of children. Similarly a crucial thing to look for when attempting to help someone in therapy is what the person says about himself – often in a roundabout manner. A patient may arrive, announcing : 'I almost didn't get here for today's session!' This statement can be taken superficially as simply conveying information. Or else one may use a Ps-explanation to help one evaluate what was said in a broader perspective. One would use generalizations about human beings in this kind of situation to re-evaluate what was said as a rather important message demanding a specific reaction on one's part. It is perfectly legitimate to extend this viewpoint to the evaluations of what people say in ordinary personal conversations. Consider some of the following everyday utterances heard around home or university :

(1) 'It's garbage-night tonight!'
(2) 'We haven't seen you for quite a while.'
(3) 'I've been quite lonely lately.'
(4) 'There isn't very much communication in the department.'
(5) 'Philosophy can be really depressing.'

What people say to one another very often is for other purposes than expressing propositions which be true or false. It is perhaps a philosophical truism that language *always* is more than just 'saying' something – it is the 'doing' of something as well.[12] The utterances listed above are typical of the sort that occur in everyday life – the specific examples no doubt reflect a specific experience. (no. 5 is very popular among our undergraduates.) It is surely obvious that evaluations are needed concerning how to react to what is said. Even the most trivial utterance (no. 1 above) has implications for possible action. As such the only proper evaluation of what is said must be based on the factors which led *that* person to say *that* thing at *that* time. And here general knowledge about human behaviour may be very helpful.

Finally, Ps-explanations may have an important bearing upon our evaluations concerning whether or not to accept or reject what a person has said. It is important to distinguish different sorts of evaluations regarding acceptance of a proposition. Let us consider a proposition p uttered by an individual x. One evaluation concerns whether or not p is true and/or well-substantiated. Here considerations about x are irrelevant and hence, *a fortiori*, so are Ps-explanations. It is important to reject the 'genetic' view that beliefs can be discredited or truth determined on the basis of some sort of genetic explanation which undermines the speaker.[13] The rule regarding *ad hominem* fallacies can be put :

> *Rule H* Whether a proposition or a theory is true must be determined independently of who thought it and under what conditions.

Rule H must be respected. There are, however, certain *ad hominem* procedures that are not fallacious. Very often our evaluation concerning whether or not to accept p may be legitimately determined by considerations other than truth and substantiation. Furthermore, considerations regarding x (the speaker) may become relevant to the evaluation. I shall attempt to show that this procedure is not necessarily fallacious. Statements uttered by philosophers afford a good example.

The need to make *ad hominem* evaluations may arise in several ways. In the first place it may be that the nature of p does not lend itself too readily to an evaluation concerning literal truth and falsehood. Philosophical utterances are notorious in just this way. Let us take the proposition 'Men are not machines'. To take this literally, at face value, would be to lose its real significance. An evaluation concerning acceptance must surely take into account that the utterance reflects a number of concerns about related issues – a deep anxiety, perhaps, about the increased mechanization of men. Where p is a moral statement it is even clearer that our evaluations must be very complicated. Consider the following examples :

(1) 'One ought to preserve the university !'
(2) 'You ought to tolerate the other person's point of view.'
(3) 'One must be committed to *some* point of view.'

Any of (1) to (3) may be the p uttered by x, who may be a professional philosopher or anyone else. It is a mistake to make decisions concerning acceptance of any one of these propositions without considering relevant factors about x. Knowledge about the background of x as well as knowledge about the situation in which the utterance was made are indispensable for a proper evaluation. The peculiar nature of p makes the *ad hominem* procedure appropriate and Ps-explanations quite applicable. This is because the quality of typical moral utterances such as (1) to (3) above is that they represent only *one* point of view. This point of view is often highly debatable with diametrically opposed views held by others. Our decisions regarding p and not-p are not easily decidable – considerations of truth and substantiation often even themselves out. It is for this reason that there is no fallacy in the *ad hominem* procedure. This may become clearer if looked at from a different perspective. Let us reconsider the example 'Men are not machines' in the context of a discussion (adapted from real life) :

A   Computers are completely unlike men.
B   But we can learn a great deal about how people reason (e.g. play chess) by developing a chess program for the computer.
A   But no chess-playing machine can ever play as a man can.
B   People shouldn't talk about things concerning which they have no competence.
A   Men are not machines.

To properly evaluate the things said in this discussion it would seem helpful to know that A was a practising philosopher concerned with the ethical implications of mechanization, and B a psychologist working in the area of artificial intelligence. A full understanding of the claim that 'men are not machines' cannot be divorced from its opposition to another claim. Therefore knowledge about A and B as well as knowledge about the particular discussion are quite pertinent. Consequently general knowledge about human beings becomes relevant as well. Ps-explanations are applicable to our evaluation.

The propositions which I have been using as examples were, of course, particularly chosen either because of their intrinsically debatable nature (e.g. 'one ought to destroy the university'), or because they often appear in the context of a discussion where considerations of truth and substantiation have been exhausted (e.g. 'men are machines'). In the kind of situation where p is argued for by individual x and not-p argued for by individual y one must rationally choose between accepting p and saying that y is wrong, or accepting not-p and saying that x is wrong. I am convinced by the point made by Donald Williams that argument *ad hominem* in this mode is not fallacious:[14] 'Evidence for or against the general integrity of either champion is logically for or against what he champions.' I would stress (what Williams does not) that the procedure does not break Rule H provided one acknowledges that whatever literal assertive truth value the proposition has must be evaluated independently of any *ad hominem* approach.[15]

III

I have proposed that Ps-explanations may radically affect the various evaluations we make of what people do and say. Behaviour of people in everyday personal relationships is seen along a continuum with adult-child and psychotherapeutic relationships. But is this view not morally objectionable and contary to basic human wishes? Does it not reduce people to mere 'objects' to be explained, spelling the end of truly personal relationships as we know them? Must this thesis not be fought against as illegitimate and dangerous? The answer to all these rhetorical questions is simply: no! Our personal relations can surely accommodate modifications of the sort suggested in this paper. My own conviction is that relations become *more* human as they make use of Ps-explanations. But convictions are not arguments; neither are fears. It is necessary to distinguish the logical and epistemological arguments from the fears. I shall concentrate on the *arguments* concerning legitimacy, and then return to consider the emotional reactions. I would like to consider in particular a number of points which are raised in Strawson's discussion about the legitimacy of adopting the 'objective attitude' in our interpersonal relations generally. When using Ps-explanations in our interpersonal relations, one is clearly adopting an attitude which Strawson would describe as objective:[16] 'To adopt the objective attitude to another human being is to see him, perhaps, as an objective of social policy; as a subject, for what, in a wide range of sense, might be called treatment.'

I have argued that it is rational to make use of Ps-explanations quite generally when involved in various forms of evaluation of other people's behaviour. The first serious objection which I must consider is that the thesis I have propounded is somehow contradictory. Strawson argues :[17]

> Personal reactive attitudes ... tend to give place, and it is judged by the civilized should give place, to objective attitudes, just in so far as the agent is seen as excluded from ordinary adult human relationships by deep-rooted psychological abnormality – or simply by being a child. But it cannot be a consequence of any thesis which is not itself contradictory that abnormality is the universal condition.

Since I have argued that Ps-explanations typically used with children and in therapy can legitimately be extended, it would seem that my thesis does entail that normal relations are universally abnormal, and is contradictory. This argument, however, is based on several possible – but questionable – assumptions. First there is the implicit acceptance of one overall normality-abnormality distinction. However, this dichotomy cannot be assumed in any simple form; it is accepted nowhere in psychopathology and has no philosophical justification.[18] Another possible assumption underlying this argument is that an explanation implies 'abnormality'. This view of explanation is surely mistaken – there is nothing in the logic of a Ps-explanation which demands that the explicandum be in any sense abnormal.[19]

Another way to consider the claim that Ps-explanations must be used in only a restricted number of cases is to consider why relationships with children or relationships in therapy are considered abnormal. Strawson, for example, discusses the 'progressive emergence of the child as a responsible being', and of the therapist's 'suspension of his ordinary moral reactive attitudes'.[20] This leads to another serious objection against my thesis; perhaps it is precisely because children are not yet responsible human beings, and because in therapy a therapist suspends his ordinary personal and moral attitudes, that Ps-explanations are legitimate in *those cases*. However, these considerations then show why it is illegitimate to extend the usage of Ps-explanations to our normal relations. I believe that this objection must be taken seriously, and I shall attempt to answer it, not by quarrelling with the reasoning, but by concentrating on the basic premises. Specifically, I believe that there are good reasons for questioning the claims about children and psychotherapy.

What claim is being made, for example, when it is said that children are not (yet) responsible? It is a claim concerning how children are actually seen by adults, or a view as to how they ought to be seen? Let us consider each interpretation in turn. I shall assume that 'responsibility' is being used in its narrow sense as equivalent to culpability and/or punishability. Now the facts are that children are viewed as responsible for their actions in the same sense as adults. Most children, it is true, lack full 'intentionality' (the ability to judge intentions, resist authority, etc.) which should affect our judgments of responsibility. But paradoxically parents do not readjust their levels of responsibility as a rule because parents – not only childen – *lack full 'intentionality'*. Piaget's theory holds that the inevitable lack of intentionality in children partly results from maturational processes and partly from parents' inevitable *lack of maturity* and lack of full 'intentionality'.[21] If Piaget is right, then there is no evidence that adults are any more 'responsible' than children (where responsibility is interpreted in terms of intentionality).

On the other hand we may view the question as one concerning what our approach to children *ought* to be. But again it is clear that we ought to see children in the same relevant sense as we do adults. For supposing we hold that parents ought to modify their evaluations concerning culpability in the case of children. They can only do this if they attempt to be truly 'intentional'. But in that case they will also modify their evaluations of culpability in the case of adults. There are of course differences between children and adults in degrees of maturity. Children often lack certain capacities and knowledge – they are, after all, 'only children'. But in our relationships with them we ought not to forget that they are people – little people, admittedly, but people nevertheless. We ought certainly to modify our tendency to blame people by using Ps-explanations, but this remains as appropriate with adults as with children. In neither case does anything follow about treating them as 'objects' because Ps-explanations are being used.

Finally, the claim that a therapist must suspend his ordinary personal and moral attitudes is also quite false. In the first place the psychotherapeutic relationship is by very definition an interpersonal relationship. As such it surely cannot involve the cancelling of human emotions and reactions. It is admittedly a special

N

kind of relationship in which there is an explicit attempt to understand, explain, and modify behaviour. Yet nothing follows from *this* about lack of involvement. On the contrary : it is a fundamental principle that one may become *more involved in a relationship by making the effort at understanding*. All good therapists acknowledge the truth of this principle and apply it in their work. I shall demonstrate that this is the case by considering each of the three main contemporary schools of therapy.

Carl Rogers has argued forcibly for this point of view, now taken for granted by clinical psychologists and psychiatrists.[22] Any therapist who would really 'suspend his emotions' just cannot be a good therapist. What Rogers teaches is that a therapist must behave and react as he does with any person : he will use his own reactions and behaviour to comment upon how emotions occur in various situations. It is not only false that a therapist can deny feeling or 'suspend his personal reactions' – it is absurd. For part of being a therapist is feeling as much as one can and as appropriately as one can (to achieve the goals of 'empathy' and 'congruence').

It might be objected that this is only one view. Perhaps Rogerian or existential therapy does not suspend emotions. But what about the older psychoanalytic views concerning the necessity for 'distancing' and 'detachment' ? And what about the newer behaviour therapies? Are not these latter excellent examples of 'objective' non-human approaches to therapy? In fact the opposite is true. Both psychoanalytic therapists and behaviour therapists accept the truth of the basic Rogerian principle. It is perhaps worthwhile quoting from leading representatives of each school. Frieda Fromm-Reichmann writes :[23]

> About technical details such as seeing patients only in the office; walking around with them, seeing them for non-scheduled interviews I *used to have strong feelings and meanings*. . . . Now I consider them unimportant as long as the therapist is aware of and alert to the dynamic significance of what he and the patient are doing and what is going on between them. . . . Successful histories of treatment . . . conducted in various and sundry *interpersonal* and environmental settings are living proof of the correctness of my present corrected attitude [my emphasis].

This point of view is now typical of the psychoanalytic school. There are no rules about 'detachment' that can override the fundamental principle which asserts that therapy *is* a relationship. The same general point is emphasized by behaviour therapists who represent the third main school. Bandura says : [24]

Therapists who do not identify with a particular school usually rely heavily on relationship factors, combined with a limited range of intervention techniques governed by trial-and-error experience. . . . The establishment of a positive relationship may enhance the value of the therapist as a model and as a dispenser of positive and negative reinforcers.

It is part of the logic of the use of social reinforcement that the therapist's relationship to the patient is crucial. For example, a patient may be urged to take strong aggressive roles and learn to assert himself despite insecurity. The primary effect is meant to increase incidents of positive interaction, and not simply aggressive responses. Thus the therapist and his involvement in the relationship is a necessary part of the procedure. This kind of argument has led one behaviour therapist to conclude : 'We suggest strongly that the variables operating in a psychotherapeutic relationship are those that operate in any social interaction.'[25]

All schools of therapy accept the principle, then, that involvement is essential. This does not mean that over-involvement is not seen as dangerous. There are specific rules about the limits of involvement, especially in regard to sexual activities and aggression. Some of these rules are in the form of ethical norms; others are codified with specific punishments for transgression. However, none of these rules in any way establishes the psychotherapeutic relationship as relevantly distinct from most other interactions. *All* interpersonal relations are governed by essentially the same rules, which cover essentially the same areas of behaviour (viz., sex and aggression) and which appear in various forms. The responsibility of a therapist to follow rules concerning over-involvement are no more – nor are they less – than any other person in relationship with human beings. One might be tempted to object at this point that a therapist *does* have an extra responsibility to avoid (say) hurting someone – perhaps because of the 'sickness' of his patient. This temptation should be resisted – it assumes the normality-abnormality dichotomy. Our everyday personal relations have sufficient potentialities for psycho-pathology to make quite general the moral injunction not to hurt people. It is *people* who ought not to be hurt, and that is why one ought sometimes to avoid 'over-involvement'.

Two conclusions can be drawn from the above discussion. First, the claim assuming 'humanless' therapy is in fact quite false. There is thus no support for the objection to the legitimacy of generalizing Ps-explanations. Second, the essence of the thera-peutic relationship does not have to be confined to client-psychologist interactions, either in theory or in fact. Therapeutic goals and methods have been taught to many people relatively quickly; these people have then done effective work.[26] This evidence should count against a commonly held view that one must be an expert to be therapeutic. It also helps support the general thesis concerning the legitimacy of Ps-explanations. Can they not be the starting-points for more therapeutic and there-fore perhaps happier human relationships?

I have concluded that the arguments here considered do not establish the illegitimacy of Ps-explanations. But there remains the question of whether it is *desirable* to extend their application. In particular there is a fear that explaining human behaviour will lead to a sort of dehumanization. This general fear can be broken down into different sorts of fears. Each should be judged independently.

One fear might be that Ps-explanations must inevitably cause pain. Much of the agony that is part of psychotherapy would be-come part of all relationships. Pain may indeed be the conse-quence of attempting to probe more deeply into relationships. However, this is not always a rational basis for fear. There is something very human about sadness and suffering being part of relationships. The so-called aversive emotions probably make relationships meaningful in the long run. As for the pain, this can be seen analogously to the pain of an operation or the pain of childbirth – the end makes it worth while.

There is a different fear, that misuse of Ps-explanations may cause more misery than happiness. Vulgar psychologizing like medical quackery represent real dangers. Furthermore, there is the possibility that people will use Ps-explanations to 'project' what is true about themselves on to others. One must admit that this is a real danger. [But it is no more a danger – and no less – than that of a surgeon with an unsteady hand.] Although there are, unfortunately, no absolute safeguards against this sort of abuse, there do exist certain measures for protection. 'Projectors' who misuse Ps-explanations can be found out in the same way as 'quacks' who misuse medical ones: we utilize the informed opinions of others. The legitimacy of any *particular* explanation can always be tested for reliability : is it also held by other people as the true explanation? In any case, the possibility of the abuse of a practice does not count against its legitimate use. The existence of 'quacks' does not mean that medical explanations are illegitimate.

Finally there is the real fear of dehumanization which should be separated from the two discussed so far. The Nazi era has shown that people can treat others as 'objects' with complete mechanization of human relationships. Furthermore, it is certainly true that psychology (like medicine and physics) can be subordinated to horrible ends. This evil state of affairs is not, however, the inevitable outcome of using Ps-explanations. Perhaps the use of Ps-explanations bears the same relationship to dehumanization as discoveries in physics do to the creation of the atomic bomb. In that case one must make the choice whether or not to run the risk of extending the use of Ps-explanations. This should be balanced against the possibility that a radical extension of Ps-explanations could change human relationships in such a way that the risk of dehumanization is lessened.

Notes

1 Sydney Hook, 'Science and Philosophy', and Raphael Demos, 'Psychoanalysis, Science and Philosophy', in S. Hook (ed.), *Psychoanalysis, Scientific Method and Philosophy*, New York University Press, New York, 1959.

2 The definition of Ps-explanations allows different sub-types which can, of course, be distinguished from one another. Thus, one may wish to contrast explanations in terms of how readily acceptable they are to the agent, or of how 'aware' (in some weak sense) he may be said to be. Or one may wish to contrast teleological and non-teleological explanations. I have preferred to de-emphasize these contrasts between sub-types and define the Ps-explanation in the more general way. I argue further in the text that this may be a more profitable way of considering the alleged incompatibility of Ps-explanations and ordinary interpersonal relations.

It should also be noted that I am not here concerned with the possible use of Ps-explanations in regard to the telling of a deliberate lie. Thus, the present discussion assumes that the 'immediately obtainable verbal answer' was sincere. The assumption of course involves certain major oversimplifications—it may, however, be justified for the purposes of immediate brevity.

(I wish to thank an anonymous reader for the opportunity to clarify these points.)

3 See, for example, D. O. Hebb, *Textbook of Psychology*, Philadelphia, Pa., W. B. Saunders, 1957, p. 7.

4 A view discussed for example in D. F. Pears (ed.), *Freedom and the Will*, London, Macmillan, 1963, pp. 59, 60 and pp. 116–21.

5 See Pears, op. cit., pp. 61 and 118.

6 This is the view maintained by B. F. Skinner. See for example his essay: 'Are Theories of Learning Necessary?' in *Psychological Review*, July 1950. Skinner's view is extreme, of course, and ultimately untenable. See for example: Michael Scriven, 'A Study of Radical Behaviourism' in the *Minnesota Studies in the Philosophy of Science*, 50, 1956, p. 88.

7 See Charles Taylor, *The Explanation of Behaviour*, London, Routledge & Kegan Paul, 1964, Part I *passim*, and especially p. 14. Also Part II, especially pp. 214–18. See also Hebb, op. cit., p. 294.

8 R. G. Collingwood, 'On the So-called Idea of Causation', *Proceedings of the Aristotelian Society*, 1938, pp. 85–108; also in H. Morris (ed.), *Freedom and Responsibility*, Stanford University Press, 1961.

9 H. L. A. Hart and A. M. Honoré, 'Causation in the Law, *Law Quarterly Review*, 72, 1956, reprinted in H. Morris, op. cit., p. 325.

10 The utilitarian justification of punishment, for example, is based upon the point of the practice.

11 I have argued elsewhere (M. Schleifer, 'The Responsibility of the Psychopath', *Philosophy*, 45, 173, July 1970) that certain views are mistaken simply because of an equivocation with different sorts of 'responsibility'. Other examples of views mistaken in that way are: J. Hospers, 'What Means this Freedom?' Part III, ch. 3, of S. Hook (ed.), *Determinism and Freedom in the Age of Science*, New York, Collier, 1961; and B. Wootton, *Social Science and Social Pathology*, London, Allen & Unwin, 1959.

12 See J. Searle, 'Austin on Locutionary and Illocutionary Acts', in *The Philosophical Review*, 77, 4, October 1968, pp. 405–24.

13 That point of view is taken by M. Lazerowitz in his article, 'The Relevance of Psychoanalysis to Philosophy' in S. Hook (ed.), *Psychoanalysis, Scientific Method and Philosophy*.

14 Donald Williams, 'Philosophy and Psychoanalysis', in Hook (ed.), op. cit., p. 158.

15 Williams in fact argues that the truth of a proposition can also be rationally influenced by *ad hominem* considerations. I quote (ibid., p. 158):

A proposition may indeed be true or proved though propounded with neurotic and ulterior motives, but it is then so much less likely to be that this will in logic tell more against it than most of the nicer evidence. The rule is that whenever individual x argues for proposition p, and y argues for not-p, we must make a rational choice between two dual conclusions: that p is true and y is wrong, and that not-p is true and x is wrong. Hence any evidence for or against the general integrity of either champion is logically for or against what he champions.

Without a further discussion concerning truth, and particularly in what sense, if any, moral propositions are true, I cannot accept Williams' thesis. As it stands, in fact, it seems to break Rule H, and therefore ought in my view to be considered fallacious. In the paper I have borrowed Williams' point only to the extent that it applies to considerations other than literal truth or falsehood.

16 P. F. Strawson, 'Freedom and Resentment', *Studies in the Philosophy of Thought and Action*, London, Oxford University Press, 1968, p. 194. I have not, of course, been concerned with arguing about determinism, and in particular whether one should adopt a completely objective attitude in the sense in which that is defined as incompatible with interpersonal relations. A main theme of Strawson's essay does concern itself with the possibility of being completely objective, because of a belief in determinism where the objective attitude 'cannot include the range of reactive feelings and attitudes which belong to involvement or participation with others in interpersonal human relationships' (ibid., p. 194). However, his arguments also count against any generalizing of the objective attitude (as in the general use of Ps-explanations which I defend) independent of the question of determinism: it is these which I consider here.

17 Ibid, p. 196.

18 See S. Hampshire, *Thought and Action*, London, Chatto & Windus, 1960, p. 179. See also H. J. Eysenck, *Uses and Abuses of Psychology*, Harmondsworth, Penguin, 1953, pp. 177–8, and R. D. Laing, *The Divided Self*, Harmondsworth, Penguin, 1960, p. 11.

19 On this point see J. Fodor, *Psychological Explanation*, New York, Random House, 1969, especially pp. 3–8.

20 P. F. Strawson, op. cit., p. 205.

21 J. Piaget, *The Moral Judgment of the Child*, London, Routledge & Kegan Paul, paperback, 1968 (originally published in 1932).

22 See Carl Rogers, 'The Process Equation of Psychotherapy', *American Journal of Psychotherapy*, 1961, 15, 1, pp. 27–45; also Carl Rogers, 'The Necessary and Sufficient Conditions of Therapeutic Personality Change', *Journal of Consulting Psychology*, 21, 1957, pp. 95–103.

23 Frieda Fromm-Reichmann, 'Psychotherapy of Schizophrenia', *American Journal of Psychiatry*, 3, 6, December 1954, pp. 410–19.

24 A. Bandura and R. Walters, *Social Learning and Personality*, New York, Holt, Rinehart and Winston, 1963, p. 249.

25 B. Maher, *Principles of Psychopathology*, New York, McGraw-Hill, 1966.
26 C. B. Truax and R. R. Carkhuff, *Counseling and Psychotherapy: Training and Practice*, Chicago, Ill., Aldine, 1967.

9 Honesty

David Wood

'Matilda told such dreadful lies, it made one gasp and stretch one's eyes.' Credibility is one problem that the dishonest man faces. Moral reprobation is another. The question I want to ask is whether it raises any serious philosophical problems.

When we say that a person is responsible for what he does, we mean not just that he was the agent, for sometimes that does not suffice (e.g. in old age, childhood, some forms of insanity[1]); we also say that the act reflects (back) on to the agent. Acts of deception are perhaps peculiar and certainly important examples. The dishonest man becomes by his actions, a deceiver. The problem of honesty and of dishonesty can be stated : how can a dishonest person have relationships with others, and if he can, what kind of relationships are these? Finally, what kind of conception of human relationships do we have that places such a high premium on honesty? We will see that these questions raise the more difficult question as to just what *is* honesty. And this is not merely an academic question.

Henri Lefèbvre ('Critique de la Vie Quotidienne') has spoken of what he calls the 'illusion of familiarity' – claiming that the things and concepts we most often use, we often know the least about (we could say 'knowledge by acquaintance' does not imply 'knowledge that'). Such was the point of the Socratic method, and the justification of the present enquiry. We profess and demand honesty while hardly beginning to understand it. I will approach what I think is an adequate account of honesty by way of an over-simple model, held by many.

On this account, honesty consists of registering, in one's words and deeds, what one knows by reflection, or would know if one were to reflect, to be the truth. There is a correspondence between

191

the external display and the internal vision of truth. Dishonesty is a deliberate misrepresentation of the facts as one believes them to be. Now, while only a statement, and not the facts themselves, can be dishonest, the fact that the statement mis-describes the world is not enough. One may mislead, unknowingly, without being dishonest. This model does give us many of the right answers. When we think of a person not speaking the truth, we think of him inwardly denying what his lips pretend. The face or even the body is conceived on the model of the mask : the ass in lion's skin. We think of the inner/outer distinction in a parallel way to common outer/outer disguises. Even if this model were not at times practically problematic – we sometimes cannot decide – it would in any case be theoretically defective. These defects can best be shown by considering examples of its failure. These cases are not just borderline cases which no theory could avoid; their occasion is quite predictable from the inherent deficiencies of the theory.

Take a marriage in which both sexual fidelity and, if necessary, truth about lapses is agreed upon by the partners. However, Mrs J does lapse. Clearly, according to the above account of honesty, to be honest, she must tell Mr J all about it. Now, in saying this we have already passed over into a positive interpretation of honesty, in which not only must one speak the truth *when* one speaks, but according to which there are occasions on which one must *without prompting* speak the truth. This, in itself, compromises the theory, as I shall explain. But the case is complicated. Mrs J was drunk, and the room was dark at the party, and, God knows how, she was seduced, she discovered later, by Mr P, Mr J's bitterest enemy.[2] Mr J is paranoid, believes his wife is often unfaithful, which is untrue, and rarely believes what she says, or her excuses, despite their truth-pact. Now the question arises, not only should she tell him what has taken place, but must she do so to be honest? The theory above must say yes, whereas I should say no. And it is not just that honesty would be inappropriate here because it would subvert the whole point of honesty, which is perhaps trust (a plausible explanation), but that the conditions for the possibility of honesty are not satisfied. It is not sufficient that she tell him what happened, it is necessary that he be able to believe her, and this he is unable to do. She can no more 'be honest with her husband' than if he was deaf and she were speaking. Certainly he can hear the words, the sentences, but he hears the whole performance as a carefully designed story. If we say that this is just a situation in which honesty would perhaps be inappropriate, we are, I think, reducing honesty to a kind of personal ritual. All that matters, then, is getting the words out. After a 'confession' one then feels at ease with oneself. But our description has already contained elements that would subvert this account. For we have said that there are occasions on which one must speak the truth to be honest, when knowledge is called for, just by virtue of the situation or the person one is speaking to. So 'confession' to the man on the bus will not do. We must acknowledge that the whole idea of honesty is situation-relative. The truth is only relevant to certain persons. This has already added considerable riders to our original account of honesty.

But to return to our case at hand. If we admit that the truth is only relevant to certain persons (e.g. Mr J), then we agree that we are talking about honesty-in-a-particular-relation. And if that relation has intrinsic to it certain assumptions, attitudes, structures, that make the conveying of certain information or feelings impossible, then these limitations must be taken account of in discussing the complexities of the interaction within the relationship. Now, Mr J knows that Mrs J knows that he will take what she is saying as a story. He has told her as much before, and he knows she understands his attitude towards her. If she then tells her tale, which is in fact true, she must tell it with the knowledge that he will not believe her. This *cannot* then be an attempt at communication, and to regard her speech as 'at least honest' is to see honesty in a barely ritualistic light and to fail to see that honesty only has significance as the quality of a social act within some social situation; within, that is, the definitions already imposed on the situation by others.

So far, it may seem that we have just added provisos to the over-simple account. I want to show that these provisos need not be regarded as extra considerations to be taken into account but, on a different account of what honesty is, fit quite coherently. This account I shall develop in the course of the paper.

I think many will feel misgivings about the example above. These may be expressed by saying that the relationship itself is not an honest one, that while they may not literally be acting, there are clearly unwritten rules by which they abide, even if they do not make these explicit. What kind of relationship is this? Is it love? Friendship? How does it differ from these? Is it a personal relationship? The last question raises the essential issue. For if we call it a personal relationship, we have no typology for distinguishing it from open and frank friendships (I leave open for the moment the status of these). Any relationship between persons – that is to say, any human relationship whatsoever – can, in a weak sense, be regarded as a personal relationship. Clearly this is not adequate for making distinctions within the category of human relations. In many such relations the person does not enter the relation *as* a person at all. The driver of the train in which I travel, for example.

We can separate two distinct elements of relationships: (*a*) their content and (*b*) their purpose. In the train-driver case, which we might nominate for the status of 'pure anonymity', the content, or how we relate – let us call it 'complementary anonymity' – fits the purpose, the anonymous performance of a function, getting me from London to Oxford. But it should not be thought that the mere fact that persons enter the relationship even *as* persons, suffices to constitute a personal relation in the strong sense to which I am leading. For there are necessarily many quasi-personal relations in which aspects of both persons' 'personality' are revealed to the other – such as my acquaintance with the grocer's wife. Here the 'content' might be regular friendly encounters between two persons as persons, and yet the purpose betrays the 'inferior' quality of the relationship. For there is no assurance that if she were not in a position to supply me with comestibles that the relationship would continue at all. That was the origin and still remains the basis of the relationship. And this distinction, between content and purpose, allows us to state the condition for a 'pure personal relationship'. Such a relationship obtains when the content of the relationship – the people doing the relating and the way they do it – *is* the purpose of the relationship, or, at the very least, is seen to be the purpose by both parties. That is, there is no known external purpose that the relationship serves. The relationship is 'about' the people in it. It is in such relationships and their complex and varied forms that honesty becomes a serious problem, because it is an *internal* problem, in a way, say, that commercial fraud is not. The whole irony of crime is that it accepts all the aims and ultimate values of business while failing to adopt the circumscribed and approved means. Dishonesty in business raises practical problems of law enforcement, restitution and so on. The clerk may not be able to get another job as a clerk. However, dishonesty in personal relationships is of a different order for it puts into question the ontological status of the person involved. Why is this a special case? Dishonesty in quasi-personal relationships is, if not to be expected, easily accommodated. It just raises problems of certainty in the future. One just cannot *use* a man who is dishonest. He is not a reliable means for the attainment of one's ends. But if a friend betrays me, a part of my world collapses.

Now, even betrayal does not raise the most serious problems. However bitter I may feel, I may at least be able to see *why* he betrayed me, I may be able to recast the whole relationship in a new light, and then come to terms with it. If, that is, the betrayal marks the end of the relationship. The spy leaves my house and defects to the East. I had made a big mistake about the relationship. But this is not insidious, betrayal is just a short, very alarming catastrophe. The kernel of the issue is to be found in cases of ongoing dishonesty, in which there is nothing outside the relation at stake (as in the case of the spy feigning friendship for my military secrets), but perhaps the very relationship itself. My relationship with the spy in my house simply loses its status as a personal relationship in the strong sense above outlined, in which the relationship is an end in itself between people who are solely ends in themselves to each other. This whole description may seem to be an idealization of ordinary personal relations. But even if this is so, it is precisely the frequent compromise of this ideal relation, for example by ongoing dishonesty, that we are investigating. It is thus defensible simply as an ideal type, which, though occasionally realized, may not be at all that common. It may still be attacked from within, by claiming that the very idea of treating others solely as ends is problematic.

The argument proceeds in a way parallel to the 'refutation' of altruism. One never does anything solely for another's good, because after all, one *wanted* to do the thing, and the satisfaction of this private want is what is really important. Similarly, if, in a given relationship, one appears to be treating another as an end in himself, this *must* somehow satisfy some private need or desire, otherwise the behaviour would be inexplicable. And so one is only appearing to treat the other as an end in himself, this very treatment making his presence a means for the satisfaction of egoistic desires. The refutation of this position which can take many forms, will be familiar. We show that the basic counter-claim is a tautology (that we always do what we want to do), and that it just does not allow as to illuminate significant differences between blatant self-seeking and genuine self-sacrifice, a distinction that the theory ought to allow us to make. But we should not miss the grain of truth in the objection. It would be absurd to suppose that personal relations are not extremely beneficial to the participants; they are noted for being emotionally and intellectually productive. But a reductionist who supposed that this was what they were all about would be mistaking the consequences for the cause. And it would seem to me unlikely that this same reductionist would be able to give a coherent account of what persons were, if he were to be totally reductionistic in his account of their relations.

Let us now look a bit closer at the role of honesty in personal relationships, in the strong sense, and then see how degenerate forms develop through its absence. There are two connected reasons why we value honesty here so highly. They may be dubbed the epistemological reason and the ontological reason.

(a) The epistemological reason   Using an example from the philosophy of perception, I want to draw an analogy between the importance of honesty in others for self-knowledge, and the use of paradigm cases in perception to banish acute doubt. In perception we are held to run up against problems of deception, illusion, doubtful appearances. This object 'looks brown', but it may just be the effect of sunset; this stick looks crooked, but it may be a worm. If the world of appearance is taken seriously, phenomenalism, or the exclusion of external cognitive contact to anything but sense-data, is the natural outcome. Now one sound objection to this position is that it does not allow us to distinguish properly the mere appearance of a tiger from the actual hungry presence of one. Instead of the complicated apparatus that phenomenalism needs to even attempt to make the distinction between the real and the illusory, the objection supplies the 'paradigm case' argument. This runs: 'If *this* isn't a bent stick, I don't know what

is.' While there may be doubtful cases, there are also certain ones; so we are not led to phenomenalism after all. It is rightly held, moreover, that phenomenalism itself implicitly rests on the existence of these clear cases, otherwise to speak of a *tiger-like* sense-datum would not make sense. To return to the case of honesty, let us suppose that a person is fundamentally concerned with his abilities, the way he strikes others, his self-image, his character traits. How does he come to know these? By self-scrutiny? But we are so easily able to flatter ourselves, or to under-value ourselves. And even when this process does occur, it is a mulling over of what people have said to us over the day or the greater parts of our lives: other people's reactions. When they do not make up a consistent picture, we have problems. A man in a position of power has the most serious problems, for few will dare to tell him anything but the most pleasant about himself. (There are some revolting tales about Louis XIV, which would not be suitable here.) All courtiers are suspect, so the king gets a jester. Ordinary mortals have close friends. If *they* are not honest, who will be? To close the analogy, the reactions of a good friend, one with whom one has a personal relationship, parallel the paradigm case argument as applied to the theory of (external) knowledge.

I must immediately admit two objections. First, it is often claimed that one can learn more from a stranger than one can from one's friends, just because the stranger has no interest in, say, maintaining one's self-image, a function sometimes attributed to friends. Second, and related to the first, friendships may get so tied up in interpersonal myths, in the intricacies of understanding the other person, that neither party is capable, if it wanted to, of being *objective* about the other. If it is then added that, after all, in any such close relationships, each is the projection of the other, X's revelation of disagreeable facts about Y might be a revelation for X as well, and might harm his image of Y. How-ever, these objections can, I think, be dealt with.

In the first case, we are in a typical dilemma, one met by art critics, historians and many others. On the one hand it is neces-sary to be detached in order to be 'objective', and on the other hand it is necessary to be sufficiently acquainted with the subject-matter to be able to pass a serious judgment. The stranger may well have the edge regarding detachment, but the friend certainly has more knowledge. Both, for different reasons, and in different ways, may not be honest. The stranger may be trying to get a free drink, the friend may not be aware of how his concern affects his judgment. This statement brings in the second objection. I think it just cannot be denied that one's friends are very often inclined to pass favourable judgments, to excuse faults, to make of one an exceptional case. But this is not an objection to my account of the epistemological reasons for valuing honesty in friendship. Rather it perfectly accounts for the distress that we have when we can no longer believe the sweet things that the friend says. On him do we rely for sincerity, and hope for insight. For he alone may be sufficiently concerned to be prepared to hurt by telling the truth, when it is in one's own interest to know it.

(*b*) *The ontological reason*   This is not unconnected to the former reason, restating a similar truth in a different way. Imagine that one evening I have identity problems. Half-seriously, I begin to list my attributes, my statuses, my feelings, hopes, memories. I begin to atomize myself, I spread myself out on the table and pick at the pieces. But could not another have just the same pieces? Am I just a collection? Who owns the pieces? I see a philosophical trap ahead, so I turn to my relationships; or my property. Perhaps, like one of Beckett's characters, I turn out my pockets to find myself. Am I a collection of my roles? Lover, political agitator, son, philosopher. . . . There are times when one sees oneself wholly within each of these relationships, in each of these roles. But none of them satisfy; nor does their sum. Let us now imagine that a very close friend enters. Now I want to say that this event can have an important effect in that it will solve my problem. How can this be? I think that what I called an identity problem is fundamentally the problem of constructing from the temporal sequence of lived experiences that a person undergoes, some sort of image or picture, not meant in a visual sense. It *might* be thought that we could do this from mere reflection on our memories. But far more important is the reflection that I can see in another person's behaviour and speech of his attitude to me. I can read off from his reactions to me, an image he has of me. As he may be just acting in this way to humour me or impress me, it is fundamentally important that his total personal reaction be genuine; for it is on the basis of such total reactions that I construct my image of myself, in a way that transcends my history. So much for Sartre's 'glance' or the 'look'. Far from there being a necessary horror of seeing myself consumed in the eyes of another, I am arrested through the eyes of others. These images precede my image of myself. What then is the ontological importance of honesty? I exist to a very great extent through the eyes of selected others. If I were to believe that their attitude to me was the same as their attitude to everyone else (thus not individuating me), or that the only 'self' she was interested in was the one that possessed the money that she was after, I would be shattered. And the metaphor is apt. Honesty in some personal relationships is thus essential for the existence of a self-image that I can recognize. And this is not just a psychological statement about other-directed people.

So far, I have been discussing what might be called ideal personal relationships, in perhaps both senses of 'ideal'. But the concern about the problem of honesty and dishonesty in relationships reflecting, I think, the reasons I have discussed for its importance, arises in less clear-cut relationships, in degenerate forms of the pure personal relationship, all of which are more common than the ideal case, but which can helpfully be discussed by reference to it. It is quite impossible to aim at completeness of examples or of understanding. The more one goes into psychoanalytic literature, the less one can maintain such pretensions. It must be borne in mind that my emphasis will be on those relations which throw a new light on the problem of honesty or give it a new twist.

Roles and deception

Lying to others does not seem at first very difficult to analyse. One person, A, tells or indicates something to another that A knows to be untrue. But what do we say in circumstances in which B knows that what A says is untrue? We say that B is not deceived, but that A still lied because he intended to deceive. A lied, but in vain. But imagine further that A knows that B knows that P, and yet asserts not-P. In some cases to be sure, B may only have a strong belief, which A is trying to alter even though it is true. But if we imagine that the evidence upon which both A and B base their knowledge is

o

present before each of them (e.g. a horse in a paddock) and A maintains that there is a cow in the paddock, what possible interpretation can we give. Is it a lie? Surely not, for there can be no intention to deceive clear-sighted B. And we are even more startled, at first, when B *agrees* that there is a cow in the paddock, asking A why it has wings. We begin to understand that 'lying' is a completely inappropriate description of the activity. For some reason, A and B are conspiring to maintain an illusion. We call it playing a game and it is played by creating a special consensus for a fiction.

This would not be so interesting were it not for the fact that such fictions are a common part of everyday life and may well be essential to its normal working. Certain polite parties, for instance, are held together by polite words, in which all concerned may take a genuine pleasure, but which should not be taken too seriously. While I cannot claim that the maintenance of the fictional relationship is so conscious as in the cattle case above (where the empirical refutation of the illusion is right there in front of the players), it only needs a careful disturbance of the situation, e.g. an attempt to 'cash' the cheques of friendliness, for the fiction to be destroyed. A person who does this is, of course, not a good player, and to be reincorporated into the game, if that is necessary, has to be given some special status such as cynic, adolescent, or genius.

Now if this disruption occurs, it is usual that one can obtain frank admissions that the meanings of the statements made within the social situation were not literal and not intended to be so taken, that everyone there knows this, at least potentially. And one cannot therefore call them lies, for there was no intention to deceive. Can we then say that the people were speaking honestly? This question points up the fact that to speak honestly and to deceive or to lie are far from exclusive alternatives. For while we may be able to conceive of such a notion as game-relative truth (and thus even of such notions as lying or being honest within the game, though this is more difficult insofar as the communication of information is perhaps the least important aspect of this activity), if we try to judge the whole activity or the game in terms of honesty/dishonesty, we are not given a clear answer. For if we say that the game is a dishonest one, in which people profess to have relationships and attitudes towards others that they do not in fact have, we may be begging the question; for it could be claimed that such relationships as they do have at the party are a separate species, worthy of consideration in their own right, and not to be equated with a liar/lied to relationship. And yet neither are these relationships honest ones, because people are presenting themselves in a false light.

It seems clear that we can usefully extend our thought if we investigate the concept of *role*. For it is just in this sense that it makes sense to say that a person is acting both honestly and dishonestly. I should make explicit here that I am applying the honesty/dishonesty dichotomy to both actions and statements. And when I speak of an honest relationship, I mean one which consists of actions and statements which have true interpretations, especially when these relate to interpersonal feeling and attitude. Certain trivial forms of dishonesty do not thereby make the relationship dishonest, but if I were dressed in 'drag', this would hardly be a hopeful beginning to an honest relationship. I shall now discuss the usefulness of the concept of role for understanding the nature of interpersonal honesty.

By a role I mean a coherent set of attitudes and actions which a person displays and which cannot be regarded as distinctively his own. The coherence of this set of traits is usually related to the fact that the role player occupies some definite place in his society or in a special social sub-group. To this position there will be attached certain rights and duties, and others usually have certain further expectations of the person 'playing' the role. I say 'usually' because there are many roles which are more transient, less related to social structure, and yet which qualify by the presence of certain standard patterns of behaviour and expectations on the part of others. It may be argued that this overextends the concept of role, but for my purpose this 'over' is not only not misleading, but useful.

The first problem is found in the fact that these actions, attitudes, etc. are not distinctively 'his own'. (This, I should say, is generally true. It is conceivable, and has in fact happened, that people have created roles for themselves perfectly tailored to their needs and aspirations. But this is not common.) But *ex hypothesi*, the man *commits* them. If they are not his, whose are they? But this is the very problem we are investigating. It is the ambiguity of ownership that makes possible the ascription of both honesty and dishonesty to the actor. For while we may say 'He was only doing his job', in many cases we insist that this occupational veil not be used as a protection against, for instance, corrupt or immoral practices. We condemned ex-Nazis at Nuremberg on such grounds, while the judges at the trial were presumably just exercising the law, and were not personally responsible for the deaths of those who received the maximum sentence. Where we approve of or have no objections to the role that a person plays, we allow him to separate his personal feelings and his private life from those incumbent on him in the role he plays. We allow, that is, that a man may only be speaking as the head of an organization and that what he says need not, though for convenience, and not by accident, it often does, correspond to what he 'really' thinks. And not only do we allow it, we often demand it. A judge *must* be fair, and not let his own opinions enter. Our society thus allows and often expects the separation of personal and public actions and attitudes. But this leads to problems of identity.

What becomes problematic is the exact status of the 'person behind the role'. Actors of the 'Method' School find it necessary to completely extinguish all fixed personality in order that they can adapt themselves to, live through, any part that comes to them without feeling any conflict. In this extreme case we may say that if a person has a personality at all, it is the sum of those parts he plays, or those he finds easiest to play. Some people find their roles tolerable only to the extent that they have a separate personality to withdraw to. What I am stressing here is that when we talk about people being divided within themselves, we would be wrong to assume that they are somehow unrelated to the world and that the division has some kind of internal genesis. For very often when we tell a person to 'come clean', to 'be honest', to 'answer sincerely', we are asking him to stop assuming the values and attitudes of his social position, or of the structured relationship that one may have built up with him. Marriages, friendships and family relationships often tend to set into certain patterns, in which certain things cannot be properly discussed, in which the possibility of getting honest answers to certain questions is limited by the definition of the relationship that is maintained by all or some members.[3] Much more on this subject has

been said by the popularizers of the 'game theory of human relationships' such as Eric Berne, Irving Goffmann and others.

Even 'honesty' can be a game; and a very terrifying one it is
when played seriously. A group of friends swear to answer truth-
fully questions that they ask each other. But quite apart from its
practical revelations, it offers us a theoretical insight. For even
if one follows the rules, one often comes up against the problem
that one just does not know what one feels towards X, or whether
one really meant Y. The theoretical consequence is that honesty
towards others, presupposes the possibility, and in particular cases
the achievement, of honesty towards oneself, at least in cases not
immediately like the horse in the field, but more tied up with
one's personal feelings. It may be objected that what is needed
is not honesty towards oneself but simply self-knowledge. But to
the extent that we have abdicated a theory of the mind that presupposes an isolated introspecting ego, in cases especially of our
feelings and attitudes to others, the problem of self-knowledge
may well be *no more than* the problem of honesty. We shall now
proceed to explore some more of the theoretical problems of
honesty.

II

In this section I shall discuss the relationship between honesty,
belief, consistency, truth and one's 'objective situation', aiming
towards a deeper understanding of what counts as honesty.

Honesty, consistency and belief

I have been forcibly struck by a common assumption that one
may be able to believe two contradictory things. Whether or not
this really stands up to analysis, it does seem to cast doubt on the
seriousness with which either belief is held. I want to make out
that inconsistency provides typical clues or hints for the diagnosis
of dishonesty, even if we have to admit that these hints may in
some cases mislead.

Without judging for the moment the precise logical relationship
they bear to belief, let us look first of all at some 'indicators' of
belief. Actions are said to express beliefs, largely because beliefs

are said to be reasons for actions, or because certain reasons presuppose certain beliefs. We often tentatively judge a man's beliefs
through his (non-verbal) actions. This is not to say that actions are
unambiguous, although context may help to rule out alternative
interpretations. Context also allows certain cases of inaction to
count as actions. But the most explicit avowals of belief, if not
always the most reliable, are made in speech. Sometimes we attribute beliefs to a person because they follow from what he says,
and sometimes from what he does. We can also distinguish a third
ground for imputing beliefs, that of a person's social position. But
while this may be reducible to the first category we will not be
concerned with it here, as we deal with it later.

I have called all these grounds on which we attribute beliefs
'indicators', because there is no guarantee that they constitute
sufficient conditions for such ascriptions, because of possible ambiguity in a number of ways, and because of the considerations
we are about to deal with.

It is quite clear that a person may say one thing and act in a
quite contrary manner. He may also act in inconsistent ways and
may say incompatible things. Now, it has been said that while
we cannot believe any complex proposition of the explicit form
(P and not-P), because we can no more believe a contradiction
than we can want what is logically impossible (e.g. to be a white
shadow), we can independently believe two things which happen
to be inconsistent. Walt Whitman,[4] for instance, elevates this to a
virtue. This is supposed to be possible as a consequence of the
variety of belief-indicators. And one certainly can commit two
actions which singly point to contradictory beliefs, and one can
say things that appear to be inconsistent. But it cannot be claimed
that the mere utterance *ipso facto* constitutes the holding of a
belief that the utterance itself might lead us to suspect. The person may be acting, drunk, under personal pressure and so on. It
makes perfect sense to say that Pierre did not really believe what
he said. But the fact that there are many different sorts of belief-
indicators does not show that a person can be rightly held to
hold contradictory beliefs. For if we admit that indications of a
belief P can be countered by contra-indications, we must admit that
the indication at another time, or in another context, of not-P
is just such a contra-indication. Far from concluding that the
person holds both P and not-P (i.e. two beliefs, not one com-

plex one), we come to doubt which of the two beliefs this person really holds, or whether the person seriously believes either. We cannot take the simple way out of seeing what he does and just ignoring what he says, because one can always add extenuating circumstances which make the action inconclusive.

I conclude that the claim that one can, on independent grounds, hold two inconsistent beliefs is open to serious objections as soon as one considers what counts as holding a belief. For whatever counts as holding not-P automatically raises epistemological doubts as to the ascription of P. And as we are not prepared to rely simply on the sincere claims of the subject we are scrutinizing, the analysis has immediate consequences for the parallel case of honesty. While the feeling of sincerity may accompany contradictory claims or actions, the very contradiction is sufficient to make us doubt whether both avowals or actions can be being made honestly. Inconsistency, then, is a powerful way of detecting dishonesty. But it does not follow that consistency assures honesty, as we shall see later.

While this view merits considerable expansion, spatial limits force us to consider only one further aspect specifically, that of the temporal extension of the subject. But first we will discuss honesty and truth.

Honesty and truth

'To be honest about my feelings towards you I must actually know what I feel first.' Is this the same as saying: 'To tell you honestly the number of pages in "Being and Time" I must know the answer myself.' Or is it like: 'To tell you honestly what coat I shall wear to the funeral, I must first decide myself.' Or what? Is telling the truth about my feelings the same as telling the truth about a matter of fact? If it is not, and if we are assuming that it is, we will be making a serious mistake. When I speak of a matter of fact, and of feelings, I am wanting to draw a sharp line between those things over which I have no control, such as the height of Everest, things with which I am not the slightest bit involved, and states of affairs, some of which may also be regarded as matters of fact in a broader sense, which are subject to my free choice, or if that be not allowed, things which I have a hand in creating. (Someone might object that I am 'ruled by my passions' and so they are not 'freely chosen'.) If we may be allowed this distinction, and I agree there will be undecidables on the fringes, we see that the problem of honesty – what IS honesty – is different in each of the two cases. The truth about Everest is not up to me, my attitude to you may be. My ignorance of the height of Everest is not the same as my not being able to tell you what I feel about you. For in the first case, Everest *has* a height that I do not know, but I will not say that I have certain feelings towards you which I just cannot pick out yet. Even if I find 'the right words' after half an hour, it does not follow that *that* was what I felt all along. We must eschew the model of the blurred image which then becomes clear. After all it might never become clear. Do I then really have certain feelings, even though I cannot state them? No. An emotional blur is not a blurred emotion. Coming to know what one feels is thus a form of creation, of decision, closer to the example above of the decision to wear a certain coat. But I can know whether I am right about Everest, by checking other sources, sources independent of my will. If we say that all these sources might be mistaken, we have at least some idea as to what is meant by a mistake here. There are only practical problems associated with establishing the truth, e.g. problems of measurement. But is there any such checking procedure possible for my feelings towards you, any form of verification? Is this just the same problem as knowing whether I am exhausted? I think not. If I am exhausted, and say so, I may come to doubt what I have said. (I cannot be exhausted after only ten minutes' walk.) So I walk on until I drop three minutes later, exclaiming 'I was right, I *was* exhausted, after all it's been a very steep hill.'

But what of my feelings towards you? There may be nothing inside to which the expression of these feelings corresponds, as there is in the case of headaches, and nothing outside, as in the case of Everest. So the truth is not, in this sense of 'correspondence' between my statement and a separate entity or state, checkable. But if to be honest we must say what we truly feel, and if we have no way of knowing what we truly feel, and nor has anyone else, how can we possibly be honest about it? And yet this is just what people are asking us to be all the time. We see again why honesty is a *problem*.

But I said earlier that we could regard 'coming to know what one feels' as an act of creation, as a decision, based to some extent on thoughts that run through one's head, the palpitation of one's heart when seeing the other (fear, or love, or hate . . .), and reflection on one's behaviour in relevant situations. This gives us a clue. A scientific hypothesis can be looked at as a leap, a going beyond the evidence, on a hunch, on an 'intuition'. Why not regard a feeling in the same light? It would follow, if we continue the analogy, that there are two strands involved in making the hypothesis plausible. First, one can deduce from it certain other feelings, other attitudes, which I may then affirm or not (the latter constituting falsification); and second, I may deduce from it the pleasurableness of certain actions, the way I will react to the other in certain situations and so on. These two types of deductions are synchronic and diachronic respectively. One may attempt to run through the diachronic ones in one's imagination or prefer to wait until the occasion arises. Each correct deduction gives added weight to the feeling. And if the truth of the feeling consists in it fitting a whole set of other feelings and reactions and so on, each of which relies in turn on a further set, or parts of the same set, we have here a perfect application of the coherence theory of truth. The analogy with the scientific hypothesis fits everything we know about our feelings. In particular, it explains why a woman will put off saying yes. She *feels* love, but she is not sure. Certainty requires time, the time to test her feelings against a whole variety of situations, against the feelings of others. So we not only say that honesty in the expression of attitudes and feelings is very important for personal relationships, but that such relationships are often a means of discovering the feelings about which one is to be honest.[5]

However, strictly speaking, this procedure does not give us a guarantee of truth, all it offers is the possible falsification of our feelings. For we cannot deny the possibility that however consistent a whole set of feelings and attitudes are, however much one is able to guess one's future reactions to a person in different situations, all one has got are admittedly convincing fulfilments of a necessary condition. It does not constitute a sufficient condition, or it arguably does not, because of the possibility that we are merely dealing with a chain of self-deceptions. But this has to be given sense. This will come later.

Honesty and time

When one says 'I believe P' one is not just saying 'it is believed that P', one is implicating a particular subject, namely oneself. And this subject is not a static entity, as I think many people have assumed. Not only is it extended in time, as for instance a table is extended, but time is an essential dimension for the very realization of the subject as the changing kind of entity it is. This is the point of saying that a person is a process. So, to the extent that we demand that a belief implicates its subject, it relates with greater or less coherence to an entity that changes and develops in time. And through that entity it is related to a whole series of completed and prospective and merely possible belief – implying actions and simple avowals. And yet we do not want to say that a person who changes his mind about P at t_2 was acting or speaking dishonestly at t_1, or at least not on that ground alone, for we recognize the possibility of genuine changes of heart, re-consideration of issues and so on, even when the new belief is not based on new evidence. We recognize and often praise internal revolutions in thought.[6]

And yet one of the obvious forms of binding oneself to the future – promising – is constituted by rules which deliberately try to prevent the person promising from changing his mind. It follows that one should not promise too far into the future, or in cases where one thinks one has rather shifting foundations for belief or commitment. However, because promising is not making a contract in the legal sense, because, that is to say, the promising relationship is still between human beings who recognize and in the last resort must allow for people changing their minds, it does make sense to say that I sincerely promised that I would P now, but that I am not going to do it and that I do not believe I should. The promising bond can be outweighed by further considerations of the rightness of the action that one has promised to do. While, in general, it is important from a practical and a logical point of view that one's attitudes towards actions do not change too easily, it remains true, I think, that all promised acts must be capable of being re-evaluated at the time of being carried out, for the person who commits them is responsible for them then, and not when he promises to do them.

Now, while all this may sound plausible, we all know of people who are predictably able to sincerely promise P and yet find some good reason not to P when the time comes. And when I say predictably, I am implying that there is something suspicious about the change of heart. One feels that the person must surely know that his good intentions always dissolve on the brink of action. He may admit that this has always or often been the case in the past – he has been weak-willed – and yet *this* time his feeling of sincerity is so strong that he is sure that . . . and yet he fails again. Such is the 'last drink' of the alcoholic. It is not just that he is deceiving others, he himself is deceived. So while honesty often has an implicit reference to the future, it really only applies to known or knowable or suspected futures, and one can honestly change one's mind, even without further evidence, as long as this change of mind was not too clearly predictable for the subject (even in principle). When there are such doubts, the only honest thing to do is to add clear temporal limitations to one's attitudes, beliefs. 'I love you now, but I cannot be sure that I will love you tomorrow.' However exasperating, it may be the most honest course. One is giving expression to a limited coherence of one attitude (love) with the rest of one's beliefs or feelings, while not claiming that this set, or this coherence, is a stable feature of one's personality. Alternatively, one might be claiming that while the set of attitudes would not change, one's attitude to the person loved might well change, because that person loved could never be quite the same again, or the situation could not be repeated. One can never step into the same affair twice, because new associations are ever flowing in. It is, I think, very arguable that the whole insistence on honesty through time (especially noticeable in pecuniary matters), and the use of 'dishonesty' as an accusatory weapon is just an attempt to 'stabilize' others, to make them into objects which persist rather than develop through time, and may well express a deeper form of malaise or, in Sartre's terms, 'bad faith'.

However, there are certain logical considerations that would put some sort of a limit on this criticism. For time and the persistence of consistency through time are often essential for establishing, even for oneself, whether a single belief was an honest expression of one's beliefs etc. And while it may well be a mistake to hold people to statements that they made years ago, a certain amount of time lapse is usually essential in order to decide if the utterance was made sincerely, seriously, with full knowledge, etc. And without *that* set of conditions being satisfied we have not established whether there is anything *there* to which we might then, albeit in 'bad faith', hold a person. The stated belief must first attain the status of a genuine belief, and this requires time. Unless one accepts that some sense can be attached to honesty, one cannot even state one's objection to honesty used as a weapon to bind people to their avowals. And as the ascription of honesty involves an extended series (limited) of actions and other assertions, it follows that either we do away with honesty altogether, or accept that certain minimum periods of consistency are logically presupposed by any criticism of their extension.

But while I am sure that consistency, at least where connections are transparent, is a necessary condition of honesty, I am equally sure that it is not a sufficient condition. As long as it makes sense to say that a person is deceiving himself about a whole set of beliefs and attitudes, their consistency supplies no more proof of honesty than sincerity. But as we have relied so heavily on consistency so far we will have to explore more deeply what is involved in gross (i.e. pervasive) dishonesty and self-deception.

Dishonesty and self-deception

The immediate problem is that another person might be quite happy to deal with me, and even say that I was 'honest', so long as he could rely on my carrying out certain promises, so long as my reactions to events and people were fairly predictable and so on. It is quite possible that my whole outer life, however, be radically denied by some inner revulsion or 'disavowal'.[7] Or alternatively, I might be leading a double public life – cynic and egoist in Paris in the spring, and philanthropist in New York in the summer. Within any period I would seem perfectly consistent and yet we would not want to say that such consistency was a sufficient condition of honesty; because one can never ignore the fact that honesty is someone's honesty, and not just a property of the internal relations between a set of statements that he utters. So while inconsistency undermines the very possibility of honesty, this is not to say that consistency of presentation of certain attitudes to certain people, or even to the public in general, in any way guarantees honesty. The whole affair may be a fabric of lies or deceits.

But there is an important difference between the two cases above. If we assume that the Paris/New York man would be willing to describe one of his attitudes (e.g. the New York philanthropy) as a pose, then we have at least some foundation on which to base an appearance/reality distinction. But in the case of, say, Melville's *Confidence Man*, there seems to be nothing left over when we subtract all the poses and disguises that the hero appears in. Each of the man's roles has an internal pattern, none of them are compatible, and none of them seem to have any greater claim to represent the con man's 'real self'. Indeed, it is Melville's intention to doubt whether there is such a thing as an underlying self, in any of our relationships. And one of the real problems that arises if we deny Melville's position, is 'What would it mean to say that a person has an identity that he never (*ex hypothesi*) displays?' Would it just mean that accompanying each affirmation to the public there was a sub-vocal 'I don't think'? But any manual that one reads on becoming a confidence man stresses the real necessity to take oneself seriously. One must live the part, the mask one is wearing. But we might want to say, inverting Kant, that the 'I don't think' must be capable of accompanying any representation. On later questioning a person would admit that he was only 'playing a role'. But in allowing this as a way of establishing the true feelings of the person involved we have to assume that this latter admission can be accorded some special revealing status. Yet we are not, for reasons given earlier, prepared to do this solely on the basis of sincere feeling, for we have shown how this may be misleading. But again, *ex hypothesi*, neither can we accord it this status on the basis of its being more representative, more typical, for simply in quantitative terms it may not be more typical at all. The weekly confession of an international gangster to his priest may seem to represent deeper parts of himself, and yet we are more likely to regard them as instalments against hell. We might be much more inclined to treat his weekly confession as the clearest pose, though in view of the universal acceptance of God's omniscience we might regard it as more likely to succeed as self-deception than as the deception of God. But on exactly what basis we come to such a conclusion, to

such a judgment of an act as a pose, is not yet clear. One 'solution' we will now deal with.

Honesty as an objective relation

In claiming that one is not necessarily being honest just by saying
what one sincerely believes to be true, even when one would also
avow a further set of beliefs or feelings that follow from the first
belief, I am saying that it may make sense to say that a person is
systematically deceived about his feelings in this area, or his beliefs about another person, or about his position in the world. One
way in which this might be demonstrated would be to show that
there is some sense in which a person occupies a social position,
or a position in a certain relationship, quite irrespective of what
he says about the matter. It is in such a way that Fingarette (*Self-
Deception*, 1969) comes to understand self-deception. It is for
him a refusal to avow engagements in the world which one quite
obviously (objectively) has. He adds that there follows a failure
to accept responsibility for the non-avowed engagements. This
would seem to supply just what we need, to establish dishonesty
in the midst of coherent sincerity. But there are serious draw-
backs. Who decides what engagements a person has? Not the person himself, *ex hypothesi*. Who, then? An unbiased observer? Or
a person to whom he is related, such as his wife? The clear
assumption behind this account is that there are objective descriptions of a person's situation and the responsibilities it carries, and
of the beliefs that are appropriate to it. Now, I think it cannot be
doubted that there *are* cases in which this account does help us.
I am not in any sense the king of England, and to think that I
am, to avow quite clear non-engagements, would be a real mistake if not a case of self-deception. But this is not yet interesting.
For what is important about disavowal of engagements is the
shedding of responsibility, the failure to identify oneself with one's
engagements. I may, for instance, refuse to consider the fact that
political agitation on my part will bring disrepute upon my
university. But all I am doing is rejecting what my engagement
involves in the way of behaviour, attitudes. Similarly, if I dis-
avow the class-consciousness that I am told is appropriate to my
position, I may well be prepared to deny that this consciousness
is appropriate, or that classes exist. This may then be seen to be

an even more pernicious avowal. My interlocutor may be able to explain all these further disavowals as deeper evidence of my failure to realize my objective position in the world. Have I not even gone so far as to rationalize this misapprehension.

But there is a fundamental difference between my claiming to be the king of England and my claiming to be, say, free to leave my aged mother in a destitute state. The former may be false as a matter of fact. If the latter is false, it requires considerable and largely contestable theoretical backing to make out the case. And to the extent that imputed responsibilities are not *willed* by me, as is true of many, I may have a very good case for refusing to assume them. If these responsibilities are attributed to me on the basis of choices I have freely made, I may yet reject the purported connections between the acts I have committed and their supposedly consequent responsibilities. There are indeed certain logical considerations that are relevant here, but I shall deal with these later. Very often, one is attributed engagements for which there may be no general consensus (which is not to say that that would really clinch the matter), and with which one may utterly disagree. These are cases of theoretical engagements, not 'objective' relations at all. And as such theories constitute their objects – people – in very general ways, allowing no ways in which the individual so treated can avoid the imputations they make, one concludes that they are not so much empirical claims as *a prioristic* theoretical projections.

There are further objections to talking of objective engagements as jointly sufficient conditions (with consistent sincerity) for honesty. For instance, if the engagement is simply claimed on the basis of one's behaviour, and as we have already agreed that behaviour is equally capable of being inauthentic, then it just falls under the original heading of systematic, consistent sincere self-illusion.

One final point : it is often assumed that if only a person avows a standardly avowed engagement in which all agree he is engaged, and does so sincerely, then, barring my cases of systematic illusion, we have all that is required for honesty. I think it should be pointed out that the mere fact that a particular form of worldly activity is common, acceptable and avowed has no bearing on the consistency or inconsistency of the beliefs that may be drawn from the various behaviours that make it up. And if we make consistency into a necessary condition for honesty as, with provisos about time, we have done, it follows that the avowal of certain engagements may *ipso facto* rule out the possibility of honesty, far from helping to ensure it. People with such sorts of engagements as, say, a novelist turned advertising executive, may be totally unable to 'avow' their professional work, and experience what is called role-distance. This final point is meant to draw off any remaining enthusiasm that there may be about the use of objective engagements as a way of finalizing a judgment of honesty or dishonesty.

III

In most discussions about self-deception there is assumed to be some need to postulate mechanisms whereby one hides from oneself what one knows in some deeper sense to be true. That is, there is some inner process within the person that, if uncovered, would explain how the person deceives himself. However, it does not seem necessary to posit any such mechanisms simply to understand what self-deception is. And indeed there is a positive advantage in *not* postulating such processes,[8] first, because they are bound to be speculative, but more importantly because this focuses too much attention on the active sense of self-deception, i.e. taken as an act that must then have an agent and a further subject and so on, which leads to all kinds of problems about the internal structure of selves. I think the answer to these dilemmas lies in looking at the social context of a person; but before I do this, I shall elaborate on the distinction between the active sense of self-deception, and the state of self-deception.

Acts and contents

I think it is important to separate the problem of what goes on in self-deception, from the question as to what are the contents about which we are deceived. 'Self-deception' – the phrase – makes for ambiguity here (just as Berkeley's use of 'perception'). For we have not yet clearly distinguished whether we are talking about the supposed act of deceiving oneself or whether we are talking about being in a state of self-deception *about* oneself. I think the latter is the real problem that people from Sartre to Fingarette have been concerned with, while they saw it in the light of the first, active formulation, i.e. how we deceive ourselves. My reasons for thinking this are: in one clear sense, any case in which another person deceives us about ourself is thereby a case of self-deception. In terms of the active formulation of the problem one is, if only implicitly, allowing oneself to be deceived. But the crucial point is that one is the *subject matter* of deception. These two aspects are not commonly distinguished, because it is easier to locate the deceiving agent within, even though its theoretical status may be suspect, when the only alternatives, other people or a whole social situation, are too complex to analyse. But others do often give us false self-images. Cases in which this does happen occur most frequently in child-rearing, mental hospitals, and in some ordinary forms of interpersonal interaction in which ordinary people confirm or implant in each other false self-images. The prostitute may give a man a false impression of his potency – that may be her chief function; the man then suffers from self-deception, despite the external agency.

It is also clear that people have been mainly interested in the self as the *content* of deception, by the way that they always focus on cases in which a person is deceived about peculiarly personal and important things,[9] e.g. the kinds of relationship that one has, as in the case of Sartre's 'young lady'. Otherwise we simply call them mistakes, for if the item is trivial, we are not interested in the agency question at all. Though if we were to pursue the active interpretation of self-deception, we might have to construe certain mistakes under the heading of self-deception. The fact that we do not want to do this shows, I think, that we are more interested in the interpretation of the problem which makes the self the object rather than the agent of deception. This does not mean that we rule out the problems of how a person can deceive himself; but I think these problems can be given a different formulation and thus a different sort of solution.

But what do we mean by saying that self-deception consists in having, for some reason, a false self-image? I think it is unproblematic *that* we have in various ways, some idea of who we are, that we have delighted in seeing how others see us, e.g. in letters or conversation, that we can describe ourselves generally,

P

and how we see particular relationships. What I want to argue is that this self-image consists almost entirely in how we (*a*) believe and (*b*) wish others to see us. It is a way of looking at ourselves as objects, though in case (*a*) not entirely objectively. And the way others see us is a function of the types of relationships we have with them. Now while there are more standard ways of looking at relationships, the revealing way from my point of view is to look at them in terms of *levels*. Not only can we speak of different relationships being conducted with different degrees of explicitness, but of different levels of explicitness within relationships, at different times and at the same time. To explain the latter, an example : if a man argues about some personal issue with another man who has power over him, such as his employer or his father, it is important that he recognizes, at least covertly, that there are certain limits over which he must not step. The argument may appear to be between equals. An innocent observer may think that the employer or father has 'won', whereas he has only won because there were certain things that the other could not say for fear of destroying the relationship. What is actually done and said, we may call the explicit level, and what was not permissible, but which could have been said, we will call an implicit level, or indicating an implicit level, for there may be more to it. And these relationships we will call *stratified*. We should not assume from this example that all stratified relationships are ones in which there is dominance. In friendships there may be things systematically unsaid, which may not even be consciously known to the comrades, and the silence may be essential for the maintenance of the relationship, quite apart from dominance. In passing we might note that Freud's id/ego/super-ego model smacks very strongly of an internalization of a social dominance relationship. And if there are other forms, as I hinted at the beginning, they may prove even more useful in understanding self-deception. I think that there *are* others and that they can generally be expressed under the title 'game', of which dominance is only an example.

Applications of the active/state distinction

A mental hospital patient thinks that he is Napoleon (erroneously). This we agree is a clear case of self-deception. It is a case of deception *about* himself. Instead of saying that he deceives himself – the active formulation – we simply say that self-deception describes his state of having an incorrect self-image. Now the problems of the 'objective interpretation of honesty' that I discussed earlier, are overcome. While the man may be quite sincere in his claims, it is simply a matter of the meaning of words, or in this case reference, that allows us to say that he is wrong about himself. Now the question arises as to whether the man himself is using the same criteria to judge his claim to be Napoleon as we are. But this is almost impossible to answer because the artificiality of the phrasing cannot escape us.

So let us take a less problematic case. A perfectly sane man watches a film of a young girl being attacked, while her boy friend stands by without interfering, too afraid to do anything. Our sane man calls him a coward. The very next night, his girl friend is attacked; he does not interfere (and there are no *obvious* reasons why he should not) and yet he refuses to be called a coward, claiming that for this and that reason, it was not right to interfere.[10] We deliberately construct the two cases so as to be indistinguishable, at least from the point of view of observable factors, and we say that the man is not being honest with himself. Why? Because he is not applying the same criteria to himself as he applies to others.

This solution reminds one of Hare's fanatic who complains about all musical instruments except his own 'trumpet, that noble instrument'. It may, of course, be claimed that a person, having insight into his own motives, has some sort of privileged access into his reasons for doing this or that, or for believing something. And yet our frequent claims to be able to spot rationalizations, excuses, show that this doctrine of privileged access has very great defects. Ryle, of course, has made similar points. Very many of our interpersonal ascriptions and descriptions are based on behavioural criteria (taken in its widest sense to include our knowledge of a person's character etc.) and so the criteria are publicly applicable, and defined. So one tentative answer as to what self-deception consists in is that it is simply a mistaken understanding of ourselves, in applying words to ourselves that have perfectly adequate public meanings, while varying these to suit our own ends. It is such an answer that can be given to someone who utterly refuses to admit that it makes sense to say that he is deceiving himself on the grounds that we would have to know, to be able to say, more about him than he does himself, which he would rule out *a priori*. We say that however much he knows about himself, to describe himself in a way that he would not describe others sharing the same objective features, is to have an incorrect self-image. And if we ask why he makes this mistake, we must admit the paradoxical result that he treats himself (as he has come to see himself) as he would others whom he sees in that way. This is why he cannot see that he is a coward, for he would not approve of another coward. It is this consistency on the level of concepts that marks out the rational man, who alone needs to be dishonest in order to retain his spurious consistency. Self-deception then is a *failure*, a failure to see oneself as one would see others, or as others see one. Of course, this does not rule out the possibility of falsely believing that someone is deceiving themselves. For when I spoke of criteria earlier, I was only using shorthand. We must still admit that concepts like cowardice, dislike, aloofness and so on, are rather loose. But this is not to say that we can *never* judge. The borders may be vague without the centrally opposed paradigms being indistinguishable.

It seems that we have avoided problems associated with theoretical imposition that I found in the 'objective theory of honesty', because here we are only appealing to the meanings of words. We are taking seriously the idea of a double standard. But this notion is itself ambiguous. A person may simply describe himself in a different way from other people. Not only, let us imagine, does he refuse in some situation to be called a coward, he refuses the description on *any* occasion. It is simply not acceptable to him. I am not thinking of people from other cultures, though they might provide useful examples, but of people who simply construct and order their lives according to quite different ideas. Are these people deceiving themselves, or are they in a state of self-deception? They may, consistently, refuse to use these concepts, except in quotes, to describe others too. But *we* are going to give entirely variant descriptions of their actions. They have not, however, invalidated the theory of the double standard, although *they* are applying quite the same standards to their own and to others' behaviour. By this example we have separated the otherwise identical criteria that :

(*a*) a person should apply the standards he applies to others to himself;

(*b*) a person should apply to himself the standards others apply to him.

It should be noted that this conjecture does not run into the problems associated with the private-language argument insofar as the man otherwise speaks English, and his particular diversions in the field of personal description are parasitic on his knowledge of English. There may be further empirical problems, particularly in the field of personal relationships, but these are not at issue here. We will assume that the man is aware of the divergences between his own person-describing concepts and those of others, so that relationships with other people do not so much deceive him as are made impossible, in many cases. I just want to doubt that we would say that this man is deceiving himself, or that he is mistaken about himself. While we could certainly *say* this, we would I think be taking conformity to ordinary usage too far, for the man adheres to what I think is a minimal and sufficient requirement for non-self-deception, i.e. rule (*a*) above. We might note in passing that the man we have described is in the typical state of conceptual isolation that is common to some schizophrenics and, more importantly, people who would formulate general theories of 'bad faith' applied to almost all their fellow men, from which they alone are emancipated. But while they may be wrong about others, I think it does make sense to claim that they are not wrong about themselves. But insofar as we are entering into or are involved in social relationships with him, we may well *say* that he is deceiving himself. But can we mean more than we disagree with his self-assessment?

IV

Games and social relationships

We have tentatively said that what is characteristic of self-deception is at least the ability to apply different standards of judgment to oneself and to others. How, we might ask, can a person fail to judge himself in the way he judges others? We may find it easy to understand his motive. Not liking to associate with, e.g. cowards, he would not like to see himself as one. But how can he avoid seeing the truth, in situations not complicated by the idiosyncratic conceptual scheme of our last example? How can he find himself not to be a coward or, more often, not find himself to be a coward (the different position of the negation is important) while finding another in an identical position to be one? We must now recall what we said about stratified relationships. These are relationships in which there is more than one level of contact between people. There is the explicit level, which is shared by each participant, and there are other levels of which one or other or both the participants may be well aware, but which cannot enter into the relationship, though they may well in fact guide its course. But this must mean that each partner can see himself in two ways, as the actor constituted according to the explicit rules, and as a subject aware, or capable of being aware, of the point of the relationship, or of at least the degree to which the relationship is a game.[11] And just as one can see oneself in these two ways when actually in some particular relationship, so one may be able to see oneself thus on reflection on a certain relationship. And if we allow that a person is capable of generalizing the notion of his relationships with other people, he may come to draw a distinction between himself as a subject and himself in relationship with what Mead[12] calls the 'generalized other'. He can see himself as an object for others.

What happens when there is a clear dissonance between these two self-images? Usually, I think, we say that a person is self-deceived, is deceived about himself, when our judgment about him diverges from his own judgment about himself. This will be represented to him as a difference between himself as an object for others, and himself as what I have called a subject. Now it seems that there are two forms of self-deception possible. In the first case, he rejects the ascription others give him, while not being willing to withhold such descriptions to like others. In the second case, he adheres to his self-as-constituted-by-others, denying what he really feels. However, this rift in the heart of being has to be given expression for it to be imputable to a person, or for it even to be recognized by him. And the characteristic way in which this is expressed is by *dissociating oneself from some particular role one is playing*. But when one does this, the second case collapses into the first. The man rejects the description that others give of him, claiming that his social actions are not representative in some way.

Now we have already supported the possibility of a person's having his interpretations which he also applies to others. The sole remaining possible form of self-deception is again found to be that of applying double-standards. For if the two cases we distinguished above both come down to disowning some social construct, oneself-for-others, while maintaining the validity of oneself-as-a-subject, and yet at the same time one judges other people in the same superficial, and one claims, erroneous way that one is being judged, then and only then do we have a case of self-deception, i.e. real deception about oneself; for the grounds on which one preserves oneself from the judgments of others, one is not willing to extend. This means that there are no criteria of a true, subjective self-image at all; and yet one has rejected the only other alternative, oneself-for-others. To think of oneself in this totally isolated way, unprepared to extend one's attitude to others, is simply a gross illusion.

But we are immediately provided with two 'problems'. One is the problem of relating to someone who treats himself as a special case, refusing to apply the same standards to himself as he applies to others. And the other is that of relating to someone who, while he applies the same standards to himself and others, diverges in his application of these standards from other people generally or has altogether different standards. But while the latter may be the most disconcerting, it is the least likely to become the seed of a dishonest relationship for, unlike the first case, there is no self-deception to be projected back, where it came from, on to one's relationships with others. It simply means that relationships with such a person are very difficult, but usually quite the reverse of dishonest, involving constant discussion, or awareness of just the divergences that mark out the person as 'strange'.

Conclusion

After sketching what I called a pure personal relationship, I proceeded to discuss the relationship of honesty to time, truth and self-deception. As it has been my implicit, if not always explicit contention that lying and deceit, while not unimportant, are not problematic in the way that self-deception is, I have tried to show

how this arises in and through certain types of social relations, such as in the playing of roles and involvement in games. Various conceptual and logical considerations led me to the conclusion that, while there are many grounds for attributing dishonesty, it is not at all easy to see what would count as sufficient criteria for honesty. In particular, we claimed that because of the possibility of gross personal illusion, sincerity and consistency could not, even when supplemented by the avowal of one's 'objective' engagements, be regarded as sufficient grounds. But this was largely due to a person's ability to fail to integrate his public self and his own view of himself. This, we said, was often due to an application of double standards of judgment.

The particular form that this paper has taken has been designed to show the inseparability of the importance of honesty in personal relationships, and of understanding what honesty is all about. This inextricability is the basis of my use of an individual's social relationships as both the field in which honesty operates and, partially, the source of its definition.

Notes

1 I agree that some may find the denial of agency to be the best way out.
2 See Giovanni Giacomo Casanova, *Memoirs* (Elek, 1958) for examples of just such situations.
3 Apart from the documentation of these phenomena by R. D. Laing, an excellent dramatic example is found in Sartre's *Altona*, full of evasions, 'truths' and defences in the family which is the subject of the play.
4 'Song of Myself', verse 51.
5 This would seem to commit me to saying that courting is necessary for the discovery of love for another. I think, however, that 'love at first sight' is possible, for reasons which are rather complicated, but which centre on the significance of a person's *style*.
6 I should stress that the kinds of beliefs I am thinking about are largely of the value, feeling, attitude kind, i.e. those in which we allow non-contradictory differences between people's opinions and which are usually intimately related to the way the person sees himself and is seen by others.
7 See Fingarette on 'Self-Deception'. He uses this term frequently.
8 We can see in the conscious/unconscious distinction an attempt to account for the difference in availability between the elements of the contradiction which are said to constitute self-deception. We believe one thing, x, consciously, and another, y, unconsciously. The difference between x and y is thus an external difference, a question of their location in a mind.

However, it seems that we could put a more revealing interpretation on the facts, if we understood that the two elements of the contradiction are different in *kind*. One is sincerely believed, is the 'property' of the believer; the other is not held by him at all, but is the judgment that another makes. As far as the believer is concerned, this judgment is potentially available to him as a belief, as are all beliefs, but we could say that it was non-conscious, not unconscious at all. It is available to him in the sense that he is capable of passing just this judgment on others. Freud (*The Ego and the Id*, p. 11) recognizes this sense of non-conscious, but requires, he thinks, a sense of 'dynamic' unconsciousness.

9 Gardiner ('Error, Faith and Self-Deception', *Proceedings of the Aristotelian Society*, April 1970) criticizes Butler for saying this, claiming that there are many other things about which we are capable of deceiving ourselves than simply our character or motives. But the examples he gives to back up this claim, e.g. a general's misconception about his chances of success, simply fail to make the point, for they are all about projects with which a person is intensely involved—not just 'misapprehensions concerning how things stand in the world confronting him'.

10 Compare Sartre's paederast (*Being and Nothingness*, trans, Barnes, London, Methuen, 1966, pp. 63–4.

11 By a game I mean a relationship ordered according to rules that allow the players to adopt distinct, but compatible roles in order that some independently desirable socially defined relation be maintained.

12 G. H. Mead, *Mind, Self and Society from the Standpoint of a Social Behaviorist*, ed. Charles W. Morris, Chicago, 1934, p. 155, etc.

Index

iothèqu
s dic

Libra